Air Fryer Cookbook for Beginners

1500 Mouthwatering Days of Easy and
Tasty Recipes for Your Air Fryer

By Charlotte Gallo

Table of Contents

Breakfast Recipes

Egg Cups with Crispy Southwestern Ham

Prep time: 5 minutes **Cooking time:** 12 minutes
Servings: 2

Ingredients
4 (1-ounce) slices deli ham
4 large eggs
2 tablespoons diced white onion
2 tablespoons diced red bell pepper
2 tablespoons full-fat sour cream
1/4 cup diced green bell pepper
1/2 cup shredded medium Cheddar cheese

Directions

Set one slice of ham on the bottom of four baking cups. In a large bowl, whisk eggs with sour cream. Stir in green pepper, red pepper, and onion.

Pour the egg mixture into ham-lined baking cups. Top with Cheddar. Place cups into the fryer basket. Adjust the temperature to 320F and set the timer for 12 minutes or until the tops are browned. Serve warm.

Buffalo Egg Cups

Prep time: 10 minutes **Cooking time:** 15 minutes
Servings: 2

Ingredients
4 large eggs
2 tbs buffalo sauce
2 ounces full-fat cream cheese
1/2 cup shredded sharp Cheddar cheese

Directions

Crack eggs into two (4") ramekins. In a small microwave-safe bowl, mix cream cheese, buffalo sauce, and Cheddar. Microwave for 20 seconds and then stir. Place a spoonful into each ramekin on top of the eggs.

Place ramekins into the air fryer basket. Adjust the temperature to 320F and set the timer for 15 minutes Serve warm.

Bacon Strips in Minutes

Prep time: 5 minutes **Cooking time:** 12 minutes
Servings: 2

Ingredients
8 slices sugar free bacon

Directions

Place bacon strips into the air fryer basket. Adjust the temperature to 400F and set the timer for 12 minutes. After 6 minutes, flip bacon and continue cooking time. Serve warm.

"Banana" Nut Cake

Prep time: 15 minutes **Cooking time:** 25 minutes
Servings: 6

Ingredients
1 cup blanched finely ground almond flour
1/2 cup powdered Erythritol
1/2 teaspoon ground cinnamon
1/4 cup unsalted butter, melted
1/4 cup chopped walnuts
2 tablespoons ground golden flaxseed
2 teaspoons baking powder
1/4 cup full-fat sour cream
2 large eggs
2 1/2 teaspoons banana extract
1 teaspoon vanilla extract

Directions

In a large bowl, merge almond flour, Erythritol, flaxseed, baking powder, and cinnamon.

Stir in butter, banana extract, vanilla extract, and sour cream. Add eggs to the mixture and gently stir until fully combined. Stir in the walnuts.

Pour into 6" nonstick cake pan and place into the air fryer basket. Adjust the temperature to 300F and set the timer for 25 minutes.

Cake will be golden and a toothpick inserted in center will come out clean when fully cooked. Allow to fully cool to avoid crumbling.

Breakfast Quiche with Mushrooms

Prep time: 10 minutes **Cooking time:** 10 minutes
Servings: 4

Ingredients

1 tablespoon flour
2 button mushrooms, chopped
1 small yellow onion, chopped

Salt and black pepper to the taste
1/2 teaspoon thyme, dried

1 tablespoon butter, soft
3 eggs
9 inch pie dough
A pinch of nutmeg, ground
2 tbsp ham, chopped
1/4 cup Swiss cheese, grated
1/3 cup heavy cream

Directions

Dust a working surface with the flour and roll the pie dough. Press in on the bottom of the pie pan your air fryer has. In a bowl, mix butter with mushrooms, ham, onion, eggs, heavy cream, salt, pepper, thyme and nutmeg and whisk well.

Add this over pie crust, spread, sprinkle Swiss cheese all over and place pie pan in your air fryer. Cook your quiche at 400 degrees F for 10 minutes. Slice and serve for breakfast. Enjoy!

Duo-Cheese Roll

Prep time: 10 minutes **Cooking time:** 20 minutes
Servings: 12

Ingredients

2 1/2 cups shredded Mozzarella cheese
2 ounces (57 g) cream cheese, softened
1/2 cup Erythritol

1 cup blanched finely ground almond flour
1/2 teaspoon vanilla extract
1 tbsp ground cinnamon

Directions

In a large microwave-safe bowl, combine Mozzarella cheese, cream cheese, and flour. Microwave the mixture on high 90 seconds until cheese is melted. Add vanilla extract and Erythritol, and mix until a dough forms.

When the dough is processed to work with your hands, about 2 minutes, spread it out into a 12-inch × 4-inch rectangle on ungreased parchment paper. Evenly sprinkle dough with cinnamon.

Begin at the long side of the dough; roll lengthwise to form a log. Slice the log into twelve even pieces. Divide rolls between two ungreased 6-inch round nonstick baking dishes. Place one dish into air fryer basket. Adjust the temperature to 375F (190C) and set the timer for 10 minutes. Cinnamon rolls will be done when golden around the edges and mostly firm. Repeat with second dish. Allow rolls to cool in dishes 10 minutes before serving.

Sausage stuffed with peppers

Prep time: 15 minutes **Cooking time:** 15 minutes
Servings: 4

Ingredients

1/2 pound (227 g) spicy ground pork breakfast sausage
1/4 cup canned diced tomatoes and green chiles, drained
1/2 cup full-fat sour cream

4 ounces (113 g) full-fat cream cheese, softened
4 large eggs
8 tablespoons shredded pepper jack cheese
4 large poblano peppers

Directions

In a skillet medium heat, crumble and brown the ground sausage until no pink remains. Detach sausage and drain the fat from the pan. Crack eggs into the pan, scramble, and cook until no longer runny.

Place cooked sausage in a large bowl and fold in cream cheese. Mix in diced tomatoes and chilies. Gently fold in eggs.
Cut a 4-inch–5-inch slit in the top of each poblano, removing the seeds and white membrane with a small knife. Separate the filling into four **Servings:** and spoon carefully into each pepper. Top each with 2 tablespoons pepper jack cheese.

Place each pepper into the air fryer basket.
Adjust the temperature to 350F (180C) and set the timer for 15 minutes.

Peppers will be soft and cheese will be browned when ready. Serve immediately with sour cream on top.

Chocolate Chip Muffin

Prep time: 5 minutes **Cooking time:** 15 minutes
Servings: 6

Ingredients

11/2 cups finely ground almond flour
1/3 cup granular brown Erythritol

4 tablespoons salted butter, melted
2 large eggs, whisked
1 tbsp baking powder
1/2 cup low-carb chocolate chips

Directions

In a large bowl, combine all Ingredients. Evenly pour batter into six silicone muffin cups greased with cooking spray.

Place muffin cups into air fryer basket. Adjust the temperature to 320°F (160°C) and set the timer for 15 minutes. Muffins will be golden brown when done.

Let muffins cool in cups 15 minutes to avoid crumbling. Serve warm.

Seasoning "Everything" Air Fryer Asparagus

Prep time: 15 minutes **Cooking time:** 20 minutes
Serve: 1

Ingredients

1-pound thin asparagus
1 tablespoon olive oil
4 wedge (blank)s lemon wedges

1 tablespoon everything bagel seasoning
1 pinch salt to taste

Directions

Rinse and trim the asparagus, removing any woody ends. Drizzle olive oil over asparagus on a platter. Toss with the bagel seasoning until well

blended. Arrange the asparagus in a single layer in the air fryer basket. If necessary, work in bunches.

Preheat the air fryer carefully carefully to 390°F (200 degrees C). 5–6 minutes, flipping with tongs halfway through, until slightly soft. If necessary, season with salt. With lemon slices, **Serve:**.

Air Fryer Fingerling Potatoes with Dip

Prep time: 20 minutes **Cooking time:** 25 minutes
Serve: 1

Ingredients

12 ounces fingerling potatoes, halved lengthwise
1 tablespoon olive oil
⅓ cup reduced-fat sour cream,
2 tablespoons mayonnaise
2 tablespoons finely grated Parmesan cheese
1 tablespoon chopped fresh parsley

1 teaspoon garlic powder,
¼ teaspoon paprika salt and ground black pepper to taste
1 ½ tablespoons ranch dressing mix (such as Hidden Valley Ranch®)
1 tablespoon white vinegar

Directions

Preheat an air fryer carefully for 5 minutes at 390 degrees F (200 degrees C).

Combine the potatoes, olive oil, garlic powder, paprika, salt, and pepper in a mixing bowl. Transfer the potatoes to the air fryer basket after tossing until coated.
Cook, shaking the basket halfway through until the potatoes are cooked through and crispy, 15 to 17 minutes in a preheated air fryer.

In a separate bowl, combine sour cream, mayonnaise, Parmesan cheese, ranch dressing mix, and vinegar while the potatoes are boiling.

Transfer the cooked potatoes to a platter and sprinkle with parsley. **Serve:** right away with dipping sauce.

Jalapeno Poppers in the Air Fryer

Prep time: 15 minutes **Cooking time:** 20 minutes
Serve: 1

Ingredients

6 jalapeno peppers, halved and seeded
6 bacon strips, halved lengthwise

7 ½ ounces garden vegetable cream cheese (such as Philadelphia®)

Directions

Preheat the air fryer carefully to 390°F (200 degrees C).
Fill each half of jalapeño with cream cheese and wrap a split bacon strip. To secure, tuck in the bacon ends or use toothpicks.

Place the jalapeno poppers in the air fryer basket, working in batches as necessary to minimize congestion.

Cook in a preheated air fryer for 10 to 12 minutes, or until the bacon is done to your preference.

Air Fryer Shortbread Cookie Fries

Prep time: 15 minutes **Cooking time:** 18 minutes
Serve: 1

Ingredients

1 ¼ cups all-purpose flour
⅓ cup strawberry jam
3 tablespoons white sugar
⅓ cup lemon curd

½ cup butter
⅛ teaspoon ground dried chipotle pepper (Optional)

Directions

In a medium mixing bowl, combine the flour and sugar. Using a pastry blender, cut in the butter until the mixture resembles fine crumbs and begins to cling. Make a ball out of the
Ingredients and knead it until smooth.

Preheat an air fryer carefully to 350°F (190 degrees C). On a lightly floured surface, roll out the dough to 1/4-inch thickness. Cut into 3- to 4-inch-long 1/2-inch-wide "fries." Sprinkle with more sugar if desired.

Arrange the fries in the air fryer basket in a single layer. Cook for 3 to 4 minutes, or until gently browned. Allow cooling in the basket until hard enough to transfer to a wire rack to finish cooling. Rep with the remaining dough.

To make strawberry "ketchup," use the back of a spoon to push jam through a fine-mesh sieve. Next, stir in the chipotle powder. Next, whip the lemon curd until it is dippable for the "mustard." Serve the strawberry ketchup and lemon curd mustard with the sugar cookie fries.

Omelet with Ham and Peppers

Prep time: 5 minutes **Cooking time:** 8 minutes
Servings: 1

Ingredients

2 large eggs
1/4 teaspoon fine sea salt
1/8 teaspoon ground black pepper
2 tablespoons diced green onions, plus more for garnish
1/4 cup diced red bell peppers
Quartered cherry tomatoes, for serving (optional)

1/4 cup unsweetened, unflavored almond milk
1/4 cup diced ham (omit for vegetarian)
1/4 cup shredded Cheddar cheese (about 1 ounce / 28g) (omit for dairy-free)

Directions

Preheat the air fryer to 350F (180C). Grease a 6 by 3-inch cake pan and set aside.
In a bowl, use a fork to whisk together the eggs, almond milk, salt, and
pepper. Add the ham, bell peppers, and green onions. Pour the mixture into the greased pan. Add the cheese on top (if using).
Set the pan in the basket of the air fryer. Cook for 8 minutes, or until
the eggs are cooked to your liking.
Detach the omelet from the sides of the pan with a spatula and place it on a serving plate. Garnish with green onions and serve with cherry tomatoes, if desired. Best served fresh.

Ham with Avocado

Prep time: 5 minutes **Cooking time:** 10 minutes
Servings: 2

Ingredients

1 large Hass avocado, halved and pitted
2 tablespoons green onions, plus more for garnish
1/4 cup Cheddar cheese (omit for dairy-free)

2 large eggs
2 thin slices ham
1/4 teaspoon ground black pepper

1/2 teaspoon fine sea salt

Directions

Preheat the air fryer to 400F (205C). Place a slice of ham into the cavity of each avocado half. Crack an egg on top of the ham, then sprinkle on the green onions, salt, and pepper.

Set the avocado halves in the air fryer cut side up and cook for 10 minutes. Top with the cheese (if using) and cook for 30 seconds more, or until the cheese is melted. Garnish with chopped green onions. Best served fresh.

Eggs Sausage with Smoky Mustard Sauce

Prep time: 20 minutes **Cooking time:** 12 minutes
Servings: 8

Ingredients

1 pound (454 g) pork sausage
1 large egg
2 tablespoons milk
1/4 cup mayonnaise
1 tablespoon Dijon mustard
1 teaspoon chipotle hot sauce

8 soft-boiled or hard-boiled eggs, peeled

1 cup crushed pork rinds
2 tablespoons sour cream
Smoky Mustard Sauce

Directions

Preheat the air fryer to 390F (199C) Divide the sausage into 8 portions. Take each portion of sausage, pat it down into a patty, and place 1 egg in the middle, gently wrapping the sausage around the egg until the egg is completely covered. (Wet your hands slightly if you find the sausage to be too sticky.) Repeat with the remaining eggs and sausage.

In a small bowl, merge the egg and milk until frothy. In another shallow bowl, place the crushed pork rinds. Working one at a time, dip a sausage-wrapped egg into the beaten egg and then into the pork rinds, gently rolling to coat evenly. Repeat with the remaining sausage- wrapped eggs.

Set the eggs in the device, and lightly spray with olive oil. Air fry for 10 to 12 minutes, pausing halfway through the baking time to turn the eggs, until the eggs are hot and the sausage is cooked. To make the sauce In a bowl, merge the mayonnaise, sour cream, Dijon, and hot sauce. Whisk until thoroughly combined. Serve with the Scotch eggs.

Pecan and Almond Granola

Prep time: 10 minutes **Cooking time:** 5 minutes
Servings: 6

Ingredients

2 cups pecans, chopped
1 cup almond slivers
1/3 cup sunflower seeds
1/4 cup golden flaxseed
2 tablespoons unsalted butter
1/4 cup granular Erythritol

1 cup unsweetened coconut flakes
1/4 cup low-carb, sugar-free chocolate chips
1 teaspoon ground cinnamon

Directions

In a large bowl, mix all Ingredients. Place the mixture into a 4-cup round baking dish. Place dish into the air fryer basket. Adjust the temperature to 320F (160C) and set the timer for 5 minutes. Allow to cool completely before serving.

Flavorful Banana Muffins

Prep time: 10 minutes **Cooking time:** 15 minutes
Serve: 10

Ingredients
1 egg	¾ cup self-rising flour
1 tsp vanilla	½ cup brown sugar
1 tsp cinnamon	1/3 cup olive oil
2 ripe bananas	

Directions

Preheat the air fryer to 320 F. mIn a mixing bowl, add ripe bananas and mash using a fork. Add oil, brown sugar, vanilla, and egg and stir until well combined.

Add cinnamon and flour and mix until just combined. Spoon batter into the silicone muffin molds. Place muffin molds into the air fryer basket and cook for 15 minutes. **Serve:** and enjoy.

Quick & Easy Granola

Prep time: 10 minutes **Cooking time:** 10 minutes
Serve: 4

Ingredients
1 cup rolled oats	2 tbsp butter, melted 3
1 tsp vanilla	tbsp honey
1 tsp cinnamon	½ cup almonds, sliced
	Pinch of salt

Directions

In a mixing bowl, mix together oats, vanilla, butter, honey, cinnamon, almonds, and salt. Add granola mixture into the parchment-lined air fryer basket and cook for 10 minutes. Stir after every 2-3 minutes. **Serve:** and enjoy.

Breakfast Hush Puppies

Prep time: 10 minutes **Cooking time:** 10 minutes
Serve: 4

Ingredients
1 egg	¼ cup onion, chopped
¾ cup milk	½ tsp garlic powder
½ tsp onion powder	¼ tsp sugar
1 ½ tsp baking powder	¾ cup all-purpose flour
½ tsp salt	1 cup yellow cornmeal

Directions

In a mixing bowl, mix together cornmeal, flour, baking powder, sugar, onion, garlic powder, onion powder, and salt Add milk and egg and mix until well combined.

Make small balls from the cornmeal mixture and place into the parchment-lined air fryer basket and cook for 10 minutes. Turn halfway through. **Serve:** and enjoy.

Delicious Breakfast Potatoes

Prep time: 10 minutes **Cooking time:** 25 minutes
Serve: 4

Ingredients
1 ½ lbs. potatoes, diced	¼ tsp fennel seed
¼ tsp garlic powder	¼ cup onion, diced
Salt	Pepper
	2 bell peppers, sliced

Directions

Preheat the air fryer to 360 F. In a mixing bowl, toss potatoes with remaining Ingredients.

Add potato mixture into the air fryer basket and cook for 20-25 minutes. Stir after every 5 minutes. **Serve:** and enjoy.

Blueberry Oatmeal

Prep time: 10 minutes **Cooking time:** 15 minutes
Serve: 2

Ingredients
1 egg	¼ cup blueberries
2 tbsp maple syrup	¼ tsp baking powder
2 tbsp butter, melted	1/3 cup milk
½ tsp vanilla	½ tsp cinnamon
¾ cup rolled oats	¼ tsp salt

Directions

In a mixing bowl, mix together oats, egg, cinnamon, vanilla, baking powder, maple syrup, milk, and salt. Add blueberries and fold well.

Pour oat mixture into the two greased ramekins. Place ramekins into the air fryer basket and cook at 300 F for 12-15 minutes. **Serve:** and enjoy.

Banana Bread

Prep time: 10 minutes **Cooking time:** 15 minutes
Serve: 6

Ingredients
1 egg	¼ cup butter, melted
1/3 cup walnuts, chopped	3 bananas, overripe &
1 cup sugar	mashed
1 ½ cups all-purpose flour	½ tsp salt
1 tsp baking soda	

Directions

In a mixing bowl, mix together flour, baking soda, sugar, walnuts, and salt. Add melted butter, egg, and mashed bananas and mix until well combined.

Pour batter into the greased loaf pan. Place loaf pan into the air fryer basket and cook at 350 F for 12-15 minutes. Slice and **Serve:**.

Roasted Bananas in the Air Fryer

Prep time: 15 minutes **Cooking time:** 25 minutes
Serve: 1

Ingredients

1 banana, sliced into 1/8-inch-thick diagonals
avocado oil cooking spray

Directions

The parchment paper should be used to line the air fryer basket.

Preheat an air fryer carefully to 375°F (190 degrees C). Place the banana slices in the basket, ensuring they don't touch; cook in batches if required. Avocado oil should be sprayed on banana slices.

Cook for 5 minutes in the air fryer. Remove the basket and carefully turn the banana slices (soft). Cook for another 2 to 3 minutes, or until the banana slices are browning and caramelized. Remove from the basket with caution.

Air Fryer Crab Rangoon

Prep time: 20 minutes **Cooking time:** 25 minutes
Serve: 1

Ingredients

1 (8 ounces) package cream cheese
1 teaspoon soy sauce
2 tbs chopped scallions
2 tbs Asian sweet chili sauce
4 ounces lump crab meat
1 serving nonstick cooking spray
1 teaspoon Worcestershire sauce
24 each wonton wrappers

Directions

In a mixing bowl, add cream cheese, crab meat, scallions, soy sauce, and Worcestershire sauce, whisk until well blended. Preheat an air fryer carefully to 350°F (175 degrees C). Coat the air fryer basket with cooking spray. Warm water should be placed in a small dish.

On a clean work area, arrange 12 wonton wrappers. 1 teaspoon cream cheese mixture should be placed in the center of each wonton wrapper. Wet the sides of each wonton wrapper with your index finger after dipping it into the warm water. Crimp the wrapper corners upwards until they meet in the middle to make dumplings.

Spray the tops of the dumplings with cooking spray and place them in the prepared basket. Cook dumplings for 8 to 10 minutes, or until desired crispness is achieved. Transfer to a plate lined with paper towels. While the first dumplings are cooking, construct the remaining dumplings using the leftover wrappers and filling.
Serve: with sweet chili sauce as a dipping sauce.

Air Fryer Fish Sticks

Prep time: 15 minutes **Cooking time:** 20 minutes
Serve: 1

Ingredients

1 pound cod fillets
½ cup panko breadcrumbs
1 egg
1 tablespoon parsley flakes,
1 teaspoon paprika
¼ cup all-purpose flour
¼ cup grated Parmesan cheese
½ teaspoon black pepper
cooking spray

Directions

Preheat an air fryer carefully to 400°F (200 degrees C). Pat the fish dry using paper towels before slicing it into 1x3-inch pieces.

In a small bowl, combine the flour and salt. In a separate shallow dish, beat the egg. In a third shallow dish, combine panko, Parmesan cheese, parsley, paprika, and pepper.
Each fish stick should be coated in flour, then dipped in beaten egg, and then coated in seasoned panko mixture.
Spray the air fryer basket with nonstick cooking spray. Arrange half of the sticks in the basket, ensuring none of them is a contact. Cooking spray should be sprayed on the top of each stick. Cook for 5 minutes in a hot air fryer. Cook for a further 5 minutes after flipping the fish sticks. Rep with the rest of the fish sticks.

Air-Fryer Asparagus Fries

Prep time: 15 minutes **Cooking time:** 22 minutes
Serve: 1

Ingredients

1 large egg
1 cup panko breadcrumbs
12 asparagus spears,
¼ cup stone-ground mustard
1 pinch cayenne pepper (Optional)
1 teaspoon honey
½ cup grated Parmesan cheese
¼ cup Greek yogurt

Directions

Preheat an air fryer carefully to 400°F (200 degrees C). In a long, thin bowl, whisk together the egg and honey. In a separate dish, combine panko and Parmesan cheese. Coat each asparagus stalk in the egg mixture before rolling in the panko mixture to coat.

Cook 6 spears in the air fryer for 4 to 6 minutes, or until desired brownness is achieved. Rep with the remaining spears.

Combine the mustard, yogurt, and cayenne pepper in a small bowl. Serve with asparagus spears and dipping sauce.

Salad of Tomatoes and Arugula

Prep time: 10 minutes **Cooking time:** 10 minutes
Servings: 4

Ingredients

4 green tomatoes
1 large egg, lightly beaten
1/2 cup peanut flour
1 cup mayonnaise
1/2 cup sour cream
2 tablespoons finely chopped fresh parsley
1/2 teaspoon garlic powder
1 (5-ounce / 142-g) bag arugula Buttermilk Dressing

1/2 teaspoon salt
1 tablespoon Creole seasoning
2 teaspoons fresh lemon juice
1 teaspoon dried chives
1/2 teaspoon salt
1/2 teaspoon onion powder
1 teaspoon dried dill

Directions

Preheat the air fryer to 400F (205C). Divide the tomatoes into 1/2-inch slices and sprinkle with the salt. Let sit for 5 to 10 minutes. Set the egg in a small shallow bowl. In another small shallow bowl, combine the peanut flour and Creole seasoning. Soak each tomato slice into the egg wash, and then dip into the peanut flour mixture, turning to coat evenly.

Working in batches if necessary, arranges the tomato slices in a single layer in the air fryer basket and spray both sides lightly with olive oil. Air fry until browned and crisp, 8 to 10 minutes.

To make the buttermilk dressing In a small bowl, whisk together the mayonnaise, sour cream, lemon juice, parsley, dill, chives, salt, garlic powder, and onion powder.
Serve the tomato slices on top of a bed of the arugula with the dressing on the side.

Herb Tomato Egg Cups

Prep time: 10 minutes **Cooking time:** 12 minutes
Serve 6

Ingredients

5 eggs
½ cup tomatoes, chopped
Salt

1 medium onion, chopped
2 tbsp fresh parsley, chopped
2 tbsp fresh basil, chopped Pepper

Directions

Preheat the air fryer to 300 F. In a mixing bowl, whisk eggs with pepper and salt. Add onion, basil, parsley, and tomatoes and stir well. Pour egg mixture into the silicone muffin molds. Place muffin molds into the air fryer basket and cook for 10-12 minutes. Serve and enjoy.

Tasty Egg Bites

Prep time: 10 minutes **Cooking time:** 12 minutes
Serve 6

Ingredients

6 eggs
2 green onions, sliced
2 bacon slices, cooked & chopped
Pepper Salt

¼ tsp mustard powder
1 tbsp milk
¼ cup cheddar cheese, shredded
1 tbsp heavy cream

Directions

Preheat the air fryer to 350 F. In a bowl, whisk eggs with mustard powder, cream, pepper, and salt until fluffy.

Add green onions, cheese, and bacon and stir well. Pour egg mixture into the silicone muffin molds. Place muffin molds into the air fryer basket and cook for 10-12 minutes or until eggs are set. Serve and enjoy.

Cheese Sandwich

Prep time: 10 minutes **Cooking time:** 5 minutes
Serve 2

Ingredients

4 bread slices
4 oz cheddar cheese slices
2 tbsp butter

¼ tsp garlic powder
1 tomato, cut into slices

Directions

Preheat the air fryer to 350 F. Spread butter on one side of each bread slice. Take two bread slices and top with cheddar cheese slices and tomato slices.

Cover with remaining bread slices. Make sure buttered side up. Sprinkle garlic powder on top of sandwiches. Place sandwiches into the air fryer basket and cook for 4-5 minutes. Serve and enjoy.

Easy French Toast

Prep time: 10 minutes **Cooking time:** 10 minutes
Serve 2

Ingredients

2 eggs
¼ tsp cinnamon
½ cup milk

4 bread slices
1 tbsp sugar
1 tsp vanilla

Directions

Preheat the air fryer to 380 F. In a shallow bowl, whisk eggs with milk, sugar, vanilla, and cinnamon. Dip bread slices in egg mixture from both sides.

Place bread slices into the air fryer basket and cook for 4 minutes. Turn bread slices and cook for 6 minutes more. **Serve:** and enjoy.

Cauliflower Tots with Cheesy Sauce

Prep time: 15 minutes **Cooking time:** 12 minutes
Servings: 16

Ingredients

1 large head cauliflower
1/2 cup grated Parmesan cheese
1 large egg

1 cup shredded Mozzarella cheese
1/4 teaspoon dried parsley
1/4 teaspoon garlic powder 1/8 teaspoon onion powder

Directions

On the stovetop, set a large pot with 2 cups water and place a steamer in the pan. Bring water to a boil. Divide the cauliflower into florets and set on steamer basket. Cover pot with lid.

Allow cauliflower to steam 7 minutes until fork tender. Remove from steamer basket and place into cheesecloth or clean kitchen towel and let cool. Squeeze over sink to remove as much excess moisture as possible. The mixture will be too soft to form into tots if not all the moisture is removed. Beat with a fork to a smooth consistency.

Put the cauliflower into a large mixing bowl and add Mozzarella, Parmesan, egg, garlic powder, parsley, and onion powder. Stir until fully combined. The mixture should be wet but easy to mold.

Take 2 tablespoons of the mixture and roll into tot shape. Repeat with remaining mixture. Place into the air fryer basket.

Adjust the temperature to 320F (160C) and set the timer for 12 minutes. Turn tots halfway through the cooking time. Cauliflower tots should be golden when fully cooked. Serve warm.

Cauliflower with Lime Juice

Prep time: 10 minutes **Cooking time:** 7 minutes
Servings: 4

Ingredients

2 cups chopped cauliflower florets
2 tbsp coconut oil, melted
2 tbsp chopped cilantro

1/2 teaspoon garlic powder
1 medium lime
2 teaspoons chili powder

Directions

In a bowl, merge cauliflower with coconut oil. Sprinkle with chili powder and garlic powder. Set seasoned cauliflower into the air fryer basket.

Set the temperature to 350F (180C). Cauliflower will be juicy and begin to turn golden at the edges. Set into serving bowl. Divide the lime into quarters and squeeze juice over cauliflower. Garnish with cilantro.

Cauliflower Rice Balls with Cheesy Sauce

Prep time: 10 minutes **Cooking time:** 8 minutes
Servings: 4

Ingredients

1 (10-ounce / 283-g) steamer bag cauliflower rice, cooked according to package instructions
2 ounces (57 g) plain pork rinds, finely crushed
1/4 teaspoon salt

1/2 cup shredded Mozzarella cheese
1 large egg
1/2 teaspoon Italian seasoning

Directions

Place cauliflower into a large bowl and mix with Mozzarella. Whisk egg in a separate medium bowl. Place pork rinds into another large bowl with salt and Italian seasoning.

Separate cauliflower mixture into four equal sections and form each into a ball. Carefully dip a ball into whisked egg, and then roll in pork rinds. Repeat with remaining balls.

Place cauliflower balls into ungreased air fryer basket. Adjust the temperature to 400F (205C) and set the timer for 8 minutes. Rice balls will be golden when done.
Use a spatula to move cauliflower balls to a large dish for serving carefully. Serve warm.

Broccoli with Sesame Dressing

Prep time: 5 minutes **Cooking time:** 10 minutes
Servings: 4

Ingredients

6 cups broccoli florets
1 tablespoon olive oil

2 tablespoons coconut aminos
1/4 tbsp red pepper flakes

2 tablespoons sesame seeds
2 tablespoons rice vinegar
1/2 teaspoon Swerve
1/4 teaspoon salt
2 tablespoons sesame oil

Directions

Preheat the air fryer to 400F (205C). In a bowl, merge the broccoli with the olive oil and salt until thoroughly coated.
Transfer the broccoli to the air fryer basket. Pausing halfway through the cooking time to shake the basket, air fry for 10 minutes.

Meanwhile, in the same large bowl, whisk together the sesame seeds, vinegar, coconut aminos, sesame oil, Serve, and red pepper flakes (if using). Transfer the broccoli to the bowl and toss until thoroughly coated with the seasonings. Serve warm or at room temperature.

Keto Thumbprint Cookies in the Air Fryer

Prep time: 15 minutes **Cooking time:** 22 minutes
Serve: 1

Ingredients

1 cup almond flour
1 egg
3 tablespoons low-calorie natural sweetener (such as Swerve®)

2 ounces cream cheese, softened
1 teaspoon baking powder
3 ½ tablespoons reduced-sugar raspberry preServe:s

Directions

In a mixing bowl, combine the flour, cream cheese, sweetener, egg, and baking powder until a moist dough forms.

Place the bowl in the freezer for 20 minutes or until the dough is cold enough to shape into balls.

According to the manufacturer's instructions, preheat an air fryer carefully to 400°F (200°C). Then, using parchment paper, line the basket.

Roll the dough into ten balls and set them in the prepared basket. In the center of each cookie, make a thumbprint. Fill each indentation with 1 spoonful of preServe:s. Cook for 7 minutes in a warm air fryer until the edges are golden brown.

Cool the cookies entirely before removing them from the parchment paper, about 15 minutes, or they will crumble.

Air Fryer Spicy Roasted Peanuts

Prep time: 10 minutes **Cooking time:** 18 minutes
Serve: 1

Ingredients

2 tablespoons olive oil
salt to taste
½ teaspoon cayenne pepper

3 teaspoons seafood seasoning
8 ounces raw Spanish peanuts

Directions

Preheat an air fryer carefully to 320°F (160 degrees C). Combine olive oil, seafood seasoning, and cayenne pepper in a large mixing bowl. Stir in the peanuts until they are equally coated.

Place the peanuts in the air fryer basket. Cook the peanuts for 10 minutes in the air fryer. Cook for a further 10 minutes, tossing occasionally.

Remove the air fryer basket and season the peanuts to taste. Cook for 5 minutes more after tossing the peanuts one last time. Allow the peanuts to cool on a dish lined with paper towels

Air Fryer Roasted Salsa Verde

Prep time: 18 minutes **Cooking time:** 20 minutes
Serve: 1

Ingredients

1-pound tomatillos
1 jalapeno pepper, halved and seeded
½ large white onion, cut
½ cup chopped cilantro
1 pinch salt to taste

1 serrano pepper, halved and seeded
1 serving cooking spray
4 cloves garlic, peeled
½ lime, juiced, or more to taste

Directions

Preheat the air fryer carefully to 390°F (200 degrees C).
Remove the husks from the tomatillos and rinse them; cut the tomatillos in half. Place the tomatillos and peppers in the air fryer basket, skin side down. Add the onion. To aid in the roasting process, lightly coat veggies with cooking spray. 5 minutes in the air fryer.

Open the basket and place the garlic cloves inside. Spray lightly with cooking spray and continue to air fry for 5 minutes.

Allow 10 minutes for the veggies to cool. Transfer to a food processor bowl. Combine the cilantro, lime juice, and salt in a mixing bowl. Pulse several times until the veggies are finely chopped, reaching the ideal consistency. Refrigerate or **Serve:** at room temperature to let flavors mingle

Air Fryer Spinach and Feta Casserole

Prep time: 15 minutes **Cooking time:** 20 minutes
Serve: 1

Ingredients

cooking spray
1 cup cottage cheese
2 eggs, beaten

¼ cup crumbled feta cheese
⅛ teaspoon ground nutmeg
1 clove garlic, minced, or more to taste

1 (13.5 ounces) can of spinach
2 tablespoons butter, melted
2 tablespoons all-purpose flour

1 ½ teaspoons onion powder

Directions

Preheat an air fryer carefully to 375°F (190 degrees C). Set aside an 8- inch pie tin sprayed with cooking spray.

In a mixing bowl, combine spinach, feta cheese, flour, butter, cottage cheese, eggs, garlic, onion powder, and nutmeg. Stir until all of the Ingredients are properly combined. Pour into the pie pan that has been prepared.
Air fry until the center is set, 15 to 20 minutes.

Vegan Recipes

Tofu Grilled in the Air

(**Ready in about** 15 minutes | **Servings:** 3)

Ingredients

8 ounces firm tofu, pressed and cut into bite-sized cubes 1 tablespoon tamari sauce
1/2 teaspoon onion powder

1 teaspoon peanut oil
1/2 teaspoon garlic powder

Directions

Toss the tofu cubes in a bowl with the tamari sauce, peanut oil, garlic powder, and onion powder.

Cook your tofu for about 13 minutes in a preheated Air Fryer at 380 degrees F, shaking the basket once or twice to ensure even browning. Good appetite!

Golden Beet Salad with Tahini Sauce

(**Ready in about** 40 minutes | **Servings:** 2)

Ingredients

2 golden beets
Sea salt and ground black pepper, to taste
2 tablespoons soy sauce
1/2 jalapeno pepper, chopped
1 clove garlic, pressed

1 tablespoon sesame oil
2 tablespoons tahini
2 cups baby spinach
1 tablespoon white vinegar
1/4 teaspoon ground cumin

Directions

Toss the golden beets with sesame oil. Cook the golden beets in the preheated Air Fryer at 400 degrees F for 40 minutes, turning them over once or twice to ensure even cooking.

Let your beets cool completely and then, slice them with a sharp knife. Place

the beets in a salad bowl and add in salt, pepper and baby spinach.

In a small mixing dish, whisk the remaining Ingredients until well combined.

Spoon the sauce over your beets, toss to combine and **Serve:** immediately. Bon appétit!

Roasted Fennel Made Simple

(**Ready in about** 25 minutes | **Servings:** 3)

Ingredients

1 pound fennel bulbs, sliced
1/2 teaspoon dried marjoram
1 tablespoon olive oil

1/2 teaspoon dried basil
1/4 cup vegan mayonnaise
Sea salt and ground black pepper, to taste

Directions

Toss the fennel slices with the olive oil and spices and transfer them to the Air Fryer cooking basket.

Roast the fennel at 370 degrees F for about 20 minutes, shaking the basket once or twice to promote even cooking. **Serve:** the fennel slice with mayonnaise and enjoy!

Asian-Style Brussels Sprouts

(**Ready in about** 20 minutes | **Servings:** 3)

Ingredients

1 pound Brussels sprouts, trimmed and halved
1 tablespoon agave syrup
1 teaspoon rice vinegar
1 clove garlic, minced
1 tbs sesame seeds, toasted

2 tablespoons Shoyu sauce
1 teaspoon coconut oil
1/2 teaspoon Gochujang paste
2 scallion stalks, chopped

Directions

Toss the Brussels sprouts with coconut oil, Shoyu sauce, agave syrup, rice vinegar, Gochujang paste and garlic. Cook the Brussels sprouts in the preheated Air Fryer at 380 degrees F for 15 minutes, shaking the basket halfway through the cooking time.

Place the roasted Brussels sprouts on a serving platter and garnish with scallions and sesame seeds. **Serve:** immediately!

Healthy Jicama & Green Beans

Prep time: 10 minutes **Cooking time:** 45 minutes
Serve: 6

Ingredients
12 oz green beans, sliced in half	1 tsp dried thyme
3 garlic cloves, minced	3 tbsp canola oil
1 tsp dried rosemary	1/2 tsp salt
	1 medium jicama, cubed

Directions

Preheat the air fryer to 400 F. Add green beans, jicama, and remaining ingredients into the mixing bowl and toss well.

Spread green beans and jicama mixture into the air fryer basket and cook for 45 minutes. Stir halfway through. **Serve:** and enjoy.

Crispy Brussels Sprouts

Prep time: 10 minutes **Cooking time:** 15 minutes
Serve: 4

Ingredients
2 cups Brussels sprouts	1/4 cup almonds, crushed
2 tbsp everything bagel seasoning Pepper	Salt
	2 tbsp canola oil

Directions

Preheat the air fryer to 375 F. Add Brussels sprouts into the saucepan with 2 cups of water. Cover and cook for 10 minutes. Drain well and let it cool completely.

Cut each Brussels sprouts in half. Add Brussels sprouts and remaining ingredients into the bowl and toss to coat. Add Brussels sprouts into the air fryer basket and cook for 15 minutes. Stir halfway through. **Serve:** and enjoy.

Flavorful Green Beans

Prep time: 5 minutes **Cooking time:** 10 minutes
Serve: 2

Ingredients
2 cups green beans	1/8 tsp cayenne pepper
1/2 tsp dried oregano	1/8 tsp ground allspice
1/4 tsp ground coriander	1/2 tsp salt
1/4 tsp ground cumin	2 tbsp canola oil
1/4 tsp ground cinnamon	

Directions

Preheat the air fryer to 370 F. Add green beans and remaining ingredients into the mixing bowl and toss well.
Add green beans into the air fryer basket and cook for 8-10 minutes. Stir halfway through. **Serve:** and enjoy.

Ratatouille Made Simple

Prep time: 10 minutes **Cooking time:** 15 minutes
Serve: 6

Ingredients
1 eggplant, diced	2 bell peppers, diced
2 tbsp herb de Provence	1 onion, diced
1 tbsp vinegar	1 1/2 tbsp olive oil
3 tomatoes, diced	2 garlic cloves, chopped
Pepper	Salt

Directions

Preheat the air fryer to 400 F. Add all ingredients into the bowl and toss well and transfer into the air fryer baking dish. Place baking dish into the air fryer basket and cook for 15 minutes. **Serve:** and enjoy.

Tasty Zucchini Chips

Prep time: 10 minutes **Cooking time:** 12 minutes
Serve: 3

Ingredients
1 large zucchini, cut into slices	3 tbsp roasted pecans, crushed
1 tbsp olive oil	1 tbsp Bagel seasoning
3 tbsp almond flour	

Directions

Preheat the air fryer to 350 F. Add zucchini slices, crushed pecans, almond flour, oil, and bagel seasoning into the mixing bowl and toss until well coated.

Arrange zucchini slices into the air fryer basket and cook for 12 minutes. Turn halfway through. **Serve:** and enjoy.

Crispy Cauliflower Tots

Prep time: 10 minutes **Cooking time:** 12 minutes
Serve: 4

Ingredients
1 large cauliflower head, cut into florets	2 tbsp arrowroot
1/4 cup extra-virgin olive oil	3 tbsp hot sauce
	1 tbsp olive oil Pepper
	Salt

Directions

Preheat the air fryer to 380 F. Toss cauliflower florets with oil and coat with arrowroot. Add cauliflower florets into the air fryer basket and cook for 6 minutes. Meanwhile, in a mixing bowl, mix together hot sauce and extra-virgin olive oil.

Once cauliflower florets are cooked then transfer them into the sauce and toss well. Return cauliflower florets into the air fryer basket and cook for 6 minutes more. Serve and enjoy.

Bok Choy with Hoisin Glaze

(**Ready in about** 10 minutes | **Servings:** 4)

Ingredients

1 pound baby Bok choy, bottoms removed, leaves separated
½ teaspoon sage
1 tbsp all-purpose flour
1 teaspoon onion powder
2 garlic cloves, minced
2 tablespoons sesame oil
2 tablespoons hoisin sauce

Directions

Place the Bok choy, garlic, onion powder, and sage in the lightly greased Air Fryer basket.

Cook in the preheated Air Fryer at 350 degrees F for 3 minutes. In a small mixing dish, whisk the hoisin sauce, sesame oil, and flour. Drizzle the sauce over the Bok choy. Cook for a further 3 minutes. Bon appétit!

Herb Roasted Potatoes and Peppers

(**Ready in about** 30 minutes | **Servings:** 4)

Ingredients

1 pound russet potatoes, cut into 1-inch chunks
1 teaspoon dried rosemary
1 teaspoon dried basil
1 teaspoon dried parsley flakes
1/2 teaspoon smoked paprika
2 bell peppers, seeded and cut into 1-inch chunks
1 teaspoon dried oregano
2 tablespoons olive oil
Sea salt and ground black pepper, to taste

Directions

Toss everything into the Air Fryer basket. Roast for 15 minutes at 400°F, tossing the basket halfway through. Working in batches is recommended. **Serve:** immediately and enjoy.

Spicy Roasted Cashew Nuts

(**Ready in about** 20 minutes | **Servings:** 4)

Ingredients

1 cup whole cashews
Salt and ground black pepper, to taste
1 teaspoon olive oil
1/2 teaspoon smoked paprika
1/2 teaspoon ancho chili powder

Directions

In a mixing bowl, combine all of the Ingredients.

Line the Air Fryer basket with parchment paper. In the basket, arrange the spiced cashews in a single layer.

Roast for 6 to 8 minutes at 350°F, shaking the basket once or twice. Working in batches is recommended. Enjoy!

Corn on the Cob with Spicy Avocado Spread

(**Ready in about** 15 minutes | **Servings:** 4)

Ingredients

4 corn cobs
1 clove garlic, pressed
1 tablespoon fresh lime juice
1/2 teaspoon cayenne pepper
1 teaspoon hot sauce
1 tablespoon soy sauce
1/2 teaspoon dried dill
1 avocado, pitted, peeled and mashed
4 teaspoons nutritional yeast
Sea salt and ground black pepper, to taste
2 heaping tablespoons fresh cilantro leaves, roughly chopped

Directions

Spritz the corn with cooking spray. Cook at 390 degrees F for 6 minutes, turning them over halfway through the cooking time.

In the meantime, mix the avocado, lime juice, soy sauce, nutritional yeast, cayenne pepper, dill, salt, black pepper, and hot sauce.

Spread the avocado mixture all over the corn on the cob. Garnish with fresh cilantro leaves. Bon appétit!

Winter Squash and Tomato Bake

(**Ready in about** 30 minutes | **Servings:** 4)

Ingredients

Cashew Cream
1/4 cup lime juice
1 tablespoon tahini
Sea salt, to taste

1/2 cup water Squash
2 ripe tomatoes, crushed
2 tablespoons olive oil
1 cup vegetable broth
2 tablespoons olive oil
1/2 teaspoon dried basil
2 garlic cloves, minced
1/2 cup sunflower seeds, soaked overnight, rinsed and drained
2 teaspoons nutritional yeast
1 pound winter squash, peeled and sliced
Sea salt and ground black pepper, to taste Sauce
6 ounces spinach, torn into small pieces
1/2 teaspoon dried rosemary

Directions

Mix the Ingredients for the cashew cream in your food processor until creamy and uniform. Re**Serve:**.

Place the squash slices in the lightly greased casserole dish. Add the olive oil, salt, and black pepper.

Mix all the Ingredients for the sauce. Pour the sauce over the vegetables. Bake in the preheated Air Fryer at 390 degrees F for 15 minutes.

Top with the cashew cream and bake an additional 5 minutes or until everything is thoroughly heated.

Transfer to a wire rack to cool slightly before sling and serving.

Air Fryer Baked Potatoes

Prep time: 18 minutes **Cooking time:** 20 minutes
Serve: 1

Ingredients

2 large russet potatoes, scrubbed

½ teaspoon coarse sea salt
1 tablespoon peanut oil

Directions

Preheat the air fryer carefully to 400°F (200 degrees C).
Potatoes should be brushed with peanut oil and seasoned with salt. Place them in the air fryer basket, then in the air fryer.

Cook until potatoes are tender, about 1 hour. Prick them with a fork to see whether they're done.

Air Fryer Vegan Buffalo Cauliflower

Prep time: 15 minutes **Cooking time:** 25 minutes
Serve: 1

Ingredients

1 ½ pound cauliflower florets
¾ cup all-purpose flour
1 teaspoon paprika
¼ teaspoon ground black pepper nonstick cooking spray

4 tbsp Egg substitute, liquid
½ teaspoon salt
1 teaspoon garlic powder
½ cup vegan Buffalo wing sauce (such as Frank's®)

Directions

Preheat the air fryer carefully to 400°F (200 degrees C).
In a large mixing basin, combine cauliflower florets. Stir the egg replacement into the florets to coat.

Combine the flour, garlic powder, paprika, salt, and pepper in a large plastic resealable bag. Shake and zip until evenly blended. 1/2 of the florets should be dipped in seasoned flour. Zip it up and shake it to coat. Fill the air fryer basket with florets. Nonstick cooking spray should be sprayed on the tops.

5 minutes in the air fryer. Cook for 5 minutes more after flipping the cauliflower and spraying any powdery places. Repeat with the rest of the cauliflower florets.

Meanwhile, prepare the buffalo wing sauce in a skillet over medium heat. Place the cauliflower in a large mixing basin. Toss the top with the wing sauce until uniformly covered. Serve right away.

Vegan Sweet Potato Fritters in the Air Fryer

Prep time: 15 minutes **Cooking time:** 20 minutes
Serve: 1

Ingredients

1 ½ cups shredded sweet potato
¼ cup finely diced onions
½ teaspoon salt
¼ teaspoon ground turmeric avocado oil

½ cup almond flour cooking spray
½ tablespoon olive oil
½ tbsp ground black pepper

Directions

Preheat an air fryer carefully to 350°F (175 degrees C). Combine the shredded sweet potato, almond flour, onions, olive oil, salt, pepper, and turmeric in a mixing bowl. Using a large cookie scoop, divide the mixture into 9 balls and shape it into patties. Place the patties in the air fryer basket, ensuring they don't touch. Coat the tops with cooking spray.

Cook in a preheated air fryer for 10 to 12 minutes, or until the cakes begin to brown on the edges. Flip the patties over, coat with cooking spray, and continue to air fry for 6 to 8 minutes. Allow for a 1-minute rest before removing from the air fryer basket.

Air Fryer Apple Dumplings

Prep time: 10 minutes **Cooking time:** 18 minutes
Serve: 1

Ingredients

2 tablespoons sultana raisins
2 small apples, peeled and cored
2 tablespoons butter, melted

2 sheets puff pastry
1 tablespoon brown sugar

Directions

Preheat an air fryer carefully to 320°F (180 degrees C). Aluminum foil should be used to line the air fryer basket.
In a mixing dish, combine sultanas and brown sugar.

Place a sheet of puff pastry on a clean work surface. Fill the core of an apple with the sultana mixture and place it on the crust. Fold the dough around the apple to cover it completely. Repeat with the rest of the pastry, apple, and filling.

Brush the dumplings with melted butter and place them in the prepared basket. Cook the dumplings for 25 minutes, or until golden brown and the apples are tender.

Roasted Garlic in the Air Fryer

Prep time: 15 minutes **Cooking time:** 20 minutes
Serve: 1

Ingredients

1 head garlic aluminum foil

1 tbsp extra-virgin olive oil

¼ teaspoon salt

¼ tbs ground black pepper

Directions

Preheat the air fryer carefully to 380°F (190 degrees C).

Remove the top of the garlic head and set it on a square piece of aluminum foil. Wrap the foil around the garlic. Season with salt and pepper and drizzle with olive oil. Fold the ends of the foil over the garlic to form a pouch.

16 to 20 minutes in the air fryer until the garlic is tender. Open the foil package with extreme caution, as hot steam will escape.

Air Fryer Latkes

Prep time: 15 minutes **Cooking time:** 25 minutes
Serve: 1

Ingredients

1 (16 ounces) package frozen shredded hash brown potatoes

1 egg

2 tablespoons matzo meal cooking spray

½ cup shredded onion avocado oil

kosher salt and ground black pepper to taste

Directions

The manufacturer's instructions preheat an air fryer carefully to 375°F (190°C). Next, prepare a piece of parchment or waxed paper.

Place the thawed potatoes and shredded onion between layers of paper towels. Cover with extra paper towels and wring out as much liquid as possible.

Combine the egg, salt, and pepper in a large mixing bowl. With a fork, mix in the potatoes and onion. Stir in the matzo meal until the ingredients are uniformly distributed. Form the mixture into ten 3- to 4- inch broad patties with your hands. Place the patties on a sheet of parchment or waxed paper.

Cooking spray should be sprayed on the air fryer basket. Place half of the patties properly in the basket and coat with cooking spray generously.

Air-fry for 10 to 12 minutes, or until the exterior is crispy and dark golden brown. (If you like a softer latke, check for doneness at 8 minutes.) Transfer the latkes to a plate. In the same manner, cook the remaining patties and coat them with cooking spray before cooking.

Air Fryer Stuffed Mushrooms

Prep time: 15 minutes **Cooking time:** 20 minutes
Serve: 1

Ingredients

1 (16 ounces) package whole white button mushrooms

4 ounces cream cheese, softened

¼ cup finely shredded sharp Cheddar cheese

¼ teaspoon ground paprika

1 pinch salt

cooking spray

2 scallions

Directions

Gently clean the mushrooms with a moist towel. Remove and discard the stems. Separate the white and green sections of the scallions. Preheat an air fryer carefully to 360°F (182 degrees C).

In a small mixing dish, combine cream cheese, Cheddar cheese, the white sections of the scallions, paprika, and salt. Stuff the filling into the mushrooms, pushing it in with the back of a small spoon to fill the cavity. Cooking sprays the air fryer basket and place the mushrooms inside. You may need to perform two batches depending on the size of your air fryer. Cook for 8 minutes or until the filling is gently browned. Rep with the remaining mushrooms.

Air Fryer Turkey Breast

Prep time: 15 minutes **Cooking time:** 25 minutes
Serve: 1

Ingredients

1 tablespoon finely chopped fresh rosemary

1 teaspoon finely minced fresh garlic

½ teaspoon salt

¼ teaspoon ground black pepper

1 teaspoon finely chopped fresh chives

2 tbsp cold unsalted butter

2 ¾ pounds skin-on, bone-in split turkey breast

Directions

Preheat the air fryer carefully to 350°F (175 degrees C).

Combine the rosemary, chives, garlic, salt, and pepper on a chopping board. Place thin slices of butter on the herbs and spices and mash until thoroughly combined.

Pat the turkey breast dry and massage it on both sides and beneath the skin with herbed butter.

Place the turkey in the air fryer basket, skin side down, and cook for 20 minutes.

Turn the turkey skin-side up and fry for another 18 minutes, or until an instant-read thermometer placed near the bone registers 165 degrees F (74 degrees C). Transfer to a dish and tent with aluminum foil for 10 minutes to rest. **Serve:** heated, sliced.

Blueberry Chimichangas in the Air Fryer

Prep time: 15 minutes **Cooking time:** 25 minutes
Serve: 1

Ingredients

½ (8 ounces) package
Neufchatel cheese,
softened
1 teaspoon vanilla extract
½ tbsp ground cinnamon
5 (7 inches) flour tortillas
avocado oil cooking spray

1 ½ tablespoon white
sugar
2 tablespoons sour cream
1 (6 ounces) container
blueberries
2 ½ tablespoons white
sugar

Directions

Combine Neufchatel cheese, sour cream, sugar, and
vanilla extract in a mixing bowl and whisk with an
electric hand mixer. Fold in the blueberries with care.

Heat tortillas until soft and malleable in a big pan or
directly on the grates of a gas burner. 1/4 cup
blueberry mixture should be placed down the center
of each tortilla. Fold the top and bottom of the
tortillas over the filling, then wrap each tortilla into a
burrito form. Mist with avocado oil and set in an air
fryer basket.

Cook the chimichangas in the air fryer at 400 degrees
F (200 degrees C) for 4 to 6 minutes, or until golden
brown. 1 to 2 minutes more, flip each chimichanga
over, spritz with cooking spray, and air fry until golden
brown. Allow cooling slightly.

In a small dish, combine the sugar and cinnamon.
Each chimichangashould be sprayed with avocado oil
and rolled with cinnamon sugar.

Air Fryer Polenta Fries

Prep time: 18 minutes **Cooking time:** 20 minutes
Serve: 1

Ingredients

1 (16 ounces) package
prepared polenta nonstick
olive oil cooking spray

salt and ground black
pepper to taste

Directions

Preheat an air fryer carefully to 350°F (175 degrees C).
Cut the polenta into long, thin slices that resemble
French fries.

Cooking spray should be sprayed on the bottom of
the basket. Place half of the polenta fries in the basket
and spritz the tops gently with cooking spray. Season
with salt and pepper to taste.

Cook for 10 minutes in a preheated air fryer. Flip the
fries with a spatula and cook for another 5 minutes, or
until crispy. Place the fries on a dish lined with paper
towels. Repeat with the other half of the fries.

Air Fryer Falafel

Prep time: 20 minutes **Cooking time:** 25 minutes
Serve: 1

Ingredients

1 cup dry garbanzo
beans
¾ cup fresh flat-leafed
parsley stems removed
¼ teaspoon baking soda
2 tbsp chickpea flour
1 tbsp ground cumin
salt and ground black
pepper to taste

1 ½ cups fresh cilantro,
stems removed
1 clove garlic
1 small red onion,
quartered
1 tbsp sriracha sauce
1 tbsp ground coriander
½ tbsp baking powder
cooking spray

Directions

Soak chickpeas for 24 hours in a large amount of cold
water. Rub your fingers through the wet chickpeas to
help loosen and remove the skins. Rinse and drain
well. To dry, spread chickpeas on a wide clean dish
towel. In a food processor, combine chickpeas,
cilantro, parsley, onion, and garlic until rough paste
forms. Transfer the mixture to a large mixing basin.
Chickpea flour, coriander, cumin, sriracha, salt, and
pepper. Allow the mixture to rest for 1 hour, covered.

Preheat an air fryer carefully to 375°F (190 degrees C).
To the chickpea mixture, add the baking powder and
baking soda. Using your hands, mix until just blended.
Create 15 equal-sized balls and softly press them to
form patties. Cooking spray should be sprayed on the
falafel patties.
Cook for 10 minutes in a preheated air fryer with 7
falafel patties. Cook for 10 to 12 minutes, transfer
cooked falafel to a platter and repeat with the
remaining 8 falafel.

Air Fryer Roasted Okra

Prep time: 15 minutes **Cooking time:** 20 minutes
Serve: 1

Ingredients

½ pound okra ends
trimmed, and pods sliced
⅛ tbsp black pepper

¼ teaspoon salt
1 teaspoon olive oil

Directions

Preheat an air fryer carefully to 350°F (175 degrees C).
Combine the okra, olive oil, salt, and pepper in a
mixing dish. Place in the air fryer basket in a single
layer. Cook for 5 minutes in the air fryer. Cook for 5
minutes more after tossing. Cook for 2 minutes more
after tossing. **Serve:** right away In a shallow dish,
combine panko breadcrumbs, salt, Italian seasoning,
and pepper. Then, in a separate dish, softly beat the
remaining egg. Each rice ball should be dipped in egg
first, then the panko mixture. Next, spray the air fryer
basket with cooking spray and place the rice balls in it.

Beef, Pork & Lamb Recipes

Air Fryer Blueberry Chimichangas

(**Ready in about** 20 minutes | **Servings:** 4)

Ingredients

1 pound Porterhouse steak, sliced
Coarse sea salt and ground black pepper, to taste
1/2 teaspoon shallot powder

1 pound cauliflower, torn into florets

1 teaspoon butter, room temperature
1/2 teaspoon porcini powder 1 teaspoon granulated garlic
1 teaspoon smoked paprika

Directions

Brush all sides of the steak with butter and season with all spices. Season the cauliflower to taste with salt and pepper.

Place the steak in the cooking basket and roast for 12 minutes at 400 degrees F, turning halfway through.

Remove the cauliflower from the basket and cook your steak for another 2 to 3 minutes, if necessary. Garnish the steak with the cauliflower. Consume while warm.

Chuck Roast with Sweet 'n' Sticky Sauce

(**Ready in about** 35 minutes | **Servings:** 3)

Ingredients

1 pound chuck roast
2 tablespoons butter softened
1 tablespoon coriander, chopped
1 tablespoon fish sauce
2 tablespoons honey

Sea salt and ground black pepper, to taste

1 tablespoon fresh scallions, chopped
1 teaspoon soy sauce

Directions

Season the chuck roast with salt and pepper; spritz a nonstick cooking oil all over the beef.

Air fry at 400 degrees F for 30 to 35 minutes, flipping the chuck roast halfway through the cooking time.

While the roast is cooking, heat the other

Ingredients in a sauté pan over medium-high heat. Bring to a boil and reduce the heat; let it simmer, partially covered, until the sauce has thickened and reduced.

Slice the chuck roast into thick cuts and **Serve:** garnished with sweet 'n' sticky sauce. Bon appétit!

Pomodoro Peperonata Pomodoro Italian Sausage

(**Ready in about** 15 minutes | **Servings:** 2)

Ingredients

2 bell peppers, sliced
1 chili pepper
2 smoked beef sausages
1 teaspoon Italian spice mix
1 garlic clove, minced

1 yellow onion, sliced
1 teaspoon olive oil
2 medium-sized tomatoes, peeled and crushed

Directions

Spritz the sides and bottom of the cooking basket with a nonstick cooking oil. Add the peppers, onion and sausage to the cooking basket.

Cook at 390 degrees F for 10 minutes, shaking the basket periodically. Re**Serve:**.

Heat the olive oil in a medium-sized saucepan over medium-high flame until sizzling; add in the tomatoes and garlic; let it cook for 2 to 3 minutes.

Stir in the peppers, onion and Italian spice mix. Continue to cook for 1 minute longer or until heated through. Fold in the sausages and **Serve:** warm. Bon appétit!

Flank Steak with Dijon Honey Butter

(**Ready in about** 15 minutes | **Servings:** 3)

Ingredients

1 pound flank steak
1/2 teaspoon olive oil
3 tablespoons butter

Sea salt and red pepper flakes, to taste
1 teaspoon Dijon mustard
1 teaspoon honey

Directions

Brush the flank steak with olive oil and season with salt and pepper.

Cook at 400 degrees F for 6 minutes. Then, turn the steak halfway through the **Cooking time:**and continue to cook for a further 6 minutes.

In the meantime, prepare the Dijon honey butter by whisking the remaining Ingredients.

Serve: the warm flank steak dolloped with the Dijon honey butter. Bon appétit!

Garlic Roasted Beef

Prep time: 15 minutes **Cooking time:** 40 minutes
Servings: 2-4

Ingredients

2 tbsp. of minced garlic
1tsp. of garlic powder
1 tsp. of black pepper (ground)
1cups of chicken stock
2yellow onions
1 lb. of beef brisket
7 oz. of mushrooms
1 tsp. of salt
1 tbsp. of extra-virgin olive oil
1 cup of chopped celery stalk

Directions

Merge garlic powder, salt and ground black pepper together in a mixing bowl and stir. Rub the beef brisket with all the spice mixture. Set the pressure cooker to Sauté mode and place the beef brisket in the pressure cooker.

Sauté the meat for about 5 minutes on them, until golden brown. Add celery stalk. Peel the onions, chop vegetables, and slice mushrooms. Detach the beef brisket from the pressure cooker. Put the vegetables into pressure the cooker. Sprinkle the constituents with the organic olive oil and sauté for 10 minutes, stirring frequently. Add the chicken stock, garlic and beef brisket.

Close the pressure cooker lid and cook the dish on Keep Warm mode roughly for about 25 minutes. When the Cooking time ends, release pressure on the cooker and open the lid. Stir the amalgamation and Serve.

Pork Satay

Prep time: 10 minutes **Cooking time:** 25 minutes
Servings: 3-5

Ingredients

12 oz. of pork loin
1tbsp. of essential olive oil
1 tbsp. of sesame oil
1 tsp. of turmeric
1 tsp. of basil
1 tsp. of cilantro
11 tbsp. of fish sauce
3 tbsp. of apple cider vinegar treatment
1/2 tsp. of red pepper cayenne
1 tsp. of Erythritol
1 tsp. of soy sauce

Directions

Chop the pork loin into medium-sized pieces. Place the pork loin in the mixing bowl.

Sprinkle the meat with apple cider vinegar, organic olive oil, sesame oil, turmeric, cayenne, cilantro, basil, Erythritol, soy sauce, and fish sauce, stir well. Thread the meat on the skewers. Set the strain cooker to Sauté mode. Place the skewers in the pressure cooker and Cook the pork satay for about 25 minutes. When cooked, transfer the satays to a wide bowl and allow them to rest before serving.

Horseradish-flavored beef

Prep time: 10 minutes **Cooking time:** 30 minutes
Servings: 4-6

Ingredients

5 oz. of horseradish
1cup of cream
1 tsp. of coriander
1 tsp. of oregano
1 tsp. of salt
1 tbsp. of olive oil
1 lb. of beef brisket
1 tbsp. of thyme
1/2 cup of chicken stock
1 tbsp. of fresh dill
1garlic cloves

Directions

Chop the beef rump and sprinkle it with salt. Peel the onions and slice them. Mix the sliced onions with the extra virgin olive oil and stir well.

Mix the burgundy or merlot wine, bay leaves, black-eyed peas, groundginger thyme, red pepper cayenne, freshly squeezed lemon juice, cilantro, oregano, and minced garlic together in a mixing bowl. Set pressure cooker to Sauté mode and add the sliced onion mixture to pressure cooker and sauté for about 10 minutes, stirring frequently.

Add the chopped beef rump and allow it marinate for a handful of minutes. Stir well and close the strain cooker lid. Cook the dish on Sauté mode for about 40 minutes. When the Cooking time ends, open pressure cooker lid and stir again. Transfer the dish to serving bowls. **Serve:** immediately and Enjoy!

Turmeric Meatballs

Prep time: 10 minutes **Cooking time:** 10 minutes
Servings: 5-7

Ingredients

1tbsp. of turmeric
1/2 tsp. of oregano
1 tsp. of salt
10 oz. of ground pork
1 egg yolk
1 tsp. of ground ginger
1 tsp. of minced garlic
1 zucchini
1 tbsp. of organic olive oil
1 tsp. of cilantro

Directions

Mix the turmeric, ground ginger, salt, oregano, and cilantro in a mixing bowl and stir well. Add ground pork into the contents and stir again. Add the egg yolk and minced garlic. Chop the zucchini and transfer it to the blender. Blend the vegetable mixture until smooth. Add zucchini into the meat mixture and stir well. Make medium-sized meatballs from your meat mixture.

Set pressure to succeed cooker to Pressure mode. Pour the organic olive oil into the pressure cooker contents. Place the meatballs in the pressure cooker and close the lid. Cook for about 10 minutes. When the dish is cooked, release pressure and open the load cooker lid. Remove the meatballs and **Serve:**.

Soup with Meatballs

Prep time: 10 minutes **Cooking time:** 15 minutes
Servings: 6- 8

Ingredients

7 oz. of ground pork
2carrot
A tbsp. of minced garlic
1 tsp. of ground black
pepper
1/2 cup of dill
An egg

1 tsp. of oregano
1 onion
6 cups of chicken stock
1 tsp. of paprika
1 tbsp. of flour

Directions

Skin the carrot and onion and chop them. Combine
the vegetables together and transfer them into the
pressure cooker. Set the load cooker to Pressure
mode. Add chicken stock and paprika. Combine the
soil pork, oregano, flour, and ground pork in a mixing
bowl.

Beat the egg and pour them into the pork mixture. Stir
the   Ingredients carefully. Make small meatballs using
the ground pork mixture place them in the pressure
cooker.

Close the cooker lid and cook for about 14 minutes.
Wash the dill and chop it. When the dish is cooked,
ladle it into serving bowls. Sprinkle the soup with the
dill and **Serve:**.

Pork Belly with Peanuts

Prep time: 10 minutes **Cooking time:** 25 minutes
Servings: 4- 6

Ingredients

5 oz. of peanut
1lb. of pork belly
1 tsp. of ground black
pepper
1 tbsp. of cilantro
1garlic cloves

1 cup of chicken stock
1 tbsp. of salt
1 tsp. of onion powder
1 tsp. of paprika
3tbsp. of fresh rosemary

Directions

Rub the pork belly with salt, ground black pepper,
onion powder, paprika, and cilantro. Set pressure
cooker to Pressure mode. Put the pork belly into the
cooker followed by rosemary and chicken stock.

Close pressure cooker lid and cook for about 25
minutes. Crush the peanuts. When the **Cooking
time:**ends, open pressure cooker lid and remove the
pork belly. Dry the pork belly with a paper towel.
After that, slice it and sprinkle crushed peanuts before
serving.

Pork with Every One of the Almonds and Sage

Prep time: 15 minutes **Cooking time:** 40 minutes
Servings: 5-7

Ingredients

3 lb. of pork loin
3 tbsp. of sage
3 garlic cloves
1 tsp. of lemon zest
1 tbsp. of almond flakes
A cup of almond milk

3 carrots
5 tbsp. of chicken stock
5tbsp. of extra-virgin olive
oil
1 tbsp. of salt

Directions

Pat the pork loin with the sage and leave them to chill
for about 10 minutes. Peel the garlic cloves and
carrots. Cut the carrots into halves. Place the garlic
cloves, halved carrots, and lemon zest into the
pressure cooker.

Add the fundamental organic olive oil, almond milk,
salt, and almond flakes. Set pressure cooker to Sauté
mode.
Put the pork into pressure cooker and close its lid.
Cook the dish on meat mode for about 40 minutes.

When the **Cooking time:**elapses, open the cooker
and remove the pork. Allow the pork-meal to cool a
bit. Slice it and **Serve:** while warm.

Rack of Lamb

Prep time: 15 minutes **Cooking time:** 25 minutes
Servings: 4-6

Ingredients

13 oz. of lamb rack
1tbsp. of Erythritol
A tsp. of ground black
pepper
3tbsp. of butter
1 tsp. of curry
1 tsp. of fresh rosemary

A cup of burgundy or
merlot wine
1 cup of chicken stock
1 onion
1 tbsp. of extra virgin
organic olive oil
1 tsp. of cilantro

Directions

Combine Erythritol, ground black pepper, cilantro,
chicken stock, curry, and rosemary in a mixing bowl
and stir.

Peel the onion and chop it. Add the chopped onion in
the mixture and stir. Place the lamb rack chicken stock
mixture and allow it to marinate for about 10 minutes
Set pressure cooker to Pressure mode. Add the butter
into pressure cooker and melt it. Add the marinated
lamb rack and sprinkle it with curry.

Secure the lid and cook for about 25 minutes. When
the **Cooking time:**elapses, remove your rack of lamb
meal from the cooker. Allow it to cool before serving.

Stew with Hawaiian Beef

Prep time: 20 minutes **Cooking time:** 25 minutes
Serve: 1

Ingredients

1 tablespoon vegetable oil	4 pounds stew beef
5 stalks celery	10 cups water
5 cloves garlic, minced	½ cup red wine
1 onion, cut into chunks	6 ounces can tomato paste
1 teaspoon ground black pepper	3 potatoes
2 tablespoons salt, or to taste	4 carrots
	3 bay leaves
¼ cup cornstarch	2 tablespoons white sugar
	¼ cup water

Directions

In a medium-high-heat saucepan, heat the oil. Cook and stir the meat for approximately 10 minutes or until browned. Cook for 2 to 3 minutes, or until the garlic is fragrant. Cook until the alcohol has cooked off, about 5 minutes. Cook until the celery and onions are soft, approximately 5 minutes.

Fill the saucepan with 10 glasses of water. Combine tomato paste, salt, sugar, bay leaves, and pepper in a mixing bowl. Bring the water to a boil. Reduce the heat to medium-low. Cook, covered, for 1 hour, or until meat is tender.

Cook until the carrots are slightly soft, about 10 minutes. Cook for 10 to 15 minutes, or until potatoes are soft. Combine the cornstarch and 1/4 cup water; add to the stew. Allow thickening for about 3 minutes.

Greek-Style Beef Pita

Prep time: 15 minutes **Cooking time:** 18 minutes
Serve: 1

Ingredients

1 pound beef sirloin tip steaks, cut 1/8 to 1/4-inch thick	3 teaspoons vegetable oil, divided
¾ cup plain or seasoned hummus	1 tbsp lemon pepper
	4 each whole-wheat pita bread, cut crosswise in half

Directions

Stack beef steaks and cut them half lengthwise, then crosswise into 1- inch broad strips. In a medium mixing dish, combine the beef and lemon pepper.

In a large nonstick pan, heat 2 teaspoons oil over medium-high heat until hot. Stir-fry 1/2 of the meat for 1 to 3 minutes, or until the outer surface of the beef is no longer pink. (Avoid overcooking.) Take out of the skillet. Repeat with the entire meat, adding the remaining 1 teaspoon oil to the skillet as needed.

Fill pita pockets equally with hummus. Fill with equal parts steak and preferred toppings.

Backyard Bourbon Beef Marinade

Prep time: 15 minutes **Cooking time:** 22 minutes
Serve: 1

Ingredients

1 cup Kikkoman Soy Sauce	¾ cup water
3 tablespoons bourbon	2 pounds beef flank steak
1 tbsp crushed garlic clove	2 tablespoons sugar
	1 tablespoon confectioners' sugar

Directions

Except for the beef flank steak, combine all Ingredients in a mixing bowl. Marinate the beef* in the marinade for 12 to 24 hours in the refrigerator. Grill using your preferred manner.

Grilled Beef Fajitas

Prep time: 18 minutes **Cooking time:** 20 minutes
Serve: 1

Ingredients

1 (1 ounces) package fajita seasoning mix	Reynolds Wrap® Heavy Duty Aluminum Foil
1-pound boneless beef top round steak	1 medium red or yellow bell pepper
1 medium green bell pepper, cut into strips	1 tablespoon vegetable oi
1 medium onion	l 8 (8 inches) flour tortillas
Salsa	

Directions

Prepare the fajita spice mix according to the package recommendations and pour over the meat. Marinate the steak for 1 to 2 hours in Reynolds Wrap® Heavy Duty Aluminum Foil.

Form two layers of foil around the outside of a 13x9x2inch baking pan to make a grill pan. Remove the foil and crimp the edges to make a tight rim, resulting in a pan with 1-inch sides. Place on a baking sheet.

Preheat the grill to high heat. Remove the steak from the marinade and discard the marinade. In a foil pan, combine the peppers, onion, and oil. Slide the foil pan from the cookie sheet onto the grill and set the steak next to it.
Grill on high for 8 to 10 minutes in a covered grill. After 5 minutes, stir the veggies and flip the steak. Remove the foil pan from the grill and place it on a cookie sheet. Thinly slice the grilled steak.

Wrap tortillas in foil and place them on the grill while carving meat. Wrap meat, peppers, and onions in warm tortillas and **Serve:** with salsa.

Lamb Chops

Prep time: 10 minutes **Cooking time:** 12 minutes
Servings: 3-5

Ingredients

14 oz. of ground lamb
2 white onions
1 tbsp. of salt
1/2 tsp. of ground rosemary
1 cup of fresh basil
1/4 tsp. of sage
1 egg

1tsp. of ground black pepper
1 tsp. of cilantro
1 tsp. of organic essential olive oil
1 tsp. of minced garlic
1 tsp. of paprika

Directions

Combine the ground lamb, ground black pepper, egg, salt, cilantro, ground rosemary, minced garlic, and paprika in a mixing bowl and stir well.

Peel the onions and dice them. Add the diced onion on the ground lamb mixture and stir well. Chop the basil and pour sage over it. Set pressure cooker to Sauté mode. Pour the virgin organic olive oil in to the pressure cooker and add basil mixture.

Sauté the amalgamation for about 2 minutes while stirring frequently. Remove the basil mixture from the cooker. Make medium-sized cutlets from the lamb mixture and hang them in the pressure cooker. Cook the cutlets for about 10 minutes or until golden brown on both sides. Remove the lamb cutlets from the cooker and allow it to cool before serving.

Lamb with Thyme

Prep time: 10 minutes **Cooking time:** 45 minutes
Servings: 6-8

Ingredients

1cup of fresh thyme
1 tbsp. of turmeric
1 tsp. of oregano
1lb. of lamb
1/4 cup of rice wine
1 tsp. of Erythritol
1/4 cup of chicken stock

1 tbsp. of essential olive oil
1 tbsp. of ground black pepper
4tbsp. of butter
1 tsp. of paprika

Directions

Chop the fresh thyme and mix it with oregano, ground black pepper, paprika, rice wine, Erythritol, chicken stock, and turmeric.

Sprinkle the lamb with the spice mixture and stir it carefully. Transfer the lamb mixture to a pressure cooker and add olive oil.

Close the pressure cooker lid and cook the dish on meat mode for about 45 minutes. When the lamb meal is cooked remove it from the pressure cooker. Allow it to rest and slice it. Enjoy!

Lamb Chops with Rosemary Sauce

Prep time: 10 minutes **Cooking time:** 52 minutes
Serving 8

Ingredients

8 lamb loin chops
Salt & black pepper to taste
For the sauce
1 tablespoon rosemary leaves
1 oz. plain flour
6 fl. oz. vegetable stock
2tablespoons cream, whipping

1small onion, peeled and chopped
1 onion, peeled and chopped
1 oz. butter
6 fl. oz. milk
Salt and black pepper, to taste

Directions

Place the lamb loin chops, and onion in a baking tray, then drizzle salt and black pepper on top. Choose "Power Button" of Air Fry Oven and turn the dial to select the "Bake" mode. Choose the Time button and again turn the dial to set the **Cooking time:**to 45 minutes.

Now press the Temp button and rotate the dial to set the temperature at 350 degrees F. Once preheated, set the lamb baking tray in the oven and close its lid.

Set the white sauce by melting butter in a saucepan the sti in onions Sauté for 5 minutes, then stir flour and stir cook for 2 minutes. Stir in the rest of the ingredients and mix well. Pour the sauce over baked chops and **Serve:**.

Garlicky Lamb Chops

Prep time: 10 minutes **Cooking time:** 45 minutes
Serving 8

Ingredients

8 medium lamb chops
2 garlic cloves, crushed
1teaspoon dried oregano
1 teaspoon salt

3 thin lemon slices
1/2 teaspoon black pepper
1/4 cup olive oil

Directions

Set the medium lamb chops in a baking tray and rub them with olive oil. Attach lemon slices, garlic, oregano, salt, and black pepper on top of the lamb chops.

Choose "Power Button" of Air Fry Oven and turn the dial to select the "Air Roast" mode. Choose the Time button and again turn the dial to set the **Cooking time:**to 45 minutes.

Now press the Temp button and rotate the dial to set the temperature at 400 degrees F. Once preheated, set the lamb baking tray in the oven and close its lid. Slice and **Serve:** warm.

Glazed Sausage

Prep time: 10 minutes **Cooking time:** 15 minutes
Servings: 4-6

Ingredients

1tbsp. of Erythritol	1 tbsp. of coconut flour
1 tbsp. of butter	6 oz. of ground chicken
1 lb. of ground pork	1 tbsp. of salt
1tbsp. of liquid stevia	1 tsp. of cilantro
1 tsp. of oregano	1 onion
1 tsp. of water	1 tbsp. of ground black pepper

Directions

Peel the onion and grate it. Pour the grated onion, ground pork, ground chicken, salt, oregano, cilantro, and ground black pepper in a mixing bowl. Add the coconut flour and mix well. Combine liquid stevia, Erythritol, and water in another bowl.

Stir the mixture well to dissolve Erythritol, make medium-sized sausages patties from the meat mixture. Set the pressure cooker to Sauté mode. Add the butter into the cooker and allow it melt. Pour the sausage patties into the pressure cooker and sauté the patties for about 4 minutes.

Sprinkle the sausage patties with liquid stevia mixture and close the lid. Cook the dish for another 10 minutes on Sauté mode. When the **Cooking time:**ends, remove the cooked sausage patties from pressure cooker and **Serve:**.

Roast Lamb Shoulder

Prep time: 10 minutes **Cooking time:** 60 minutes
Serving 2

Ingredients

1lb. boneless lamb shoulder roast	1 tablespoon rosemary, chopped
4 cloves garlic, minced	2teaspoon thyme leaves
3tablespoon olive oil, divided Salt	Black pepper
2 lb. baby potatoes halved	

Directions

Toss potatoes with all the herbs, seasonings, and oil in a baking tray. Choose "Power Button" of Air Fry Oven and turn the dial to select the "Air Roast" mode.

Choose the Time button and again turn the dial to set the Cooking time to 60 minutes.

Now rest the Temp button and rotate the dial to set the temperature at 370 degrees F. Once preheated, set the lamb baking tray in the oven and close its lid. Slice and **Serve:** warm.

Chops of Ginger Pork

Prep time: 10 minutes **Cooking time:** 35 minutes
Servings: 3-5

Ingredients

2 tbsp. of ground ginger	1 cup of soy sauce
1lb. of pork chop	1 tsp. of parsley
1 tsp. of ground black pepper	1 tbsp. of freshly-squeezed lemon juice
1 tsp. of garlic powder	1 cup of water

Directions

Combine the soy sauce and water in a mixing bowl. Add fresh lemon juice and mix.

Sprinkle the mixture with ground ginger, parsley, ground black pepper, and garlic powder. Add freshly squeezed lemon juice and stir well.

Cut the pork chop roughly using a sharp object. Put the pork on the soy sauce mixture and allow it to sit for about 15 minutes.

Set pressure cooker to Sauté mode. Place the amalgamation into the cooker and close its lid. Cook the dish for about 35 minutes. When cooked, open pressure cooker lid and **Serve:** the ginger pork chops while hot.

Salisbury Steak

Prep time: 10 minutes **Cooking time:** 15 minutes
Servings: 3-5

Ingredients

1/2 cup of onion soup mix	2eggs
A cup of water	1 tsp. of tomato paste
1lb. of ground beef	A tbsp. of mustard
A tsp. of ground white pepper	1 tsp. of salt
	1 tbsp. of extra virgin organic olive oil

Directions

Whisk the eggs in the mixing bowl and whisk them. Add the mustard, salt, and ground white pepper, stir well until smooth. Dip the beef in the egg mixture and ensure it mixes well. Make mid-sized balls from the meat mixture and flatten them.

Set the pressure cooker to Sauté mode and pour the olive oil into pressure and preheat it in sauté mode. Add the steaks and sauté the dish for 2 minutes on both sides. Combine the tomato paste and onion soup together and stir well.

Pour the soup mixture to the pressure cooker and close the lid. Cook the dish on Pressure mode for about 5 minutes. When the Cooking time elapses, remove Salisbury steak from the pressure cooker and **Serve:** with gravy.

Almond Flour 'n Egg Crusted Beef

Prep time: 10 Minutes **Cooking time:** 15 minutes
Servings: 1

Ingredients

1/2 cup almond flour
1 egg beaten
1 slice of lemon to **Serve:**

1/2-pound beef schnitzel
2 tablespoons vegetable oil

Directions

Preheat the air fryer for 5 minutes. Mix the oil and almond flour together. Dip the schnitzel into the egg and dredge in the almond flour mixture.

Press the almond flour so that it sticks on to the beef. Set in the air fryer and cook for 15 minutes at 3500F. **Serve:** with a slice of lemon.

Easy Teriyaki BBQ Recipe

Prep time: 10 Minutes **Cooking time:** 15 minutes
Servings: 2

Ingredients

1 tablespoon honey
1 tablespoon mirin
14 oz. lean diced steak, with fat trimmed

1 tablespoon soy sauce
1 thumb-sized piece of fresh
ginger, grated

Directions

Merge all Ingredients in a bowl and marinate for at least an hour. Turning over halfway through marinating time.
Thread mead into skewers. Place on skewer rack.
Cook for 5 minutes at 390oF or to desired doneness.
Serve: and enjoy.

Apricot Glazed Pork Tenderloins

Prep time: 10 Minutes **Cooking time:** 30 minutes
Servings: 3
Ingredients

1/2 teaspoon salt
2 tablespoons minced fresh rosemary or 1 tablespoon dried rosemary, crushed
3 tablespoons lemon juice
1 cup apricot

1/2 teaspoon pepper
2 tablespoons olive oil, divided
4 garlic cloves, minced
Apricot Glaze Ingredients
2 garlic cloves, minced
1-lb pork tenderloin

Directions

Mix well pepper, salt, garlic, oil, and rosemary. Brush all over pork. If needed cut pork crosswise in half to fit in air fryer. Lightly grease baking pan of air fryer with cooking spray. Add pork. For 3 minutes per side, brown pork in a preheated 390F air fryer. Meanwhile, mix well all glaze Ingredients in a small bowl. Baste pork every 5 minutes. Cook for 20 minutes at 330F.
Serve: and enjoy.

Kansas City Baby Back Rib Recipe

Prep time: 10 Minutes **Cooking time:** 50 minutes
Servings: 2

Ingredients

1/4 cup apple cider vinegar 1/4 cup molasses
1 tablespoon brown sugar
1 tbsp Worcestershire sauce
1 teaspoon dry mustard
1-pound pork ribs, small
2 cloves of garlic

1/4 teaspoon cayenne pepper
1 tablespoon liquid smoke seasoning, hickory
Salt and pepper to taste
1 cup ketchup

Directions

Bring all ingredients in a Ziploc bag and allow marinating in the fridge for at least 2 hours. Preheat the air fryer to 390F. Place the grill pan accessory in the air fryer.

Grill meat for 25 minutes per batch. Flip the meat halfway through the cooking time.

Bacon, Spinach and Feta Quiche

Prep time: 10 Minutes **Cooking time:** 30 minutes
Servings: 3

Ingredients

6 EGGS
1/2-pound fresh spinach
3 slices bacon, chopped
1 1/2 teaspoons butter
1-1 /2 ounces crumbled feta cheese

salt and freshly ground pepper to taste
1/2 pinch cayenne pepper
1/2 pinch salt
1/4 onion, diced

Directions

Lightly grease baking pan of air fryer with butter. Add spinach and for 2 minutes, cook on 360F.
Drain well the spinach and squeeze dry. Chop and set aside.

Add bacon in air fryer pan and cook for 6 minutes or until crisped. Discard excess fat.
Stir in onion and season with salt. Cook for another 5 minutes. Stir in chopped spinach and cook for another 5 minutes to heat through.

Meanwhile, in a bowl whisk well eggs, cayenne pepper, black pepper, and salt. Remove basket, evenly spread mixture in pan, and pour in eggs. Sprinkle feta cheese on top.

Cook for another 15 minutes, until eggs are cooked to desired doneness. **Serve:** and enjoy.

Casserole with Bacon and Cheeseburgers

Prep time: 10 Minutes **Cooking time:** 35 minutes
Servings: 6

Ingredients

1small onion, chopped
1 tablespoon Worcestershire sauce
1/2 can (15 ounces) tomato sauce
1/4 cup sliced dill pickles
6 bacon strips, cooked and crumbled
8-ounces frozen Tater Tots
1 tbsp ground mustard
1-pound ground beef
1/2 cup grape tomatoes, chopped
1/2 cup shredded cheddar cheese
4-ounces process cheese (Velveeta)

Directions

Lightly grease baking pan of air fryer with cooking spray. Add beef and half of onions. For 10 minutes, cook on 390F. Halfway through cooking time, stir and crumble beef.

Stir in Worcestershire, mustard, Velveeta, and tomato sauce. Mix well. Cook for 4 minutes until melted. Mix well and evenly spread in pan. Top with cheddar cheese and then bacon strips.

Evenly top with tater tots. Cover pan with foil. Cook for 15 minutes at 390F. Uncover and bake for 10 minutes more until tops are lightly browned. **Serve:** and enjoy topped with pickles and tomatoes and remaining onion.

Baked Cheese 'n Pepperoni Calzone

Prep time: 10 Minutes **Cooking time:** 25 minutes
Servings: 4

Ingredients

1cup chopped pepperoni
1 to 2 tablespoons 2% milk
1 tablespoon grated Parmesan cheese
1/4 cup shredded part-skim mozzarella cheese
1 loaf frozen bread dough, thawed
1/2 teaspoon Italian seasoning, optional
1/2 cup pasta sauce with meat

Directions

In a bowl mix well mozzarella cheese, pizza sauce, and pepperoni. On a lightly floured surface, divide dough into four portions. Set each into a 6-in. circle; top each with a scant 1/3 cup pepperoni mixture. Fold dough over filling; pinch edges to seal.

Lightly grease baking pan of air fryer with cooking spray. Place dough in a single layer and if needed, cook in batches. For 25 minutes, cook on 330F preheated air fryer or until dough is lightly browned. **Serve:** and enjoy.

Beef Recipe Texas-Rodeo Style

Prep time: 10 Minutes **Cooking time:** 1 hour **Servings:** 6

Ingredients

1/2 cup honey
1/2 teaspoon dry mustard
1clove of garlic, minced
Salt and pepper to taste
1/2 cup ketchup
3pounds beef steak sliced
1 tablespoon chili powder
2onion, chopped

Directions

Stick all Ingredients in a Ziploc bag and allow marinating in the fridge for at least 2 hours. Preheat the air fryer to 390F. Place the grill pan accessory in the air fryer.

Grill the beef for 15 minutes per batch making sure that you flip it every 8 minutes for even grilling. Meanwhile, pour the marinade on a saucepan and allow simmering over medium heat until the sauce thickens. Baste the beef with the sauce before serving.

Beef Roast in Worcestershire-Rosemary

Prep time: 10 Minutes **Cooking time:** 2 hours **Servings:** 6

Ingredients

1onion, chopped
1 tbs Worcestershire sauce
3 stalks of celery, sliced
1-pound beef chuck roast
2cloves of garlic, minced
1 tablespoon butter
1 teaspoon thyme
1 teaspoon rosemary
2cups water
3tablespoons olive oil

Directions

Preheat the air fryer for 5 minutes. Set all Ingredients in a deep baking dish that will fit in the air fryer. Bake for 2 hours at 350F. Braise the meat with its sauce every 30 minutes until cooked.

Beefy Bell Pepper 'n Egg Scramble

Prep time: 10 Minutes **Cooking time:** 30 minutes
Servings: 4

Ingredients

1green bell pepper, seeded and chopped
3tablespoons olive oil
6 cups eggs, beaten
1-pound ground beef
2cloves of garlic, minced
Salt and pepper to taste
1 onion, chopped

Directions

Preheat the air fryer for 5 minutes with baking pan insert.
In a baking dish mix the ground beef, onion, garlic, olive oil, and bell pepper. Season with salt and pepper to taste.
Pour in the beaten eggs and give a good stir. Place the dish with the beef and egg mixture in the air fryer. Bake for 30 minutes at 330F.

Tenders of Pork with Bell Peppers

Prep time: 5 minutes **Cooking time:** 15 minutes
Servings: 4

Ingredients

11 Oz Pork Tenderloin
1 Bell Pepper, in thin strips
Pepper to taste
1/2 tbsp. Mustard

1 tbsp. Olive Oil
1 Red Onion, sliced
1 Tsps. Provencal Herbs
Black

Directions

Preparing the Ingredients. Preheat the Pro Breeze air fryer to 390 degrees. In the oven dish, mix the bell pepper strips with the onion, herbs, and some salt and pepper to taste.

Attach half a tablespoon of olive oil Divide the pork tenderloin into four pieces and rub it with salt, pepper, and mustard.
Thinly coat the pieces with remaining olive oil and place them upright in the oven dish on top of the pepper mixture

Air Frying. Place the bowl into the Air fryer. Set the timer to 20 minutes and roast the meat and the vegetables
Turn the meat and mix the peppers halfway through
Serve: with a fresh salad

Wonton Meatballs

Prep time: 15 minutes **Cooking time:** 10 minutes
Servings: 4

Ingredients

1-pound ground pork
2 large eggs
fresh ginger cloves garlic, minced
1 teaspoons soy sauce

1/2 teaspoon kosher salt

1/4 cup chopped green onions
1/4 cup chopped fresh cilantro tablespoon minced
1 teaspoon oyster sauce
1 teaspoon black pepper

Directions

Preparing the Ingredients, merge the pork, eggs, green onions, cilantro, ginger, garlic, soy sauce, oyster sauce, salt, and pepper.

Merge on low speed until all of the ingredients are incorporated, 2 to 3 minutes. Form the mixture into 12 meatballs and arrange in a single layer in the air fryer basket.

Air Frying. Set the Pro Breeze air fryer to 350F for 10 minutes. Use a meat thermometer to ensure the meatballs have reached an internal temperature of 145F. Set the meatballs to a bowl and **Serve**

Easy Air Fryer Marinated Pork Tenderloin

Prep time: 1 hour and 10 minutes **Cooking time:** 30 minutes
Servings: 4 to 6

Ingredients

1/4 cup olive oil
1/4 cup freshly squeezed lemon juice

1/2 teaspoon freshly ground black pepper

1/4 cup of soy sauce
1 tablespoon Dijon mustard
1 teaspoon salt
1 pounds pork tenderloin
1 garlic clove, minced

Directions

Preparing the Ingredients. In a mixing bowl, make the marinade. Mix the olive oil, soy sauce, lemon juice, minced garlic, Dijon mustard, salt, and pepper. Re**Serve:** 1/4 cup of the marinade.

Place the tenderloin in a large bowl and pour the remaining marinade over the meat. Cover and marinate in the refrigerator for about 1 hour. Place the marinated pork tenderloin into the air fryer basket.

Air Frying. Set the temperature of your Pro Breeze AF to 400F. Set the timer and roast for 10 minutes. Using tongs flip the pork and baste it with half of the re**Serve:**d marinade. Reset the timer and roast for 10 minutes more.
Using tongs, flip the pork, and then baste with the remaining marinade.

Reset the timer and roast for another 10 minutes, for a total Cooking time of 30 minutes.

Barbecue Flavored Pork Ribs

Prep time: 5 minutes **Cooking time:** 15 minutes
Servings: 6

Ingredients

1/4 cup honey, divided
3/4 cup BBQ sauce
1 tablespoon soy sauce
13/4 pound pork ribs
1/2 teaspoon garlic powder

2 tablespoons tomato ketchup
1 tablespoon Worcestershire sauce
Freshly ground white pepper, to taste

Directions

Preparing the Ingredients. In a large bowl, merge 3 tablespoons of honey and the remaining ingredients except for the pork ribs. Refrigerate to marinate for about 20 minutes.

Preheat the Pro Breeze air fryer to 355 degrees F. Place the ribs in an Air fryer basket.

Air Frying. Cook for about 13 minutes. Detach the ribs from the Air fryer and coat with remaining honey.
Serve: hot.

Fried Egg Rolls with Beef Tacos

Prep time: 10 minutes **Cooking time:** 15 minutes
Serving 8

Ingredients

1tsp. cilantro	1chopped garlic cloves
1 C. shredded Mexican cheese	1/2 can cilantro lime rote
	1/2 chopped onion
1/2 packet taco seasoning	1 tbsp. olive oil
16 egg roll wrappers	1 pound lean ground beef

Directions

Ensure that your air fryer is preheated to 400 degrees. Add onions and garlic to a skillet, cooking till fragrant. Then add taco seasoning, pepper, salt, and beef, cooking till beef is broke up into tiny pieces and cooked thoroughly. Add rotel and stir well.

Lay out egg wrappers and brush with water to soften a bit.
Load wrappers with beef filling and add cheese to each.
Fold diagonally to close and use water to secure edges. Brush filled egg wrappers with olive oil and add to the air fryer. Cook 8 minutes, flip, and cook another 4 minutes.
Serve:d sprinkled with cilantro.

Lamb Baked with Tomato Topping

Prep time: 10 minutes **Cooking time:** 1hr 40 minutes
Serving 8

Ingredients

8 lamb shoulder chops, trimmed	1tablespoon olive oil
	1/4 cup plain flour
1 large brown onion, chopped	2medium carrots, peeled and diced
2garlic cloves, crushed	2 tablespoons tomato paste
2 1/2 cups beef stock	1 cup frozen peas
2cups potato gems	2 dried bay leaves

Directions

Dust the lamb chops with flour and sear it in a pan layered with olive oil. Sear the lamb chops for 4 minutes per side. Transfer the chops to a baking tray.

Add onion, garlic, and carrot to the same pan. Sauté for 5 minutes, then stir in tomato paste, stock and all other Ingredients. Stir cook for 4 minutes then pour this sauce over the chops.

Choose "Power Button" of Air Fry Oven and turn the dial to select the "Bake" mode. Choose the Time button and again turn the dial to set the **Cooking time:**to 1 hr. 30 minutes. Now press the Temp button and rotate the dial to set the temperature at 350 degrees F. Once preheated, place the baking pan in the oven and close its lid. **Serve:** warm.

Pub Style Corned Beef Egg Rolls

Prep time: 10 minutes **Cooking time:** 5 minutes
Serving 10

Ingredients

Olive oil	1/2 C. orange marmalade
4 C. corned beef and cabbage	10 egg roll wrappers
	Brandy Mustard Sauce
1egg	1/16th tsp. pepper
1tbsp. whole grain mustard 1 tsp. dry mustard powder	1/2 C. chicken stock
	1/4 C. brandy
	5 slices of Swiss cheese
1 C. heavy cream	
1/4 tsp. curry powder	1 minced shallot
1/2 tbsp. cilantro	3/4 C. dry white wine
2tbsp. ghee	

Directions

To make mustard sauce, add shallots and ghee to skillet, cooking until softened. Then add brandy and wine, heating to a low boil. Cook 5 minutes for liquids to reduce. Add stock and seasonings. Simmer 5 minutes.
Turn down heat and add heavy cream. Cook on low till sauce reduces and it covers the back of a spoon. Place sauce in the fridge to chill.

Crack the egg in a bowl and set to the side. Lay out an egg wrapper with the corner towards you. Brush the edges with egg wash. Place 1/3 cup of corned beef mixture into the center along with 2 tablespoons of marmalade and 1/2 a slice of Swiss cheese.

Fold the bottom corner over filling. As you are folding the sides, make sure they are stick well to the first flap you made. Place filled rolls into prepared air fryer basket. Spritz rolls with olive oil. Cook 10 minutes at 390 degrees, shaking halfway through cooking. **Serve:** rolls with Brandy Mustard sauce and devour!

Roasted Stuffed Peppers

Prep time: 10 minutes **Cooking time:** 5 minutes
Serving 4

Ingredients

4 ounces shredded cheddar cheese	1/2 tsp. salt
	1/2 tsp. pepper
1tsp. Worcestershire sauce	1/2 C. tomato sauce
8 ounces lean ground beef	1 tsp. olive oil
1 minced garlic clove	1/2 chopped onion
2green peppers	

Directions

Ensure your air fryer is preheated to 390 degrees. Spray with olive oil. Cut stems off bell peppers and remove seeds. Cook in boiling salted water for 3 minutes.
Sauté garlic and onion together in a skillet until golden in color. Take skillet off the heat. Mix pepper, salt,

Poultry Recipes

Turkey with Chili Mayo for the Holidays

(**Ready in about** 45 minutes | **Servings:** 4)

Ingredients

3 teaspoons olive oil
1/2 teaspoon marjoram
Coarse salt and ground black pepper, to taste
1/4 cup mayonnaise
1 tablespoon chili sauce
1 teaspoon basil
1/2 tbsp garlic powder
1 teaspoon shallot powder
2 pounds turkey breast, boneless Chili mayo
1/4 cup sour cream
1/2 teaspoon stone-ground mustard

Directions

Start by preheating your Air Fryer to 360 degrees F.

In a mixing bowl, thoroughly combine the olive oil with spices. Rub the turkey breast with the spice mixture until it is well coated on all sides. Air fry for 40 minutes, turning them over halfway through the cooking time.

Your instant-read thermometer should read 165 degrees.

Meanwhile, mix all of the Ingredients for the chili mayo. Place in your refrigerator until ready to **Serve:**.

Place the turkey breast skin-side up on a cutting board and slice it against the grain; **Serve:** with chili mayo and enjoy!

Garlic Butter Chicken Wings

(**Ready in about** 20 minutes | **Servings:** 3)

Ingredients

1 pound chicken wings
1 teaspoon garlic paste
1 lemon, cut into slices
Salt black pepper, to taste
2 tablespoons butter

Directions

Pat dry the chicken wings with a kitchen towel and season all over with salt and black pepper. In a bowl, mix together butter and garlic paste. Rub the mixture all over the wings.

Cook in the preheated Air Fryer at 380 degrees F for 18 minutes. **Serve:** garnished with lemon slices. Bon appétit!

Chicken Burgers from Scratch

(**Ready in about** 20 minutes | **Servings:** 4)

Ingredients

1 ¼ pounds chicken white meat, ground
1/2 white onion, finely chopped
Sea salt and ground black pepper, to taste
1 ½ cups breadcrumbs
2 small pickles, sliced
1 teaspoon fresh garlic, finely chopped
1 teaspoon paprika
4 burger buns
1/2 cup cornmeal
2 tablespoons ketchup
4 lettuce leaves
1 teaspoon yellow mustard

Directions

Thoroughly combine the chicken, onion, garlic, salt and black pepper in a mixing dish. Form the mixture into 4 equal patties. In a shallow bowl, mix paprika with cornmeal and breadcrumbs. Dip each patty in this mixture, pressing to coat well on both sides.

Spritz a cooking basket with a nonstick cooking spray. Air fry the burgers at 370 degrees F for about 11 minutes or to your desired degree of doneness.

Place your burgers on burger buns and **Serve:** with toppings. Bon appétit!

Italian-Style Turkey Meatballs

(**Ready in about** 20 minutes | **Servings:** 5)

Ingredients

1 ½ pounds ground turkey
1/2 cup tortilla chips, crumbled
1 egg, beaten
2 tablespoons Italian parsley, finely chopped
1 teaspoon Italian seasoning mix
1/2 cup parmesan cheese, grated
1 yellow onion, finely chopped
2 cloves garlic, minced
1 tablespoon soy sauce
1 teaspoon olive oil

Directions

Combine all of the Ingredients listed above until thoroughly combined. Form the mixture into 10 meatballs.

Spritz a nonstick cooking spray into a cooking basket. Cook at 360°F for about 10 minutes, or until done to your liking. Good appetite!

Spanish Chicken with Golden Potatoes

(**Ready in about** 25 minutes | **Servings:** 4)

Ingredients

2 tablespoons butter, melted

1 pound Yukon Gold potatoes, peeled and diced

1 teaspoon dried rosemary, crushed

1 teaspoon dried thyme, crushed

1/3 teaspoon freshly ground black pepper

4 chicken drumsticks bonein

1 teaspoon fresh garlic, minced

1 teaspoon cayenne pepper

1 lemon, 1/2 juiced, 1/2 cut into wedges

2 tablespoons sherry

Kosher salt, to taste

Directions

Start by preheating your Air Fryer to 370 degrees F. Then, grease a baking pan with the melted butter. Arrange the chicken drumsticks in the baking pan. Bake in the preheated Air Fryer for 8 minutes. Add the diced potatoes.

Drizzle chicken and potatoes with lemon juice. Sprinkle with garlic, rosemary, thyme, cayenne pepper, black pepper, and salt. Turn the temperature to 400 degrees F and cook for a further 12 minutes. Make sure to shake the basket once or twice. Remove from the Air Fryer basket and sprinkle sherry on top. **Serve:** with the lemon wedges. Enjoy

Pizza Spaghetti Casserole

(**Ready in about** 30 minutes | **Servings:** 4)

Ingredients

8 ounces spaghetti

2 tomatoes, pureed

1/2 cup Asiago cheese, shredded

3 tablespoons Romano cheese, grated

1 pound smoked chicken sausage, sliced

1 tablespoon Italian seasoning mix

1 tablespoon fresh basil leaves, chiffonade

Directions

Bring a large pot of lightly salted water to a boil. Cook your spaghetti for 10 minutes or until al dente; drain and re**Serve:**, keeping warm.

Stir in the chicken sausage, tomato puree, Asiago cheese, and Italian seasoning mix.

Then, spritz a baking pan with cooking spray; add the spaghetti mixture to the pan. Bake in the preheated Air Fryer at 325 degrees F for 11 minutes.

Top with the grated Romano cheese. Turn the temperature to 390 degrees F and cook an additional 5 minutes or until everything is thoroughly heated and the cheese is melted.

Garnish with fresh basil leaves. Bon appétit!

Breakfast Frittata with Turkey

(**Ready in about** 50 minutes | **Servings:** 4)

Ingredients

1 tablespoon olive oil

3 tablespoons Greek yogurt

1/4 teaspoon red pepper flakes, crushed Himalayan salt, to taste

1 green bell pepper, seeded and sliced

1 pound turkey breasts, slices

3 tablespoons Cottage cheese, crumbled

1 red bell pepper, seeded and sliced

1/4 teaspoon ground black pepper

6 large-sized eggs

Directions

Grease the cooking basket with olive oil. Add the turkey and cook in the preheated Air Fryer at 350 degrees F for 30 minutes, flipping them over halfway through. Cut into bite-sized strips and re**Serve:**.

Now, beat the eggs with Greek yogurt, cheese, black pepper, red pepper, and salt. Add the bell peppers to a baking pan that is previously lightly greased with a cooking spray. Add the turkey strips; pour the egg mixture over all Ingredients. Bake in the preheated Air Fryer at 360 degrees F for 15 minutes. **Serve:** right away!

Nana's Turkey Chili

(**Ready in about** 1 hour | **Servings:** 4)

Ingredients

1/2 medium-sized leek, chopped

1 jalapeno pepper, seeded and minced

2 cups tomato puree

1 pound ground turkey, 85% lean 15% fat

1/2 teaspoon black peppercorns

1 teaspoon mustard seeds

2 garlic cloves, minced

1/2 red onion, chopped

2 tablespoons olive oil

1 bell pepper, seeded and chopped

2 cups chicken stock

Salt, to taste

1 teaspoon chili powder

1 teaspoon ground cumin

1 (12-ounce) can kidney beans, rinsed and drained

Directions

Start by preheating your Air Fryer to 365 degrees F.

Place the leeks, onion, garlic and peppers in a baking pan; drizzle olive oil evenly over the top. Cook for 4 to 6 minutes. Add the ground turkey. Cook for 6 minutes more or until the meat is no longer pink.

Now, add the tomato puree, 1 cup of chicken stock, black peppercorns, salt, chili powder, mustard seeds, and cumin to the baking pan. Cook for 24 minutes, stirring every 7 to 10 minutes. Stir in the canned beans and the remaining 1 cup of stock; let it cook for a further 9 minutes; make sure to stir halfway through. Bon appétit!

Filets of Asian Chicken with Cheese

(**Ready in about** 50 minutes | **Servings:** 2)

Ingredients

4 rashers smoked bacon
1 teaspoon garlic, minced
1/4 tbsp black pepper, preferably freshly ground
1 tbsp mild curry powder
1 tbsp black mustard seeds
1/2 cup Pecorino Romano cheese, freshly grated

1/2 tbsp coarse sea salt
1/2 cup coconut milk
1 (2-inch) piece ginger, peeled and minced
2 chicken filets
1/3 cup tortilla chips, crushed

Directions

Start by preheating your Air Fryer to 400 degrees F. Add the smoked bacon and cook in the preheated Air Fryer for 5 to 7 minutes. Re**Serve:**.

In a mixing bowl, place the chicken fillets, salt, black pepper, garlic, ginger, mustard seeds, curry powder, and milk. Let it marinate in your refrigerator about 30 minutes.

In another bowl, mix the crushed chips and grated Pecorino Romano cheese.

Dredge the chicken fillets through the chips mixture and transfer them to the cooking basket. Reduce the temperature to 380 degrees F and cook the chicken for 6 minutes.

Turn them over and cook for a further 6 minutes. Repeat the process until you have run out of Ingredients.

Serve: with re**Serve:**d bacon. Enjoy!

Roasted Citrus Turkey Drumsticks

(**Ready in about** 55 minutes | **Servings:** 3)

Ingredients

3 medium turkey drumsticks, bone-in
1 teaspoon cayenne pepper
1 teaspoon dried parsley flakes
Zest of one orange
1/4 cup orange juice

Sea salt and ground black pepper, to taste
1 teaspoon fresh garlic, minced
1 teaspoon onion powder
1/2 butter stick, melted

Directions

Rub all Ingredients onto the turkey drumsticks.

Preheat your Air Fryer to 400 degrees F. Cook the turkey drumsticks for 16 minutes in the preheated Air Fryer.

Loosely cover with foil and cook an additional 24 minutes.

Once cooked, let it rest for 10 minutes before slicing and serving. Bon appétit!

Turkey Bacon with Scrambled Eggs

(**Ready in about** 25 minutes | **Servings:** 4)

Ingredients

1/2 pound turkey bacon
2 tablespoons yogurt
1/2 teaspoon sea salt
2 green onions, finely chopped
4 eggs

1/3 cup milk
1 bell pepper, finely chopped
1/2 cup Colby cheese, shredded

Directions

Place the turkey bacon in the cooking basket.

Cook at 360 degrees F for 9 to 11 minutes. Work in batches. Re**Serve:** the fried bacon.

In a mixing bowl, thoroughly whisk the eggs with milk and yogurt. Add salt, bell pepper, and green onions.

Brush the sides and bottom of the baking pan with the re**Serve:**d 1 teaspoon of bacon grease.

Pour the egg mixture into the baking pan. Cook at 355 degrees F about 5 minutes. Top with shredded Colby cheese and cook for 5 to 6 minutes more. **Serve:** the scrambled eggs with the re**Serve:**d bacon and enjoy!

Chinese Duck (Xiang Su Ya)

(**Ready in about** 30 minutes + marinating time | **Servings:** 6)

Ingredients

2 pounds duck breast, boneless
1 teaspoon Chinese 5-spice powder
1 teaspoon Szechuan peppercorns
1 teaspoon coarse salt
1/4 cup molasses

1 tbsp light soy sauce
2 green onions, chopped
1/2 teaspoon ground black pepper Glaze
3 tablespoons Shaoxing rice wine
1 tablespoon soy sauce
3 tablespoons orange juice

Directions

In a ceramic bowl, place the duck breasts, green onions, light soy sauce, Chinese 5-spice powder, Szechuan peppercorns, and Shaoxing rice wine. Let it marinate for 1 hour in your refrigerator.

Preheat your Air Fryer to 400 degrees F for 5 minutes.

Now, discard the marinade and season the duck breasts with salt and pepper. Cook the duck breasts for 12 to 15 minutes or until they are golden brown.

Repeat with the other Ingredients. In the meantime, add the re**Serve:**d marinade to the saucepan that is preheated over medium-high heat. Add the molasses, orange juice, and 1 tablespoon of soy sauce. Bring to a simmer and then, whisk constantly until it gets syrupy. Brush the surface of duck breasts with glaze so they are completely covered. Place duck breasts back in the Air Fryer basket; cook an additional 5 minutes. Enjoy!

Chicken with Golden Roasted Cauliflower

(**Ready in about** 30 minutes | **Servings:** 4)

Ingredients

2 pounds chicken legs
2 tablespoons olive oil
1 teaspoon sea salt
1 teaspoon dried marjoram
2 garlic cloves minced
1/3 cup Pecorino Romano cheese, freshly grated

1/2 teaspoon ground black pepper
1 tbsp smoked paprika
1 (1-pound) head cauliflower, broken into small florets
1/2 teaspoon dried thyme
Salt, to taste

Directions

Toss the chicken legs with the olive oil, salt, black pepper, paprika, and marjoram.

Cook in the preheated Air Fryer at 380 degrees F for 11 minutes. Flip the chicken legs and cook for a further 5 minutes.

Toss the cauliflower florets with garlic, cheese, thyme, and salt.

Increase the temperature to 400 degrees F; add the cauliflower florets and cook for 12 more minutes. **Serve:** warm.

Adobo Seasoned Chicken with Veggies

(**Ready in about** 1 hour 30 minutes | **Servings:** 4)

Ingredients

2 pounds chicken wings, rinsed and patted dry
1/2 teaspoon red pepper flakes, crushed
1 teaspoon granulated onion 1 teaspoon ground turmeric
2 cloves garlic, peeled but not chopped
2 tbsp tomato powder
2 bell peppers, seeded and sliced
4 carrots, trimmed and halved

1/4 teaspoon ground black pepper
1 teaspoon paprika
1 teaspoon coarse sea salt
1 tablespoon dry Madeira wine
2 stalks celery, diced
1 large Spanish onion, diced
1 teaspoon ground cumin
2 tablespoons olive oil

Directions

In a large mixing bowl, combine all of the Ingredients. Cover and place in the refrigerator for 1 hour.

Place the chicken wings in a baking dish.

Cook the chicken wings for 7 minutes in a preheated Air Fryer at 380 degrees F.

Cook for 15 minutes more after adding the vegetables, shaking the basket once or twice. **Serve:** hot.

Baked Chicken and Brown Rice

(**Ready in about** 50 minutes | **Servings:** 3)

Ingredients

1 cup brown rice
1 tablespoon butter, melted
Kosher salt and ground black pepper, to taste
1 onion, chopped
1 cup tomato puree

2 cups vegetable broth
2 garlic cloves, minced
1/2 cup water
3 chicken fillets
1 tbsp cayenne pepper
1 tablespoon fresh chives, chopped

Directions

Heat the brown rice, vegetable broth and water in a pot over high heat. Bring it to a boil; turn the stove down to simmer and cook for 35 minutes.

Grease a baking pan with butter.

Spoon the prepared rice mixture into the baking pan. Add the onion, garlic, salt, black pepper, cayenne pepper, and chicken. Spoon the tomato puree over the chicken.

Cook in the preheated Air Fryer at 380 degrees F for 12 minutes. **Serve:** garnished with fresh chives. Enjoy!

Sticky Exotic Chicken Drumettes

(**Ready in about** 25 minutes | **Servings:** 4)

Ingredients

2 tablespoons peanut oil
1 tablespoon yellow mustard
2 tablespoons honey
1/2 teaspoon sambal oelek
1/4 cup chicken broth
1 ½ pounds chicken drumettes, bone-in
Salt and ground white pepper, to taste

1 tablespoon tamari sauce
1 clove garlic, peeled and minced
2 tablespoons fresh orange juice

1/2 cup raw onion rings, for garnish

Directions

Start by preheating your Air Fryer to 380 degrees F.

Line the cooking basket with parchment paper. Lightly grease the parchment paper with 1 tablespoon of peanut oil. In a mixing bowl, thoroughly combine the remaining 1 tablespoon of oil honey, tamari sauce, mustard, garlic, orange juice, and sambal oelek. Whisk to combine well.

Arrange the chicken drumettes in the prepared cooking basket. Season with salt and white pepper.

Spread 1/2 of the honey mixture evenly all over each breast. Pour in the chicken broth. Cook for 12 minutes.

Turn them over, add the remaining 1/2 of the honey mixture, and cook an additional 10 minutes. Garnish with onion rings and **Serve:** immediately.

Asian Style Salt and Pepper Chops

Prep time: 10 minutes **Cooking time:** 20 minutes
Servings: 2

Ingredients

1egg white
1/4 teaspoon ground black pepper
2to 3 boneless pork chops
3tablespoons peanut oil
2 jalapeno peppers, stems removed, seeded and sliced 1 teaspoon sea salt

1/2 teaspoon sea salt
3/4 cup potato starch (can use cornstarch) Oil in an oil mist bottle (I used peanut)
2 green onions,
1/4 teaspoon ground black pepper

Directions

Whisk the egg white, salt and pepper in a bowl until it is foamy. Cut the pork chops in pieces and place in the bowl making sure to coat each piece well.

Cover and refrigerate 20 minutes. Remove the chop pieces from the egg white bowl and drop into the potato starch. Coat evenly.Warmth the air fryer to 390 degrees F.
Spray the air fryer basket with the oil in the mist bottle and place the chop pieces in the basket. Spray them liberally with the oil as well.

Cook for 9 minutes shaking the basket frequently. Turn the chop pieces, spray with oil and put in for another 4 to 6 minutes or until brown and crispy. Heat up a wok on the stove and spray some oil into it. Sauté the onions, jalapenos, salt and pepper for about 1 minute.
Add the pork and sauté 2 to 3 minutes. **Serve:** with rice.

Paprika Pork Ribs

Prep time: 30 minutes **Cooking time:** 15 minutes
Servings: 2

Ingredients

1pound ribs, cut apart so they fit in the air fryer
1 1/2 tablespoons paprika

21/2 tablespoons olive oil
1 teaspoon salt

Directions

Place the ribs in a large bowl. Pour in the paprika, olive oil and salt and stir around or mix with your hands to make sure the ribs are all coated.

Set the basket of the air fryer with cooking spray and place the coated ribs in. Cook at 360 degrees F – Do not preheat the air fryer! Cook for 20 minutes, removing the basket and shaking the ribs around 2 times during those 20 minutes. They should be done and the meat should pull away from the bone.

Finger-licking-good BBQ Pork Ribs

Prep time: 5 minutes **Cooking time:** 15 minutes
Servings: 2

Ingredients

1tablespoon dark brown sugar
1 tablespoon paprika (sweet) 1 teaspoon poultry seasoning
1/2 teaspoon ground black pepper

1 teaspoon garlic powder
1 teaspoon onion powder
1/2 teaspoon prepared mustard powder
1 tablespoon kosher salt
21/4-pounds St Louis-style pork spareribs

Directions

In a bowl, whisk the brown sugar, onion powder, garlic powder, paprika, poultry seasoning, mustard powder, salt and pepper. Rub this mixture into the ribs on both sides until it is completely covered.

Set the basket of the air fryer with cooking spray and place the ribs in on end leaning against the basket crossing each other.

Set the heat to 350 degrees F and cook 35 minutes. The ribs come out brown and crispy.

Garlic Butter Pork Chops

Prep time: 10 minutes **Cooking time:** 15 minutes
Servings: 4

Ingredients

2 teaspoons parsley
1/4 teaspoon pepper
1 tablespoon coconut butter
1tablespoon coconut oil

1/2 teaspoon kosher salt
2 teaspoons grated garlic pork chops

Directions

Mix the parsley, salt, pepper, garlic, coconut oil and coconut butter and mix with a rubber spatula squishing everything together so it is well mixed. Take your hands and rub the mixture in all pork chops on both sides.

Fold into aluminum foil and refrigerate at least 2 hours or overnight. When ready to cook, preheat the air fryer to 350 degrees F for 5 minutes. Unwrap the chops from the aluminum and place 2 of them in a pan that
fits inside of the air fryer that has been sprayed with cooking spray. Spread them out as well as possible. Cook 7 minutes, turn and cook another 8 minutes. Remove and repeat with the other two chops

Chicken Kebabs

Prep time: 10 minutes **Cooking time:** 6 minutes
Servings: 3

Ingredients

1lb. ground chicken	1 tbsp. fresh lemon juice
1green onion, chopped	1/4 cup almond flour
3garlic cloves	1 egg, lightly beaten
1/3 cup fresh parsley, chopped	4oz. onion, chopped
1/4 tsp. turmeric powder	1/2 tsp. pepper

Directions

Attach all ingredients into the food processor and process until well combined. Transfer chicken mixture to the bowl and place in the refrigerator for 1 hour.

Divide mixture into the 6 equal portions and roll around the soaked wooden skewers. Spray air fryer basket with cooking spray. Place skewers into the air fryer basket and cooks at 400 F for 6 minutes. **Serve:** and enjoy.

Mediterranean Chicken

Prep time: 10 minutes **Cooking time:** 35 minutes
Servings: 6

Ingredients

4 lbs. whole chicken, cut into pieces	2 garlic cloves, minced
2 tbsp. olive oil	2 lemons, sliced
1tsp. lemon zest	2tsp. kosher salt
	2 tsp. ground sumac

Directions

Rub chicken with oil, sumac, lemon zest, and salt. Place in the refrigerator for 2-3 hours. Add lemon sliced into the air fryer basket top with marinated chicken. Cook at 350 for 35 minutes. **Serve:** and enjoy.

Asian Chicken Wings

Prep time: 10 minutes **Cooking time:** 30 minutes
Servings: 2

Ingredients

4 chicken wings	3/4 tbsp. Chinese spice
1 tsp. mixed spice Pepper	Salt
1tbsp. soy sauce	

Directions

Add chicken wings into the bowl. Add remaining ingredients and toss to coat. Set chicken wings into the air fryer basket. Cook at 350 f for 15 minutes.

Turn chicken to another side and cook for 15 minutes more. **Serve:** and enjoy.

Delicious Chicken Fajitas

Prep time: 10 minutes **Cooking time:** 15 minutes
Servings: 4

Ingredients

4 chicken breasts	1 bell pepper, sliced
1 1/2 tbsp. fajita seasoning	3/4 cup cheddar cheese, shredded
2tbsp olive oil	
1onion, sliced	

Directions

Preheat the air fryer at 380 F. Coat chicken with oil and rub with seasoning. Place chicken into the air fryer baking dish and top with bell peppers and onion.

Cook for 15 minutes. Top with shredded cheese and cook for 1-2 minutes until cheese is melted. **Serve:** and enjoy.

Juicy and Spicy Chicken Wings

Prep time: 10 minutes **Cooking time:** 25 minutes
Servings: 4

Ingredients

2 lbs. chicken wings	1tsp. Worcestershire sauce
12 oz. hot sauce	1 tsp. Tabasco
6 tbsp. butter, melted	

Directions

Spray air fryer basket with cooking spray. Add chicken wings into the air fryer basket and cook at 380 F for 25 minutes. Shake basket after every 5 minutes.

Meanwhile, in a bowl, mix together hot sauce, Worcestershire sauce, and butter. Set aside. Add chicken wings into the sauce and toss well. **Serve:** and enjoy.

Curried Drumsticks

Prep time: 10 minutes **Cooking time:** 22 minutes
Servings: 2

Ingredients

2 turkey drumsticks	11/2 tbsp. ginger, minced
1/4 tsp. cayenne pepper	1 tsp. kosher salt
2 tbsp red curry paste	1/3 cup coconut milk
1/4 tsp. pepper	

Directions

Add all ingredients into the bowl and stir to coat. Place in refrigerator for overnight. Spray air fryer basket with cooking spray. Place marinated drumsticks into the air fryer basket and cook at 390 F for 22 minutes. **Serve:** and enjoy.

Tenderloin of Pork Wrapped in Bacon

Prep time: 10 minutes **Cooking time:** 20 minutes
Servings: 4-6

Ingredients

1 to 2 tablespoons Dijon mustard
2 tablespoons butter, divided
2 to 3 Granny Smith apples, peeled, cored and cut in slices
1 cup vegetable broth

3 to 4 strips bacon
1 pork tenderloin
1 small onion, peeled and chopped
1 tablespoon flour
Garnish with fresh chopped rosemary
salt and pepper to taste

Directions

Preheat the air fryer to 360 for about 5 minutes. Spread the mustard onto the pork loin and wrap it with uncooked bacon.

Place it in the air fryer basket that has been treated with cooking spray and cook 15 minutes. Turn the roast and cook another 10 to 15 minutes until brown and crisp on the outside. Check that internal temperature is around 145 degrees F.

Heat 1 teaspoon of the butter in a saucepan and sauté the onions 1 to 2 minutes. Add the apple slices and sauté 3 to 5 minutes or until soft. Pour the onions and apples into a bowl and set it aside. Use the same pan and add the remaining butter, melting it. Stir in the flour to make a roux

Slowly add the broth while stirring until it is well combined and not lumpy. Let it come to a simmer with bubbles forming around the edges. It will thicken. Add the apple and onion mixture and stir in well. Slice the roast after it rests about 5 to 8 minutes and pour the gravy over top.

Almond-Crusted Chicken

Prep time: 15 minutes **Cooking time:** 25 minutes
Servings: 4

Ingredients

1/4 cup slivered almonds
2 tablespoons full-fat mayonnaise

2 (6-ounce) boneless, skinless chicken breasts
1 tablespoon Dijon mustard

Directions

Pulse the almonds in a food processor or chop until finely chopped. Place almonds evenly on a plate and set aside. Completely slice each chicken breast in half lengthwise. Mix the mayonnaise and mustard in a small bowl and then coat chicken with the mixture.

Lay each piece of chicken in the chopped almonds to fully coat. Carefully move the pieces into the device.

Brown Sugar Ham Steak

Prep time: 10 minutes **Cooking time:** 15 minutes
Servings: 8

Ingredients

1-8 ounce bone in fully cooked ham steak

5 tablespoons brown sugar
5 tbsp butter, in slices

Directions

Lay a piece of foil big enough to completely fold the ham steak in on a flat surface and place the steak in the middle.
Melt the butter (I do it in the microwave) and add the brown sugar. Stir until combined.

Spread half the thick butter/brown sugar spread on the ham steak and turn it over.

Spread the rest on the side of the ham steak.
Pre heat the air fryer to 380 degrees F for 4 minutes.
Fold the foil up and over the ham steak creating an envelope that will not leak over the steak.
Place the folded ham steak in the basket of the air fryer and cook for 8 minutes.

Remove from the air fryer and carefully unfold the foil watching for steam. The ham steak should be done and coated with the rich brown sugar and butter sauce.
If you are making more than one ham steak, be careful. It might not take as long to cook subsequent steaks because the air fryer will be hot.

Pepperoni and Chicken Pizza Bake

Prep time: 10 minutes **Cooking time:** 15 minutes
Servings: 4

Ingredients

2 cups cubed cooked chicken
20 slices pepperoni
1/4 cup grated Parmesan cheese

1 cup low-carb, sugar-free pizza sauce
1 cup shredded mozzarella cheese

Directions

In a 4-cup round baking dish add chicken, pepperoni, and pizza sauce. Stir so meat is completely covered with sauce.
Top with mozzarella and grated Parmesan. Place dish into the air fryer basket.

Adjust the temperature to 375F and set the timer for 15 minutes. Dish will be brown and bubbling when cooked. **Serve:** immediately.

Spicy Chicken Jerky in the Air Fryer

Prep time: 15 minutes **Cooking time:** 18 minutes
Serve: 1

Ingredients

2 (5 ounces) boneless chicken breasts, cut into strips

wooden skewers

½ cup mojo criollo marinade (such as Goya®)
2 teaspoons Cajun seasoning

Directions

Combine the chicken strips, marinade, and Cajun spice in a resealable plastic bag. Refrigerate for at least 8 hours and up to overnight. Skewers should be measured to fit across the air fryer basket, barely overlapping the edge. Remove any surplus length. Preheat the air fryer carefully for 10 minutes at 180 degrees F (80 degrees C).

While the air fryer is heating, thread chicken strips onto skewers, allowing space between each piece. 1 hour 15 minutes in the air fryer **Cooking time:** should be adjusted because most air fryers have a maximum of 32 minutes. During the reset time, rearrange the skewers. Increase the temperature to 200°F (95°C) and air fry for 15 minutes. Transfer the strips to a storage container lined with paper towels. Seal. Allow resting for at least an overnight before serving.

Crispy Keto Fried Chicken in the Air Fryer

Prep time: 15 minutes **Cooking time:** 22 minutes
Serve: 1

Ingredients

½ cup whole-milk plain kefir (such as Lifeway®)
2 (3.25 ounce) packages pork rinds, crushed
½ tbs sweet smoked paprika
¾ teaspoon Catanzaro herbs

1 ½ pounds chicken tenders
1 ½ teaspoon garlic powder
3 ounces finely grated Parmesan cheese
1 tablespoon hot sauce

Directions

In a small bowl, combine the kefir and spicy sauce. Marinate the chicken tenders for 30 minutes to an hour, or longer if desired.

Fill a small resealable container halfway with crumbled pork rinds. Combine the Parmesan cheese, garlic powder, Catanzaro herbs, and paprika in a mixing bowl.

Preheat the air fryer carefully to 390°F (200°C) for about 3 minutes. Remove the chicken from the kefir mixture and dredge it in the pork rind mixture. Air fried the chicken for 17 minutes in a preheated fryer, flipping halfway through.

Stuffed Chicken Breasts in the Air Fryer

Prep time: 10 minutes **Cooking time:** 18 minutes
Serve: 1

Ingredients

2 tbsp extra-virgin olive oil
½ cup crumbled feta cheese
1 teaspoon minced garlic
½ cup diced red bell pepper
½ cup chopped fresh spinach
1 pinch salt and ground black pepper
¾ cup grated Parmesan cheese

1 egg, beaten

½ cup diced red onion

4 boneless, skinless chicken breasts

½ cup diced fresh mushrooms
½ teaspoon dried Italian seasoning
12 toothpicks
4 slices prosciutto
¾ cup fine dry breadcrumbs 1 teaspoon dried parsley
1 serving avocado oil cooking spray

Directions

In a small pan over medium heat, heat the olive oil until hot. Cook and stir for 3 minutes, or until the onion is softened. Cook, stirring periodically, for 3 minutes more after adding the red bell pepper and mushrooms. Remove the skillet from the heat and toss in the chopped spinach and garlic. Continue to stir until the spinach has wilted somewhat. Allow cooling for 10 minutes after seasoning with Italian seasoning, salt, and pepper.

Mix in the feta cheese crumbles, breaking up any large pieces as you go. Place the chicken pieces on a secure cutting board and pat dry. Insert a knife into the thickest section of each breast and slice parallel to the cutting board, leaving about 1 inch at each tip. Be cautious not to cut through the breast's thinnest edge.

If the manufacturer recommends it, preheat the air fryer carefully to 370 degrees F (190 degrees C). Place the prosciutto slices on a clean prep surface. Place 2 tablespoons of the vegetable-feta mixture on top and twist up into an oblong bundle. Tuck one prosciutto-wrapped bundle into each cut chicken breast and secure with toothpicks.

Combine the Parmesan cheese, breadcrumbs, parsley, salt, and pepper on a dish. Dredge each filled chicken breast in the breadcrumb mixture after dipping it in the beaten egg. Use avocado oil spray to coat the pan.

Cook until browned in the air fryer basket, about 15 minutes on each side. In the middle, an instant-read thermometer should read at least 165 degrees F. (74 degrees C).

Chicken Wings

Prep time: 20 minutes **Cooking time:** 30 minutes
Servings: 6

Ingredients

Ginger crushed 1 inch
Plain Yoghurt 200g
Garlic cloves crushed 3
Ground Cumin 1 tbsp.
Garam masala Powder1
tbsp.
Ground Coriander 1 tbsp.

Ground Cardamom 1/2
tbsp. Paprika 2 tsp.
Chili Powder 1/2 tbsp.
Salt 1 tbsp.
Lemon Juice 2 tbsp.
Ground Black Pepper 2
tbsp.

Directions

Put the basket of air fryer in and close the machine's door.
At 200 C, select an Air Fry. Set a timer of 20 minutes. Insert chicken wings to guarantee they don't really smoke and turn after 5 minutes.

Mix all ingredients in a bowl for marinade and whisk them together. Toss the wings into the marinade. Put the wings again to the air fryer on the grill set at 260 C for a minute or two.

Chicken, Mushroom, Leek, and Pie of Puff Pastry

Prep time: 25 minutes **Cooking time:** 65 minutes
Servings: 4

Ingredients

Light olive oil 2 tbsp.
Egg yolk 1

Chopped tarragon 1 1/2
tbsp. Chestnut
mushrooms 300g
Sprigs thyme 4, leaves
picked
Chunky smoked bacon
pancetta lardoons 60g
Chopped chives 1 1/2
tbsp.
To taste, salt and pepper

Skinless, boneless chicken
thighs 300g, cut into of
2cm
Large leek 1, cut into 1
1/2cm slices Chopped flat
parsley 1 1/2 tbsp.
Ready-made
béchamel/white sauce
275ml
Dijon mustard 2 tbsp.
All-butter puff pastry 200g
(preferably in a block),
kept fridge cold

Directions

Put the basket of air fryer in and close the machine's door.
At 200 C, select an Air Fry. Set a timer of 20 minutes. Insert chicken wings to guarantee they don't really smoke and turn after 5 minutes. Mix all ingredients in a bowl for marinade and whisk the together. Toss the wings into the marinade. Put the wings again to the air fryer on the grill setting at 260 C for a minute or two.

Bowl of Chicken Couscous

Prep time: 10 minutes **Cooking time:** 25 minutes
Servings: 2

Ingredients

Water 120ml
Couscous 120g
Sriracha sauce 1 tbsp.
Chicken breasts, sliced 2
Paprika 1 tsp.
Garlic powder 1 tsp.
Bell pepper 1, deseeded
and diced

Tomato purees 2 tbsp.
Vegetable stock cube 1/2
Tomatoes 2, diced
Oil 1 tbsp.
Onion 1, peeled and diced
Salt and pepper
For garnishing parsley feta
and cheese

Directions

Boil 120 ml of water and transfer some of the vegetable stock. Stir until the stock dissolves. In a bowl put the couscous and pour over it with vegetable stock. Cover and set the bowl on the side. Ensure that a pot is placed, but remove the grill plate. Choose ROAST, set the temp to 200 ° C, and set the timer for 15 minutes. To commence preheating, click START/STOP.

Mix the chicken, paprika, oil, garlic powder, pepper, and salt together in a dish. Once the device beeps to signal that it has preheated, insert the seasoned chicken and close the lid to start cooking. Open the cover and put bell pepper, tomatoes and onion when 10 minutes are remaining on the timer. To keep cooking, close the lid. Insert Sriracha, tomato puree and already cooked couscous and mix well when there are 3 minutes left on the timer.

Juicy Turkey Breast

Prep time: 10 minutes **Cooking time:** 60 minutes
Serve: 8

Ingredients

4 lbs. turkey breast,
boneless 1 tbsp canola oil
1 1/2 tsp garlic powder
1/2 tsp pepper

1/2 tsp cinnamon
1 1/2 tsp paprika
2 tsp salt

Directions

Preheat the air fryer to 350 F. In a small bowl, mix together paprika, garlic powder, cinnamon, pepper, and salt.

Brush turkey breast with oil and rub with spice mixture. Place turkey breast into the air fryer basket and cook for 60 minutes. Turn after 25 minutes. Slice and **Serve:**.

Chicken Fajitas in the Air Fryer

Prep time: 20 minutes **Cooking time:** 25 minutes
Serve: 1

Ingredients

1 medium red bell pepper
1 large onion, slice petals
3 teaspoons olive oil, divided salt and pepper to taste
8 (6 inches) flour tortillas, warmed
1 medium green bell pepper, cut into thin strips
1 pound chicken tenders, cut into strips
2 teaspoons fajita seasoning

Directions

Combine the bell pepper strips and onion petals in a large mixing basin. Drizzle with 2 tablespoons olive oil and season with salt and pepper. Stir until everything is well blended. In a separate dish, toss the chicken strips with the fajita spice. Drizzle with the remaining 1 teaspoon olive oil and stir with your fingertips until evenly incorporated.

Preheat the air fryer carefully to 350 degrees Fahrenheit (175 degrees C). Cook for 12 minutes, shaking halfway through, with the chicken in the basket. Transfer to a platter and set aside while you prepare the veggies. Cook for 14 minutes, shaking halfway through, in the air fryer basket with the vegetable mixture. Distribute the chicken and veggie mixture among the tortillas.

Air Fryer Chimichangas

Prep time: 15 minutes **Cooking time:** 20 minutes
Serve: 1

Ingredients

1 tablespoon vegetable oil
2 cups shredded cooked chicken
¼ cup chicken broth
1 (4 ounces) can hot fire-roasted diced green chiles
½ teaspoon salt
1 cup shredded Mexican cheese blend
½ cup diced onion
½ (8 ounces) package Neufchatel cheese,
1 ½ tablespoons chicken taco seasoning mix
6 (10 inches) flour tortillas
¼ tbsp black pepper
avocado oil cooking spray

Directions

In a medium skillet, heat the oil. Cook until the onion is tender and transparent, 4 to 6 minutes. Combine the chicken, Neufchatel cheese, diced chiles, chicken broth, taco seasoning, salt, and pepper in a mixing bowl. Cook and stir until the mixture is fully mixed and the Neufchatel has softened.

Heat tortillas until soft and malleable in a big pan or directly on the grates of a gas burner. Fill each tortilla with a third of the chicken mixture and a heaping spoonful of Mexican cheese

Air Fryer Buffalo Chicken Wings

Prep time: 15 minutes **Cooking time:** 18 minutes
Serve: 1

Ingredients

2 ½ pounds chicken wings
½ cup butter
1 teaspoon garlic powder
1 tablespoon olive oil
⅔ cup cayenne pepper sauce
2 tablespoons vinegar
¼ teaspoon cayenne pepper

Directions

Preheat the air fryer carefully to 360°F (182 degrees C). Place the wings in a large mixing basin. Drizzle oil over the wings and massage until evenly covered. Cook for 25 minutes with half of the wings in the air fryer basket. Flip the wings with tongs and cook for another 5 minutes. Place the cooked wings in a large mixing dish. Rep with the remaining wings.

In a small saucepan over medium heat, mix hot pepper sauce, butter, vinegar, garlic powder, and cayenne pepper while the second batch is cooking. Keep stirring and heating until the wings are done. Toss cooked wings with sauce to coat.

Air Fryer Chicken Nuggets

Prep time: 15 minutes **Cooking time:** 22 minutes
Serve: 1

Ingredients

1 cup buttermilk
1 cup flour
1 tablespoon paprika
3 tablespoons grated Parmesan cheese
1 teaspoon ground black pepper
2 eggs
2 pounds chicken tenderloins, cut into nugget size
1 tablespoon parsley flakes
1 teaspoon salt
2 cups panko breadcrumbs cooking spray

Directions

In a large mixing basin, combine the buttermilk and chicken and set aside while you make the seasoned flour.
Combine the flour, Parmesan cheese, paprika, parsley, salt, and pepper
in a large mixing bowl. Separately, beat the eggs. On a flat dish, spread out the breadcrumbs. Each chicken nugget should be dredged in flour, then in beaten egg, and finally in breadcrumbs.
Preheat the air fryer carefully to 400°F (200 degrees C). Cooking spray should be sprayed on the basket. Fill the basket with as many nuggets as you can without overflowing it. Spray the tops of the nuggets lightly with cooking spray.
The **Cooking time:** is 10 minutes. Cook for a further 2 minutes after flipping the chicken nuggets. Repeat with the remaining nuggets.

Air Fryer Wings with Honey-Sriracha Sauce

Prep time: 15 minutes **Cooking time:** 20 minutes
Serve: 1

Ingredients

12 fresh chicken wing drumettes
½ teaspoon garlic powder
2 teaspoons rice vinegar

½ teaspoon salt
1 tablespoon butter
¼ cup honey
1 tablespoon sriracha sauce

Directions

Preheat the air fryer carefully to 360°F (182 degrees C). Toss the chicken wings in a basin with the salt and garlic powder to coat. Fill the air fryer basket halfway with wings. Cook the wings for 25 minutes, shaking the basket every 7 to 8 minutes. When the timer goes off, switch off the air fryer and leave the wings in the basket for another 5 minutes. Meanwhile, in a small saucepan over medium heat, melt the butter. Bring butter, honey, rice vinegar, and sriracha sauce to a boil. Reduce the heat to medium-low and cook the sauce for 8 to 10 minutes, stirring regularly. Remove from fire and set aside; the sauce will thicken as it cools. In a mixing dish, combine the cooked wings and the sauce. Next, make the extra sauce to **Serve:** with the wings.

Healthier Bang Bang Chicken in the Air Fryer

Prep time: 15 minutes **Cooking time:** 25 minutes
Serve: 1

Ingredients

1 egg
1 tbsp hot pepper sauce
½ cup tapioca starch

½ teaspoon cumin
1 teaspoon garlic granules
¼ cup plain Greek yogurt
cooking spray

½ cup milk
½ cup flour
1 ½ teaspoon seasoned salt
1-pound boneless, skinless chicken breasts
3 tablespoons sweet chili sauce
1 teaspoon hot sauce

Directions

Preheat the air fryer carefully to 380°F (190 degrees C).
Whisk together the egg, milk, and spicy sauce in a small bowl. Combine the flour, tapioca starch, salt, garlic, and cumin in a separate bowl. Dredge the chicken pieces in the dry mix first, then in the egg mixture, brushing off excess. Place the chicken in the air fryer basket in batches, be careful not to overcrowd it, and lightly spritz with oil.
Cook for about 10 minutes per batch, shaking the basket every 5 minutes until the chicken is no longer pink in the middle and the juices flow clear. Combine Greek yogurt, sweet chili sauce, and spicy sauce in a small bowl. **Serve:** the sauce beside the chicken.

Air Fryer Old Bay® Chicken Wings

Prep time: 20 minutes **Cooking time:** 20 minutes
Serve: 1

Ingredients

2 pounds chicken wings
4 tablespoons butter
½ cup cornstarch

1 teaspoon seafood seasoning

2 tablespoons seafood seasoning
¼ tbsp freshly black pepper

Directions

Preheat the air fryer carefully to 400°F (200 degrees C).
Toss the chicken wings with 2 tablespoons Old Bay® seasoning and black pepper in a large mixing dish. Toss the wings in the cornstarch until well covered. Shake each wing before placing it in the air fryer basket, making sure they don't contact; cook in batches if necessary.
Fry for 10 minutes in a hot air fryer, then shake the basket and cook for another 8 minutes. Fry the wings for 5 to 6 minutes longer, or until the chicken is cooked through and the juices flow clear.

Meanwhile, add butter and 1 teaspoon Old Bay® in seasoning for the sauce in a small saucepan. Bring to a boil, frequently stirring, over medium heat. Each wing should be dipped in the sauce. **Serve:** with any leftover sauce on the side.

Air Fryer Cornflake Chicken Fingers

Prep time: 15 minutes **Cooking time:** 20 minutes **Serve:** 1

Ingredients

1 pound chicken tenders
1 teaspoon salt
½ teaspoon ground black pepper
1 serving avocado oil cooking spray

1 teaspoon poultry seasoning
1 cup corn flakes, crushed
1 large egg, beaten

Directions

Preheat the air fryer carefully to 375°F (190 degrees C).
Chicken tenders should be seasoned with poultry seasoning, salt, and black pepper. Dip in the egg, then in the crumbled cornflakes. Spray with avocado oil and place in the air fryer basket.

Cook for 7 to 8 minutes in an air fryer. Flip the chicken tenders, spritz with avocado oil again, and air fry for 3 to 5 minutes more. In the middle, an instant-read thermometer should read at least 165 degrees F. (74 degrees C).

Chicken Kyiv Balls in the Air

Prep time: 20 minutes **Cooking time:** 20 minutes
Serve: 1

Ingredients

½ cup unsalted butter softened
1 (19.1 ounces) package ground chicken breast
2 eggs, beaten
1 teaspoon salt
½ tbsp ground black pepper
2 tablespoons chopped fresh flat-leaf parsley
1 cup panko breadcrumbs
1 teaspoon paprika
2 cloves garlic, crushed
cooking spray

Directions

Blend the butter, parsley, and garlic until well incorporated into a mixing dish. On a baking sheet, divide the mixture into 12 equal sections. Freeze for approximately 20 minutes or until solid.

Make 12 balls out of the ground chicken. In the middle of each ball, make a deep imprint. Place a slice of frozen herbed butter in the indentation and wrap the meat around it until it is completely enclosed. Rep with the remaining balls.

In a mixing dish, combine the beaten eggs. Next, combine panko, paprika, salt, and pepper in a separate bowl. 1 ground chicken ball should be dipped in the beaten eggs first, then in the seasoned breadcrumbs. Re-dunk the ball in the egg and then in the seasoned breadcrumbs. Rep with the remaining balls. Place on a baking sheet and place in the freezer for 10 minutes.

Preheat the air fryer carefully to 400°F (200 degrees C). Spray half of the balls with nonstick cooking spray and place them in the air fryer. 5 minutes in the oven with tongs, turn the balls over and re-spray with nonstick cooking spray. Cook for another 5 minutes. Repeat with the rest of the chicken balls.

Air Fryer Sweet and Sour Chicken Wings

Prep time: 15 minutes **Cooking time:** 25 minutes
Serve: 1

Ingredients

1 ½ pounds chicken wings, tips discarded
1 teaspoon ground black pepper
¼ cup pineapple juice
1 tablespoon brown sugar
1 teaspoon paprika
1 teaspoon sesame oil
1 tablespoon cornstarch
¾ teaspoon sesame seeds
1 stalk green onion, sliced
2 tablespoons baking powder
½ cup white vinegar
1 teaspoon salt
¼ cup ketchup
1 tablespoon reduced-sodium soy sauce
1 tablespoon water
1 teaspoon Sriracha sauce

Directions

Preheat the air fryer carefully to 380°F (190 degrees C). Coat the basket with cooking spray. Using a paper towel, pat dries the chicken wings. Combine baking powder, salt, pepper, and paprika in a resealable plastic bag. Place some chicken wings in the bag and shake vigorously until the wings are fully covered. Shake off any extra baking powder mixture, then repeat with the remaining wings until all of them are covered.

Cook the chicken wings in the air fryer basket for 22 to 23 minutes, turning halfway through. Meanwhile, add vinegar, pineapple juice, ketchup, brown sugar, soy sauce, Sriracha, and sesame oil in a small saucepan over medium heat. Bring to a boil, stirring constantly. For around 2 minutes, bring the water to a boil. Then, reduce the heat to a low simmer. In a small bowl, mix the cornstarch and water. Pour into the pot and stir vigorously until the sauce thickens about 1 minute. Thin the sauce with a little water if it's too thick.

Increase the temperature of the air fryer to 400 degrees F (200 degrees C) and cook the wings for another 2 minutes, or until they are cooked through and crispy brown.

Pour the sauce into a large mixing dish and toss in the cooked wings. Toss well to coat. **Serve:** immediately, garnished with sesame seeds and green onion.

Vegetables & Side Dishes Recipes

Tahini-Sauced Roasted Broccoli and Cauliflower

(**Ready in about** 15 minutes | **Servings:** 3)

Ingredients

1/2 pound broccoli, broken into florets
1/2 pound cauliflower, broken into florets
1 teaspoon onion powder
1 tablespoons tahini
Salt and chili flakes, to taste

1/2 teaspoon porcini powder 1/4 teaspoon cumin powder 1/2 teaspoon granulated garlic
1 teaspoon olive oil
2 tablespoons soy sauce
1 teaspoon white vinegar

Directions

Start by preheating your Air Fryer to 400 degrees F.

Now, toss the vegetables with the onion powder, porcini powder cumin powder, garlic and olive oil. Transfer your vegetables to the lightly greased cooking basket.

Air Fry your veggies in the preheated Air Fryer at 400 degrees F for 6 minutes. Remove the broccoli florets from the cooking basket. Continue to cook the cauliflower for 5 to 6 minutes more.

Meanwhile, make the tahini sauce by simply whisking the remaining Ingredients in a small bowl. Spoon the sauce over the warm vegetables and **Serve:** immediately. Bon appétit!

Sweet & Sticky Baby Carrots

(**Ready in about** 45 minutes | **Servings:** 3)

Ingredients

1 tablespoon coconut oil
1 pound baby carrots
2 lemongrasses, finely chopped
3 tablespoons honey

1 teaspoon fresh ginger, peeled and grated
1 teaspoon lemon thyme

Directions

Toss all Ingredients in a mixing bowl and let it stand for 30 minutes. Transfer the baby carrots to the cooking basket.

Cook the baby carrots at 380 degrees F for 15 minutes, shaking the basket halfway through the **Cooking time:**to ensure even cooking.

Serve: warm and enjoy!

Salad of Green Beans, Goat Cheese, and Almonds

(**Ready in about** 15 minutes | **Servings:** 3)

Ingredients

1 ½ pounds green beans, trimmed and cut into small chunks
1 teaspoon deli mustard
2 bell peppers, deseeded and sliced
1 tablespoon Shoyu sauce
Dressing
2 tbs extra-virgin olive oil

1 small-sized red onion, sliced
Sea salt black pepper to taste
1/4 cup almonds
1/2 cup goat cheese, crumbled
1 tbsp champagne vinegar
1 clove garlic, pressed

Directions

Season the green beans with salt and black pepper to your liking. Brush them with a nonstick cooking oil.

Place the green beans in the Air Fryer cooking basket. Cook the green beans at 400 degrees F for 5 minutes and transfer to a salad bowl. Stir in the onion and bell peppers.

Then, add the raw almonds to the cooking basket. Roast the almonds at 350 degrees F for 5 minutes, shaking the basket periodically to ensure even cooking.

In the meantime, make the dressing by blending all Ingredients until well incorporated. Dress your salad and top with goat cheese and roasted almonds. Enjoy!

Roasted Asparagus with Pecorino Romano Cheese

(**Ready in about** 10 minutes | **Servings:** 3)

Ingredients

1 pound asparagus spears, trimmed
1/2 tbsp shallot powder
1/4 tsp cumin powder
1/2 tsp dried rosemary
1 tbs sesame seeds, toasted

1/2 tbsp garlic powder
1 teaspoon sesame oil
Coarse sea salt and ground black pepper, to taste 4 tablespoons Pecorino Romano cheese, grated

Directions

Begin by preheating your Air Fryer to 400°F.

Toss the asparagus with the sesame oil, spices, and cheese before placing it in the Air Fryer cooking basket.

Cook the asparagus for 5 to 6 minutes in a preheated Air Fryer, shaking the basket halfway through to ensure even browning. **Serve:** warm, garnished with toasted sesame seeds. Good appetite!

Rainbow Vegetable and Parmesan Croquettes

(**Ready in about** 40 minutes | **Servings:** 4)

Ingredients

1 pound potatoes, peeled	2 tablespoons butter
Salt and black pepper, to taste	1 carrot, grated
1/2 cup mushrooms, chopped	4 tablespoons milk
1 clove garlic, minced	1/2 teaspoon cayenne pepper
1/2 cup panko bread crumbs	3 tablespoons scallions, minced
1/2 cup all-purpose flour	1/2 cup parmesan cheese, grated
2 eggs	2 tablespoons olive oil
1/4 cup broccoli, chopped	

Directions

In a large saucepan, boil the potatoes for 17 to 20 minutes. Drain the potatoes and mash with the milk, butter, salt, black pepper, and cayenne pepper.

Add the mushrooms, broccoli, carrots, garlic, scallions, and olive oil; stir to combine well. Shape the mixture into patties. In a shallow bowl, place the flour; beat the eggs in another bowl; in a third bowl, combine the breadcrumbs with the parmesan cheese.

Dip each patty into the flour, followed by the eggs, and then the breadcrumb mixture; press to adhere.

Cook in the preheated Air Fryer at 375 degrees F for 16 minutes, shaking halfway through the cooking time. Bon appétit!

Fried Asparagus with Goat Cheese

(**Ready in about** 15 minutes | **Servings:** 3)

Ingredients

1 bunch of asparagus, trimmed	1/2 teaspoon kosher salt
1/4 teaspoon cracked black pepper, to taste	1 tablespoon olive oil
1/2 teaspoon dried dill weed	1/2 cup goat cheese, crumbled

Directions

Place the asparagus spears in the lightly greased cooking basket. Toss the asparagus with the olive oil, salt, black pepper, and dill.

Cook in the preheated Air Fryer at 400 degrees F for 9 minutes. **Serve:** garnished with goat cheese. Bon appétit!

Casserole of Tater Tots and Vegetables

(**Ready in about** 40 minutes | **Servings:** 6)

Ingredients

1 tablespoon olive oil	2 cloves garlic, minced
1 red bell pepper, seeded and sliced	1 yellow bell pepper, seeded and sliced
1 shallot, sliced	1 ½ cups kale
1 (28-ounce) bag frozen tater tots	1 cup milk
Sea salt and ground black pepper, to your liking	6 eggs
1 cup Swiss cheese, shredded	4 tablespoons seasoned breadcrumbs

Directions

Heat the olive oil in a saucepan over medium-high heat. Sauté the shallot, garlic, and peppers for 2 to 3 minutes. Add the kale and cook until wilted.

Arrange the tater tots evenly over the bottom of a lightly greased casserole dish. Spread the sautéed mixture over the top.

In a mixing bowl, thoroughly combine the eggs, milk, salt, pepper, and shredded cheese. Pour the mixture into the casserole dish. Lastly, top with the seasoned breadcrumbs. Bake at 330 degrees F for 30 minutes or until top is golden brown. Bon appétit!

Roasted Brussels Sprout Salad

(**Ready in about** 35 minutes + chilling time | **Servings:** 2)

Ingredients

1/2 pound Brussels sprouts	Coarse sea salt and ground black pepper, to taste
1 tablespoon olive oil	
2 ounces baby arugula	2 ounces pancetta, chopped
Lemon Vinaigrette	2 tablespoons extra virgin olive oil
1 shallot, thinly sliced	
1 teaspoon Dijon mustard	2 tbsp fresh lemon juice
1 tablespoon honey	

Directions

Start by preheating your Air Fryer to 380 degrees F.

Add the Brussels sprouts to the cooking basket. Brush with olive oil and cook for 15 minutes. Let it cool to room temperature about 15 minutes.

Toss the Brussels sprouts with the salt, black pepper, baby arugula, and shallot.

Mix all Ingredients for the dressing. Then, dress your salad, garnish with pancetta, and **Serve:** well chilled. Bon appétit!

Patatas Bravas in Spanish

(**Ready in about** 15 minutes | **Servings:** 3)

Ingredients

1 pound russet potatoes, cut into 1-inch cubes
1 cup tomatoes, crushed
1/2 teaspoon paprika
2 garlic cloves, crushed
A pinch of brown sugar
Salt and ground black pepper, to taste
1/2 teaspoon chili powder
2 teaspoons canola oil

Directions

Toss the potatoes with 1 teaspoon of oil, salt and black pepper. Transfer the potato chunks to the lightly oiled Air Fryer cooking basket.

Cook the potatoes in your Air Fryer at 400 degrees F for 12 minutes total, shaking the basket halfway through the cooking time.

In the meantime, heat the remaining teaspoon of oil in a saucepan over medium-high heat. Once hot, stir in the other Ingredients cook for 8 to 10 minutes until cooked through.

Spoon the sauce over roasted potatoes and **Serve:** immediately. Enjoy!

Vegetable Oatmeal Fritters

(**Ready in about** 20 minutes | **Servings:** 3)

Ingredients

1 cup rolled oats
1/2 teaspoon shallot powder 1/2 teaspoon porcini powder 1/2 teaspoon garlic powder
1/2 cup celery, grated
1/2 teaspoon mustard seeds
1 ½ cups water
2 tablespoons soy sauce
1 cup white mushrooms, chopped
1 carrot, grated

1/2 teaspoon cumin
2 tablespoons tomato ketchup

Directions

Start by preheating your Air Fryer to 380 degrees F.

Thoroughly combine all Ingredients. Shape the batter into equal patties and place them in the cooking basket. Spritz your patties with a nonstick cooking spray.

Cook the fritters in the preheated Air Fryer for 15 minutes, turning them over halfway through the cooking time.

Serve: with your favorite dipping sauce. Bon appétit!

Favorite Winter Bliss Bowl

(**Ready in about** 25 minutes | **Servings:** 3)

Ingredients

1 pound cauliflower florets
9 ounces frozen crab cakes
1 cup iceberg lettuce
1 red bell pepper, deseeded and sliced
2 tbsp fresh lemon juice
2 tbsp cilantro leaves, chopped
Sea salt and freshly ground black pepper, to taste
1 cup quinoa
1 cup baby spinach
1 tablespoon extra-virgin olive oil
1 teaspoon yellow mustard
1 teaspoon olive oil

Directions

Brush the cauliflower and crab cakes with olive oil; season them with salt and black pepper and transfer them to the cooking basket.
Cook the cauliflower at 400 degrees F for about 12 minutes total, shaking the basket halfway through the cooking time. Then, cook the crab cakes at 400 degrees F for about 12 minutes total, flipping them halfway through the cooking time.
In the meantime, rinse your quinoa, drain it and transfer to a soup pot with 2 cups of lightly salted water; bring to a boil.
Turn heat to a simmer and continue to cook, covered, for about 20 minutes; fluff with a fork and transfer to a serving bowl.
Add the cauliflower and crab cakes to the bowl. Add your greens and bell pepper to the bowl. In a small mixing dish, whisk the lemon juice, extra- virgin olive oil and yellow mustard.
Drizzle the dressing over all Ingredients, garnish with fresh cilantro and **Serve:** immediately. Bon appétit!

Mexican-Style Roasted Corn Salad

(**Ready in about** 15 minutes | **Servings:** 2)

Ingredients

2 ears of corn, husked
4 ounces Cotija cheese crumbled
1/2 red onion, chopped
1/2 teaspoon Mexican oregano
1 cup Mexican Escabeche
2 tablespoons extra-virgin olive oil
Fresh juice of 1 lime
Kosher salt and freshly ground black pepper, to taste

Directions

Start by preheating your Air Fryer to 390 degrees F.

Place the corn on the cob in the lightly greased cooking basket; cook the corn on the cob for 10 minutes, turning over halfway through the cooking time.

Once the corn has cooled, use a sharp knife to cut off the kernels into a salad bowl. Toss the corn kernels with the remaining Ingredients and **Serve:** immediately. Enjoy!

Fish & Seafood Recipes

Salad with Salmon and Fennel

(**Ready in about** 20 minutes | **Servings:** 3)

Ingredients

1 pound salmon
Sea salt and ground black pepper, to taste
1/2 teaspoon paprika
1 tablespoon lime juice
1 tablespoon sesame seeds, lightly toasted
1 cucumber, sliced

1 fennel, quartered
1 tablespoon balsamic vinegar
1 teaspoon olive oil
1 tablespoon extra-virgin olive oil
1 tomato, sliced

Directions

Toss the salmon and fennel with 1 teaspoon olive oil, salt, black pepper, and paprika in a mixing bowl.

Cook for 12 minutes in a preheated Air Fryer at 380 degrees F, shaking the basket once or twice.

Transfer the salmon to a salad bowl and cut it into bite-sized strips.

Combine the fennel, balsamic vinegar, lime juice, 1 tablespoon extra-virgin olive oil, tomato, and cucumber in a mixing bowl.

Toss well to combine and **Serve:** topped with lightly toasted sesame seeds. Enjoy!

Parmesan Chip-Crusted Tilapia

(**Ready in about** 15 minutes | **Servings:** 3)

Ingredients

1 ½ pounds tilapia, slice into 4 portions Sea salt and ground black pepper, to taste
1/4 cup parmesan cheese, preferably freshly grated
2 tablespoons buttermilk

1 teaspoon granulated garlic
1/4 cup almond flour
1/2 tbsp cayenne pepper
1 egg, beaten
1 cup tortilla chips, crushed

Directions

Generously season your tilapia with salt, black pepper and cayenne pepper.
Prepare a bread station. Add the granulated garlic, almond flour and parmesan cheese to a rimmed plate.
Whisk the egg and buttermilk in another bowl and place crushed tortilla chips in the third bowl.
Dip the tilapia pieces in the flour mixture, then in the egg/buttermilk mixture and finally roll them in the crushed chips, pressing to adhere well.
Cook in your Air Fryer at 400 degrees F for 10 minutes, flipping halfway through the cooking time. **Serve:** with chips if desired. Bon appétit!

Fillets of Keto Cod

(**Ready in about** 15 minutes | **Servings:** 2)

Ingredients

2 cod fish fillets
1 teaspoon Old Bay seasoning 1 egg, beaten

1 teaspoon butter, melted
2 tablespoons coconut milk, unsweetened
1/3 cup coconut flour, unsweetened

Directions

Place the cod fish fillets, butter and Old Bay seasoning in a Ziplock bag; shake until the fish is well coated on all sides.

In a shallow bowl, whisk the egg and coconut milk until frothy.

In another bowl, place the coconut flour. Dip the fish fillets in the egg mixture, then, coat them with coconut flour, pressing to adhere.

Cook the fish at 390 degrees F for 6 minutes; flip them over and cook an additional 6 minutes until your fish flakes easily when tested with a fork. Bon appétit!

Easiest Lobster Tails Ever

(**Ready in about** 10 minutes | **Servings:** 2)

Ingredients

2 (6-ounce) lobster tails
1/2 teaspoon dried rosemary
1/2 teaspoon garlic, pressed
1 teaspoon deli mustard
1 teaspoon olive oil

1 teaspoon fresh cilantro, minced

Sea salt and ground black pepper, to taste

Directions

Toss the lobster tails with the other Ingredients until they are well coated on all sides.

Cook the lobster tails at 370 degrees F for 3 minutes. Then, turn them and cook on the other side for 3 to 4 minutes more until they are opaque.

Serve: warm and enjoy!

Parcel Salmon

Prep time: 15 minutes **Cooking time:** 23 minutes
Servings: 2

Ingredients

2 (4-oz.) salmon fillets
6 asparagus stalks
1/4 cup champagne

1/4 cup white sauce
1 teaspoon oil
Salt and ground black pepper, as required

Directions

In a bowl, merge together all the Ingredients. Divide the salmon mixture over 2 pieces of foil evenly. Seal the foil around the salmon mixture to form the packet.

Choose "Power Button" of Air Fry Oven and turn the dial to select the "Air Fry" mode. Choose the Time button and again turn the dial to set the **Cooking time:** to 13 minutes.

Now press the Temp button and rotate the dial to set the temperature at 355 degrees F. Press "Start/Pause" button to start.

When the unit beeps to show that it is preheated, open the lid. Arrange the salmon parcels in "Air Fry Basket" and insert in the oven. **Serve:** hot.

Ranch Tilapia

Prep time: 15 minutes **Cooking time:** 13 minutes
Servings: 4

Ingredients

3/4 cup cornflakes, crushed
2 1/2 tbsp vegetable oil
2 eggs

1 (1-oz.) packet dry ranch-style dressing mix

4 (6-oz.) tilapia fillets

Directions

In a shallow bowl, beat the eggs. In another bowl, add the cornflakes, ranch dressing, and oil and mix until a crumbly mixture form.

Dip the fish fillets into egg and then, coat with the breadcrumb's mixture.

Choose "Power Button" of Air Fry Oven and turn the dial to select the "Air Fry" mode. Choose the Time button and again turn the dial to set the cooking time to 13 minutes.

Now press the Temp button and rotate the dial to set the temperature at 356 degrees F. Press "Start/Pause" button to start. When the unit beeps to show that it is preheated, open the lid.

Arrange the tilapia fillets in greased "Air Fry Basket" and insert in the oven. **Serve:** hot.

Salmon with Broccoli

Prep time: 15 minutes **Cooking time:** 12 minutes
Servings: 2

Ingredients

11/2 cups small broccoli florets
Salt and ground black pepper, as required
1 teaspoon light brown sugar
1 scallion, thinly sliced
1/4 teaspoon cornstarch

2 tablespoons vegetable oil, divided
1 tablespoon soy sauce
1 teaspoon rice vinegar
2 (6-oz.) skin-on salmon fillets
1 (1/2-inch) piece fresh ginger, grated

Directions

In a bowl, merge together the broccoli, 1 tablespoon of oil, salt, and black pepper. In another bowl, mix well the ginger, soy sauce, vinegar, sugar, and cornstarch.

Coat the salmon fillets with remaining oil and then with the ginger mixture. Choose "Power Button" of Air Fry Oven and turn the dial to select the "Air Fry" mode.

Choose the Time button and again turn the dial to set the **Cooking time:** to 12 minutes. Now press the Temp button and rotate the dial to set the temperature at 375 degrees F.
Press "Start/Pause" button to start.

When the unit beeps to show that it is preheated, open the lid. Arrange the broccoli florets in greased "Air Fry Basket" and top with the salmon fillets. Insert the basket in the oven. **Serve:** hot.

Sesame-Crusted Tuna Steak

Prep time: 5 minutes **Cooking time:** 8 minutes **Servings:** 2

Ingredients

2 (6-ounce) tuna steaks
1/2 teaspoon garlic powder
2 teaspoons white sesame seeds

1 tablespoon coconut oil, melted

2 teaspoons black sesame seeds

Directions

Brush each tuna steak with coconut oil and sprinkle with garlic powder. In a large bowl, mix sesame seeds and then press each tuna steak into them, covering the steak as completely as possible. Place tuna steaks into the air fryer basket.

Adjust the temperature to 400F and set the timer for 8 minutes. Flip the steaks halfway through the cooking time. Steaks will be well-done at 145F internal temperature. **Serve:** warm.

Tilapia Grilled with Portobello Mushrooms

(**Ready in about** 20 minutes | **Servings:** 2)

Ingredients

2 tilapia fillets
1/2 teaspoon red pepper flakes, crushed
1/2 teaspoon dried sage, crushed
1 tsp dried parsley flakes

1 tablespoon avocado oil
1/4 teaspoon lemon pepper 1/2 teaspoon sea salt
A few drizzles of liquid smoke
4 medium-sized Portobello mushrooms

Directions

Toss all Ingredients in a mixing bowl; except for the mushrooms.

Transfer the tilapia fillets to a lightly greased grill pan. Preheat your Air Fryer to 400 degrees F and cook the tilapia fillets for 5 minutes.

Now, turn the fillets over and add the Portobello mushrooms. Continue to cook for 5 minutes longer or until mushrooms are tender and the fish is opaque. **Serve:** immediately.

Authentic Mediterranean Calamari Salad

(**Ready in about** 15 minutes | **Servings:** 3)

1 pound squid, cleaned, sliced into rings
2 tablespoons sherry wine
1/2 teaspoon ground black pepper
1 cup grape tomatoes
1 teaspoon yellow mustard
1/3 cup Kalamata olives, pitted and sliced
1/2 cup mayonnaise

1/2 teaspoon granulated garlic Salt, to taste
1/2 teaspoon basil
1/2 teaspoon dried rosemary
1 small red onion, thinly sliced
1/2 cup fresh flat-leaf parsley leaves, coarsely chopped

Directions

Start by preheating the Air Fryer to 400 degrees F. Spritz the Air Fryer basket with cooking oil.

Toss the squid rings with the sherry wine, garlic, salt, pepper, basil, and rosemary. Cook in the preheated Air Fryer for 5 minutes, shaking the basket halfway through the cooking time.

Work in batches and let it cool to room temperature. When the squid is cool enough, add the remaining

Ingredients.

Gently stir to combine and **Serve:** well chilled. Bon appétit!

Filet of Flounder Cutlets

(**Ready in about** 15 minutes | **Servings:** 2)

Ingredients

1 egg
1/2 cup Pecorino Romano cheese, grated
2 flounder fillets
1 teaspoon dried parsley flakes

1/2 cup cracker crumbs
1/2 teaspoon cayenne pepper
Sea salt and white pepper, to taste

Directions

To make a breading station, whisk the egg until frothy.

In another bowl, mix the cracker crumbs, Pecorino Romano cheese, and spices.

Dip the fish in the egg mixture and turn to coat evenly; then, dredge in the cracker crumb mixture, turning a couple of times to coat evenly.

Cook in the preheated Air Fryer at 390 degrees F for 5 minutes; turn them over and cook another 5 minutes. Enjoy!

King Prawns with Lemon Butter Sauce

(**Ready in about** 15 minutes | **Servings:** 4)

Ingredients

King Prawns
2 cloves garlic, minced
1/2 cup Pecorino Romano cheese, grated
1 teaspoon garlic powder
1 teaspoon mustard seeds
2 tablespoons olive oil

2 tbs fresh lemon juice
1/2 teaspoon Worcestershire sauce

1 ½ pounds king prawns, peeled and deveined
Sea salt and ground white pepper, to your
2 tablespoons butter liking
1/2 teaspoon onion powder
1/4 teaspoon ground black pepper
Sauce

Directions

All Ingredients for the king prawns should be thoroughly combined in a plastic closeable bag; shake to combine well.

Place the coated king prawns in the Air Fryer basket that has been lightly greased.

Cook for 6 minutes at 390°F in a preheated Air Fryer, shaking the basket halfway through. Working in batches is recommended.

Meanwhile, melt the butter in a small saucepan over medium heat and add the remaining Ingredients.

Reduce the heat to low and whisk for 2 to 3 minutes, or until thoroughly heated. Pour the sauce over the hot king prawns. Good appetite!

Salmon with Prawns and Pasta

Prep time: 20 minutes **Cooking time:** 18 minutes
Servings: 4

Ingredients

14 oz. pasta (of your
choice) 4 (4-oz.) salmon
steaks
1/2 lb. cherry tomatoes,
chopped
2 tablespoons fresh thyme,
chopped

2 tablespoons olive oil
4 tablespoons pesto,
divided
8 large prawns, peeled and
deveined
2 tablespoons fresh lemon
juice

Directions

Set a large pan of salted boiling water, add the pasta
and cook for about 8-10 minutes or until desired
doneness. Meanwhile, in the bottom of a baking pan,
spread 1 tablespoon of pesto.

Place salmon steaks and tomatoes over pesto in a
single layer and drizzle with the oil. Arrange the
prawns on top in a single layer. Drizzle with lemon
juice and sprinkle with thyme.

Choose "Power Button" of Air Fry Oven and turn the
dial to select the "Air Fry" mode. Choose the Time
button and again turn the dial to set the **Cooking
time:** to 8 minutes. Now press the Temp button and
rotate the dial to set the temperature at 390 degrees F.

Press "Start/Pause" button to start. When the unit
beeps to show that it is preheated, open the lid.
Arrange the baking pan in "Air Fry Basket" and insert
in the oven. Rinse the pasta and transfer into a large
bowl. Add the remaining pesto and toss to coat well.
Divide the pasta onto serving plate and top with
salmon mixture. **Serve:** immediately.

Salmon in Papillote with Orange

Prep time: 20 Minutes **Cooking time:** 30 Minutes
Servings: 4

Ingredients

600g salmon fillet
4 oranges
1 lemon

2 cloves of garlic
Chives to taste

Directions

Pour the freshly squeezed orange juice, the lemon
juice, the zest of the two oranges into a bowl. Add two
tablespoons of oil, salt, and garlic. Dip the previously
washed salmon fillet and leave it in the marinade for
one hour, preferably in the refrigerator Place the steak
and part of your marinade on a sheet of foil. Salt and
sprinkle with chives and a few slices of orange.

Set to 160C. Simmer for 30 minutes. Open the sheet
let it evaporate, and **Serve:** with a nice garnish of fresh
orange.

Burgers with smoked salmon

Prep time: 20 minutes **Cooking time:** 22 minutes
Servings: 6

Ingredients

3 large russet potatoes,
peeled and cubed
3/4 cup frozen vegetables
(of your choice), parboiled
and drained
Salt and ground black
pepper, as required
1/4 cup olive oil

1 egg
6-oz. cooked salmon fillet
1 teaspoon fresh dill,
chopped
2 tbsp parsley, chopped
1 cup breadcrumbs

Directions

In a pan of the boiling water, cook the potatoes for
about 10 minutes. Drain the potatoes well. Set the
potatoes into a bowl and mash with a potato masher.

Set aside to cool completely. In another bowl, add the
salmon and flake with a fork. Add the cooked
potatoes, egg, parboiled vegetables, parsley, dill, salt
and black pepper and mix until well combined.

Make 6 equal-sized patties from the mixture. Coat
patties with breadcrumb evenly and then drizzle with
the oil evenly. Choose "Power Button" of Air Fry
Oven and turn the dial to select the "Air Fry" mode.

Choose the Time button and again turn the dial to set
the **Cooking time:** to 12 minutes. Now press the
Temp button and rotate the dial to set the temperature
at 355 degrees F.

Press "Start/Pause" button to start. When the unit
beeps to show that it is preheated, open the lid.
Arrange the patties in greased "Air Fry Basket" and
insert in the oven.
Flip the patties once halfway through. **Serve:** hot.

Shrimp, Zucchini and Cherry Tomato Sauce

Prep time: 10 Minutes **Cooking time:** 30 Minutes
Servings: 4

Ingredients

2 zucchinis
7 cherry tomatoes
Salt to taste

300 shrimp
1 clove garlic

Directions

Pour the oil, add the garlic clove, and diced zucchini.
Cook for 15 minutes at 150C.

Add the shrimp and the pieces of tomato, salt, and
spices.
Cook for another 5 to 10 minutes or until the shrimp
water evaporates.

Cornmeal Coated Catfish

Prep time: 15 minutes **Cooking time:** 14 minutes
Servings: 4

Ingredients

2 tablespoons cornmeal	2 teaspoons Cajun seasoning
1/2 tbs garlic powder Salt	2 (6-oz.) catfish fillets
1 tablespoon olive oil	1/2 teaspoon paprika

Directions

In a bowl, mix together the cornmeal, Cajun seasoning, paprika, garlic powder, and salt. Add the catfish fillets and coat with the mixture. Now, coat each fillet with oil.

Choose "Power Button" of Air Fry Oven and turn the dial to select the "Air Fry" mode. Choose the Time button and again turn the dial to set the cooking time to 14 minutes. Now press the Temp button and rotate the dial to set the temperature at 400 degrees F.

Press "Start/Pause" button to start. When the unit beeps to show that it is preheated, open the lid. Arrange the catfish fillets in greased "Air Fry Basket" and insert in the oven. After 10 minutes of cooking, flip the fillets and spray with the cooking spray. **Serve:** hot

Breaded Flounder

Prep time: 15 minutes **Cooking time:** 12 minutes
Servings: 3

Ingredients

1 egg	1 cup dry breadcrumbs
3 (6-oz.) flounder fillets	1 lemon, sliced
1/4 cup vegetable oil	

Directions

In a bowl, beat the egg In another bowl, attach the breadcrumbs and oil and merge until crumbly mixture is formed. Dip flounder fillets into the beaten egg and then, coat with the breadcrumb mixture.

Choose "Power Button" of Air Fry Oven and turn the dial to select the "Air Fry" mode. Choose the Time button and again turn the dial to set the **Cooking time:**to 12 minutes. Now press the Temp button and rotate the dial to set the temperature at 356 degrees F. Press "Start/Pause" button to start.

When the unit beeps to show that it is preheated, open the lid. Arrange the flounder fillets in greased "Air Fry Basket" and insert in the oven. Season with the lemon slices and **Serve:** hot.

Salmon with Vegetables Roasted

Prep time: 15 Minutes **Cooking time:** 14 Minutes
Servings: 2

Ingredients

1 large carrot, peeled and sliced	1 small onion, thinly sliced
	1/4 cup low-fat sour cream
2 (5-ounce / 142-g) salmon fillets	1 fennel bulb, thinly sliced

Directions

Preheat the air fryer to 400F (205C).
In a bowl, mix the carrot, fennel bulb, and onion. Toss well.
Transfer the vegetable mixture to a 6-inch metal pan, and then put the pan in the air fryer basket.

Roast in the preheated air fryer for 4 minutes, or until the vegetables are fork-tender. Remove the pan from the air fryer. Add the sour cream to the pan and season with ground pepper, and then spread the salmon fillets on top.

Set the pan to the air fryer and roast for an additional 10 minutes or until the fish flakes easily when tested with a fork.
Let the salmon and vegetables cool for 5 minutes before serving.

Quick Coconut Shrimp

Prep time: 10 Minutes **Cooking time:** 8 Minutes
Servings: 4

Ingredients

1/4 cup all-purpose flour	1/3 cup shredded unsweetened coconut
1 egg	1/4 cup panko bread crumbs
1 pound (454 g) raw shrimp, peeled, deveined, and patted dry	

Directions

Heat the air fryer to 400F (20°C). On a plate, place the flour. In a small bowl, toss the egg until frothy.

In a separate bowl, mix the coconut, bread crumbs, salt, and pepper. Dredge the shrimp in the flour, shake off any excess, dip them in the egg, and finally coat them in the coconut-bread mixture.

Set the air fryer basket with cooking spray. Put the breaded shrimp in the basket and spray with cooking spray.

Cook in the warmed air fryer for 8 minutes, flipping the shrimp once during cooking, or until the shrimp are opaque and crisp. Remove from the basket and **Serve:** on a plate.

Skewers of Shrimp with Vermouth

Prep time: 10 Minutes **Cooking time:** 5 Minutes
Servings: 4

Ingredients

11/2 pounds (680 g) shrimp	2 cloves garlic, crushed
1 lemon, cut into wedges	1/4 cup vermouth

Directions

Warm the air fryer to 400F (205C).
Toss the shrimp with the vermouth, olive oil, garlic, salt, and pepper in a bowl and then set it in the fridge to marinate for 1 hour.

Remove the shrimp from the refrigerator and discard the marinade. Skewer the shrimp by piercing through the center and transfer to the basket.

Cook in the warmed air fryer for 5 minutes, flipping the shrimp halfway through. Relish with the lemon wedges and **Serve:** hot.

Fish Sticks

Prep time: 15 minutes **Cooking time:** 12 minutes
Servings: 4

Ingredients

4 (4 ounces) fillets of frozen cod or tilapia thawed	1/4 cup of whole wheat flour
1 tsp. of garlic powder	1 tsp. of salt plus more for sprinkling after air frying
1/2 tsp. of pepper	
2 large eggs	1 large lemon juiced, plus more for serving after air frying
1 cup of panko breadcrumbs	
2 tsp. of old bay	1 tsp. of paprika
	Tarter sauce (recommended for serving)

Directions

Firstly, on your Air-fryer. Then preheat at 400F and set the timer to 10 to 12 minutes.

Then press "Start", the Air-fryer will notify at you when it's finished preheating.
Once warmth set the basket with cooking spray and place in approximately 6 pieces of fish and make sure they aren't touching.

After 5 minutes, carefully flip each piece of fish, and then continue cooking for the remaining 5 minutes.

Remove from Air-fryer, sprinkle with more salt (if necessary) and a generous squeeze of lemon. Repeat with remaining fish. **Serve:** and enjoy with tarter sauce!

Zesty Ranch Fish Fillets

Prep time: 5 minutes **Cooking time:** 12 minutes
Servings: 2 - 4

Ingredients

3/4 cup of bread crumbs or panko	130g packet of dry ranch-style dressing mix
2 eggs beaten	4 tilapia salmon or other fish fillets
2 1/2 tbsp. of vegetable oil	Lemon wedges to garnish

Directions

Preheat your Air-fryer at 180C. Merge the panko/breadcrumbs and the ranch dressing mix together. Attach in the oil and keep stirring until the mixture becomes loose and crumbly.

After that, soak the fish fillets into the egg, letting the excess drip off, dip the fish fillets into the crumb mixture, making sure they are coated evenly and thoroughly. Now place fish fillets into your Air-fryer carefully and cook for 12 to 13 minutes, depending on the thickness of the fillets. Remove and **Serve:** immediately. Press the lemon wedges over the fish if desired.

Fish and Chips

Prep time: 5 minutes **Cooking time:** 10 minutes
Servings: 2 - 4

Ingredients

1 lb. of cod fillet cut into strips	2 tsp. paprika
	1/2 cup of all-purpose flour
1/2 tsp. of garlic powder	1/4 tsp. of black pepper
1/4 tsp. of salt	Large egg beaten
2 cups of panko breadcrumbs Tartar sauce for serving	Lemon wedges for serving

Directions

Mix-up flour with the paprika, garlic powder and salt in a small bowl. Set the egg in another bowl and the panko breadcrumbs in a third bowl.

Set the fish dry using a paper towel. After that, dredge the fish in the flour mixture, then the egg and finally the panko breadcrumbs.

Press it down lightly until the crumbs sticks. Then spray both sides with oil. Now Air-fry at 400F for about for 10 to 12 minutes, turning halfway through cooking until it's crispy and lightly golden. **Serve:** immediately with fries and tartar sauce, and enjoy!

Fish Tacos from Reynolds Wrap

Prep time: 15 minutes **Cooking time:** 20 minutes
Serve: 1

Ingredients

Reynolds Wrap® Non-Stick Aluminum Foil
1 teaspoon olive oil
1 tablespoon fresh lime juice
½ teaspoon salt
1 clove garlic, minced
Mango salsa

4 (4 ounces) tilapia fillets, fresh or frozen (thawed)
1 teaspoon seafood seasoning
⅛ teaspoon red pepper flakes
Sliced avocado

Directions

Preheat the oven carefully to 400°F. Line a 13x9x2-inch baking sheet with Reynolds Wrap® Nonstick Foil, nonstick (dull) side up.

Place the tilapia in a pan lined with foil. Combine lime juice, olive oil, seafood seasoning, garlic, salt, and red pepper flakes in a medium mixing bowl. Pour over the fish. Bake for 18 to 20 minutes, or until the salmon flakes easily with a fork. Fill each tortilla with 1/2 fillet, lettuce, salsa, and avocado.

Corn Crusted Red Fish

Prep time: 15 minutes **Cooking time:** 20 minutes
Serve: 1

Ingredients

1 ½ cups fresh corn kernels
1 tbsp red onion, chopped
1 tablespoon cornstarch
1 cup all-purpose flour
1 teaspoon Creole seasoning, or to taste
1 tablespoon vegetable oil

1 tablespoon red bell pepper, chopped

4 (5 ounces) red snapper fillets
3 egg whites, lightly beaten

Directions

Preheat the oven carefully to 350°F (175 degrees C). In a mixing dish, combine corn kernels, bell pepper, onion, and cornstarch; put aside.

Season the red snapper with the Creole seasoning. Dip the fish in the flour, then in the egg whites. Coat both sides of the fish with the corn mixture by pushing it into the egg whites.

In an oven-safe skillet, heat the vegetable oil over medium-high heat. Fry the fillets in the pan until brown, about 5 minutes per side. Place the pan in the preheated oven and cook for another 5 minutes, or until the fish flakes easily with a fork.

Tacos de Halibut

Prep time: 15 minutes **Cooking time:** 18 minutes
Serve: 1

Ingredients

1 lime, juiced
¼ cup chopped cilantro
1 jalapeno pepper, diced
¼ teaspoon ground cumin
½ pound halibut fillets
8 corn tortillas
1 cup shredded pepper Jack cheese

¼ cup olive oil
1 tablespoon ground ancho chili powder
salt and black pepper to taste
2 cups shredded cabbage
1 (8 ounces) jar salsa
1 avocado, sliced

Directions

In a large mixing bowl or resealable zip-top bag, combine lime juice, olive oil, cilantro, jalapeño, chili powder, cumin, salt, and pepper. Marinade the halibut for 20 to 25 minutes. Do not over marinate the fish since the lime juice will begin to 'cook' it.

Preheat an outside grill to medium heat and brush the grate gently with oil. Drain marinade and cook fillets for 5 minutes on each side. Cook for another 2 minutes, or until the salmon flakes easily with a fork.

Warm the tortillas on the grill or in the oven. Top tortillas with fish, cabbage, salsa, pepper Jack cheese, and avocado.

Beer Batter for Fish

Prep time: 15 minutes **Cooking time:** 22 minutes
Serve: 1

Ingredients

3 eggs, ¾ cup beer
4 cups pastry flour
½ teaspoon baking soda
.063 teaspoon garlic powder
2 quarts of vegetable oil for frying

1 ½ cups milk
1 tablespoon baking powder
ground black pepper to taste
1 ½ pounds cod fillets
2 tablespoons cornstarch
salt to taste

Directions

Combine flour, baking powder, baking soda, and cornstarch in a medium mixing basin. In a large mixing basin, combine eggs and milk. Pour in the beer.

Mix in the flour mixture. Season with salt, pepper, and garlic powder to taste. Heat the oil to 375 degrees F in an electric deep fryer or a heavy saucepan (190 degrees C).

Coat the fish with batter and place it in the heated oil. Fry for 4 to 5 minutes, or until golden brown. **Serve:**.

Slaw on Crispy Fish Tacos

Prep time: 15 minutes **Cooking time:** 18 minutes
Servings: 2 - 4

Ingredients

1 serving nonstick of cooking spray	1 tbsp. of chopped fresh jalapeno pepper
4 cups of cabbage slaw mix	1 tbsp. of lime juice
1 tbsp. of olive oil	1 tbsp. of apple cider vinegar
1/4 cup of all-purpose flour	
1/4 tsp. of ground black pepper	1/4 cup of yellow cornmeal
1/4 tsp. of ground cayenne pepper	2 tbsp. of taco seasoning mix
1 pound of cod fillets, cut into bite-sized pieces	8 (6 inch) corn tortillas
	1/2 tsp. of salt

Directions

Preheat an air fryer to 400 F and spray the basket of the Air-fryer with cooking spray. Merge cabbage slaw, jalapeno pepper, lime juice, olive oil, vinegar, salt, pepper, and cayenne pepper in a large bowl. Then mix until evenly combined and set it aside.

Merge together flour, cornmeal, and taco seasoning in a separate bowl. Attach fish pieces and toss until evenly coated, discarding any remaining seasoning mix. Set in the prepared Air-fryer basket and mist lightly with cooking spray.

Cook fish in the preheated air fryer and shake the basket, then cook until fish is crispy and flakes easily with a fork, for about 5 minutes more.

Crumbed Fish

Preparation 10 minutes **Cooking time:** 12 minutes
Servings: 2 - 4

Ingredients

1 cup of dry bread crumbs	4 each of flounder fillets
1/4 cup of vegetable oil	1 egg, beaten
1 sliced lemon	

Directions

Preheat your Air-fryer at 350F in a bowl, mix bread crumbs and oil together and stir until mixture. Soak fish fillets into the egg; shake off any excess. Dip fillets into the

bread crumb mixture; coat evenly and fully. Set coated fillets gently in the preheated air fryer and cook for about 12 minutes until fish flakes easily with a fork. Garnish with lemon slices. **Serve:** and enjoy!

Healthy White Fish with Garlic and Lemon

Prep time: 5 minutes **Cooking time:** 12 minutes
Servings: 2 - 4

Ingredients

12 oz. of tilapia filets or 2 filets (6 oz. each)	1/2 tsp. of lemon pepper seasoning (2.5 ml)
1/2 tsp. of garlic powder (2.5 ml)	1/2 tsp. of onion powder (optional)
Kosher salt or sea salt , to taste	Lemon wedges
Fresh chopped parsley	Fresh cracked black pepper , to taste

Directions

Pre-heat your Air-fryer at 360F for 5 minutes. Wash and pat dry the fish filets. Cover or coat with olive oil spray and season with garlic powder,

lemon pepper, and/or onion powder, salt and pepper. Lay perforated Air-fryer baking paper inside base of air fryer and lightly spray the paper. If you are not using a liner, spray enough olive oil spray at the base of the Air-fryer basket to make sure fish does not stick.

Set the fish on top of the paper and add a few lemon wedges next to fish. Line with Parchment Paper.

After that, Air-Fry at 360F for about 6 to12 minutes. Sprinkle with chopped parsley and **Serve:** warm with the toasted lemon wedges.

Southern Fried Catfish Nuggets

Prep time: 5 minutes **Cooking time:** 17 minutes
Servings: 2

Ingredients

2 pounds of catfish nuggets 1/4 cup of oil	10 ounces box of fish fry mix

Directions

Firstly, wash fish and set aside. Whisk half the box of fish fry mix into a large Ziploc bag.

Attach the Catfish Nuggets into the bag with the fish fry mix. Secure the bag and shake well to coat. Using the tongs, detach the nuggets one at a time, shaking off excess batter. Attach the catfish nuggets to the basket of the Air-fryer. Check the Directions of your Air-fryer for filling the basket in case it requires no over filling of basket.

Toss the oil into a small bowl, dip your basting brush into the oil and baste a small amount of oil onto the top of each catfish nugget. Set your Air-fryer on to 380F and set timer for 17 minutes. Start checking at about 12 minutes.
Detach from basket when done and drain on paper toweling. Attach the next batch to the basket and repeat. **Serve:** when ready and enjoy!

Beer Battered Fish

Prep time: 10 minutes **Cooking time:** 12 minutes
Servings: 5

Ingredients

1 cup of all-purpose flour	1/2 tsp. of baking soda 6
2 tbsp. of cornstarch	oz. of beer
1 egg beaten	3/4 cup of all flour
1 tsp. of salt	1/4 tsp. of ground black
1/2 tsp. of paprika	pepper
11/2 lb. of cod cut into 4	Vegetable oil
or 5 pieces	Pinch of cayenne pepper

Directions

Merge the 1 cup of flour, cornstarch and baking soda in a large bowl and add the beer and egg, stir until it's smooth. Seal the bowl of batter with plastic wrap and refrigerate for at least 20 minutes. Combine the 3/4 cup of flour, paprika, salt, black pepper and cayenne pepper in a shallow dredging pan.

Set the cod fish fillets dry with a paper towel. Now dip the fish into the batter, coating all sides and allow the excess batter to drip off and then coat each fillet with the seasoned flour.

Whisk any leftover flour on the fish fillets and pat gently to adhere the flour to the batter. After that, pre-heat your air fryer at 390F. Air-fry for 12 minutes at 390F. **Serve:** with lemon wedges, malt vinegar and tartar sauce.

Breaded Sea Scallops

Prep time: 10 minutes **Cooking time:** 5 minutes
Servings: 2 - 4

Ingredients

1/2 cup of finely crushed buttery crackers	1/2 tsp. of seafood seasoning
1 lb. of sea scallops, patted dry	1 serving cooking spray 1/2 tsp. of garlic powder
2 tbsp. of butter, melted	

Directions

Preheat the Air-fryer to 390F. Merge cracker crumbs, garlic powder, and seafood seasoning together in a bowl.
Place dissolved butter in a second bowl. Then start to dip each scallop in the melted butter and roll in the breading until it's completely coated.

Bring on a plate and repeat with the remaining scallops. Set the air fryer basket with cooking spray. Set scallops in the prepared basket so that they don't touching each other. You may require working in batches. Cook in the preheated air-fryer. Turn scallops over gently with a small spatula and cook.

Cakes of Crab

Prep time: 15 minutes **Cooking time:** 10 minutes
Servings: 4 - 5

Ingredients

1 large egg, beaten	2 tbsp. of mayonnaise
1 tsp. of Worcestershire sauce	1 tsp. of seafood seasoning 1/2 tsp. of hot pepper sauce
2 tbsp. of finely chopped green onion	1 lb. of lump crabmeat, drained and picked over
1 pinch of salt and black pepper to taste	3 tbsp. of milk
11 crackers saltine crackers, crushed	4 wedges lemon 1 serving olive oil cooking spray
1 tsp. of baking powder	1 tsp. of Dijon mustard

Directions

Mix-up egg, mayonnaise, Worcestershire sauce, mustard, seafood seasoning, and hot pepper sauce in a small mixing bowl and stir in green onion and set aside.

Set crab meat in a medium bowl and break up with a fork. Then add milk, salt, and pepper and toss to coat. Attach crushed saltines and baking powder and toss lightly to combine. Attach to the egg mixture, stirring gently and being careful not to break apart the crab lumps.
Spoon crab with a 1/3-cup measure and form into 8 patties. Set patties on a plate, cover, and refrigerate for about 1 hour or until its firm.

Preheat your Air-fryer at 400F then spray crab cakes on both sides with cooking spray and place them in the air fryer basket. Cook and then gently turn the cakes over, and cook 5 minutes longer until it turns crispy brown. **Serve:** immediately!

Lemon Pepper Shrimp

Prep time: 5 minutes **Cooking time:** 10 minutes
Servings: 2 -4

Ingredients

1 tbsp. of olive oil	1 tsp. of lemon pepper
1 lemon, juiced	1/4 tsp. of paprika
1/4 tsp. of garlic powder	12 oz. of uncooked medium shrimp, peeled and deveined 1 Lemon, sliced

Directions

Preheat your Air-fryer to 400F. Then mix olive oil, lemon juice, lemon pepper, paprika, and garlic powder in a bowl. Add shrimp and toss until it's coated.

Set shrimp in the air fryer and cook until it turns pink and firm for about 6 to 10 minutes. **Serve:** with lemon slices.

Casserole of Tuna and Zoodles

Prep time: 15 minutes **Cooking time:** 15 minutes
Servings: 4

Ingredients

2 tablespoons salted butter
1/4 cup diced white onion
1/2 cup heavy cream
1/2 cup vegetable broth
2 stalks celery, finely chopped
1/2 teaspoon red pepper flakes
2 (5-ounce) cans albacore tuna

1/4 cup chopped white mushrooms
2 tablespoons full-fat mayonnaise
1/4 teaspoon xanthan gum
1 ounce pork rinds, finely ground
2 medium zucchini, spiralized

Directions

In a skillet, dissolve the butter. Add onion, mushrooms, and celery and sauté until fragrant, about 3–5 minutes.
Pour in heavy cream, vegetable broth, mayonnaise, and xanthan gum.

Reduce heat and continue cooking an additional 3 minutes, until the mixture begins to thicken. Add red pepper flakes, zucchini, and tuna. Turn off heat and stir until zucchini noodles are coated.

Pour into 4-cup round baking dish. Top with ground pork rinds and cover the top of the dish with foil. Place into the air fryer basket.Adjust the temperature to 370F and set the timer for 15 minutes. When 3 minutes remain, remove the foil to brown the top of the casserole. **Serve:** warm

Shrimp Scampi

Prep time: 10 minutes **Cooking time:** 8 minutes
Servings: 4

Ingredients

4 tablespoons salted butter
1/2 medium lemon
1/4 cup whipping cream
1/4 teaspoon red pepper flakes

1 teaspoon minced roasted garlic
1/4 tbsp xanthan gum
1 pound medium peeled and deveined shrimp
1 tbs chopped parsley

Directions

In a saucepan over medium heat, melt butter. Zest the lemon, and then squeeze juice into the pan. Add garlic. Pour in the cream, xanthan gum, and red pepper flakes. Whisk until the mixture begins to thicken, about 2–3 minutes.

Place shrimp into a 4-cup round baking dish. Pour the cream sauce over the shrimp and cover with foil. Place the dish into the air fryer basket. Adjust the temperature to 400F and set the timer for 8 minutes. Stir twice during cooking. When done, garnish with parsley and **Serve:** warm.

Fried Tuna Salad Bites

Prep time: 10 minutes **Cooking time:** 7 minutes
Servings: 12

Ingredients

1(10-ounce) can tuna, drained
1 medium avocado, peeled, pitted, and mashed
1/4 cup full-fat mayonnaise

1 stalk celery, chopped
1/2 cup blanched finely ground almond flour, divided
2 teaspoons coconut oil

Directions

In a large bowl, mix tuna, mayonnaise, celery, and mashed avocado. Form the mixture into balls. Roll balls in almond flour and spritz with coconut oil. Place balls into the air fryer basket.

Adjust the temperature to 400F and set the timer for 7 minutes. Gently turn tuna bites after 5 minutes. **Serve:** warm.

Fish Taco Bowl with Jalapeño Slaw

Prep time: 10 minutes **Cooking time:** 10 minutes
Servings: 2

Ingredients

1cup shredded cabbage
1/4 cup full-fat sour cream
1/4 cup chopped pickled jalapeños
1 teaspoon chili powder
1/4 teaspoon garlic powder
1/2 medium lime

2tablespoons full-fat mayonnaise
2(3-ounce) cod fillets
1 teaspoon cumin
1/2 teaspoon paprika
1 medium avocado, peeled, pitted, and sliced

Directions

In a large bowl, place cabbage, sour cream, mayonnaise, and jalapeños. Mix until fully coated. Let sit for 20 minutes in the refrigerator.

Sprinkle cod fillets with chili powder, cumin, paprika, and garlic powder. Place each fillet into the air fryer basket. Adjust the temperature to 370F and set the timer for 10 minutes. Turn over the fillets halfway through the cooking time. When fully cooked, fish should have an internal temperature of at least 145F.

To **Serve:**, divide slaw mixture into two serving bowls, break cod fillets into pieces and spread over the bowls, and top with avocado. Squeeze lime juice over each bowl. **Serve:** immediately.

Homemade Fish Stock

Prep time: 15 minutes **Cooking time:** 20 minutes
Serve: 1

Ingredients

3 pounds fish heads, bones, and trimmings
2 tablespoons unsalted butter
1 rib celery, chopped
1 cup dry white wine
10 whole black peppercorns

2 leeks, white part only, thinly sliced
1 carrot, chopped
2 ½ quarts water
1 bouquet garni
3 thick slices of lemon

Directions

Fish should be washed in cold water and thoroughly drained. Melt the butter in a saucepan over low heat. Cook until the leeks, carrots, and celery are cooked, 5 to 7 minutes. Bring the fish portions, wine, and water to a boil for about 5 minutes. Residuum should be skimmed and discarded. After adding the bouquet garni, peppercorns, and lemon, return to a boil.

Sexy Fish Stew

Prep time: 15 minutes **Cooking time:** 18 minutes
Serve: 1

Ingredients

2 tablespoons butter
salt and pepper to taste
½ cup sliced shallots salt
1 ¼ cups chicken broth
1 pound baby red potatoes, trimmed
½ cup heavy whipping cream
1 tbs chopped fresh tarragon

1 large leek, cleaned and thinly sliced
¾ cup white wine
½ cup thinly sliced fennel bulb
1 pinch cayenne pepper
1-pound boneless rockfish filets, cut into 1-inch pieces

Directions

In a large saucepan over medium-low heat, melt the butter. Cook and stir the leek, shallots, and 1/2 teaspoon salt in the melted butter for 10 to 15 minutes, or until softened. Stir the wine into the leek mixture, turn the heat up to medium and cook for 2 minutes. Bring the chicken broth to a boil. Stir in the fennel and potatoes and cook, occasionally turning, until the potatoes are nearly cooked about 10 minutes. Season with salt, pepper, and cayenne pepper to taste. Stir in the cream to mix.
Cover and heat for 3 minutes after adding the fish and tarragon to the soup. Reduce heat to medium-low, stir gently, and cook until fish flakes easily with a fork, about 6 minutes. Season with salt and black pepper to taste.

Sliders with Fish and Chips

Prep time: 15 minutes **Cooking time:** 22 minutes
Serve: 1

Ingredients

cooking spray
3 egg whites
1 tbs. apple cider vinegar
1 pound cod fillets
2 green onions, chopped
1 pinch salt and ground black pepper 8 slider buns

1 (8.5 ounces) bag malt vinegar-and-sea salt chips
½ teaspoon celery seed
⅓ cup plain Greek yogurt
2 tbs honey mustard
3 cups coleslaw mix

Directions

Preheat the oven carefully to 450 degrees Fahrenheit (230 degrees C). Spray a wire rack with cooking spray and place it on a rimmed baking sheet.
Blend the chips in batches until they have the consistency of breadcrumbs. Place the chips on a flat platter.
In a mixing basin, combine egg whites. Place a piece of fish on the prepared rack after dipping it in egg white and coating it with chip crumbs. Rep with the leftover fish. Coat the fish with frying spray. Bake for 15 minutes in a preheated oven. Turn on the broiler and broil
the salmon for 5 minutes, or until it is golden and crispy.
In a large mixing bowl, combine coleslaw mix and green onions while the fish is cooking. Combine the yogurt, honey mustard, vinegar, celery seed, salt, and pepper in a separate dish. Toss the coleslaw mix with the dressing to blend.

Cod Fish Cakes

Prep time: 18 minutes **Cooking time:** 20 minutes
Serve: 1

Ingredients

2 large potatoes, peeled and halved
1 tablespoon grated onion
1 egg

1 tablespoon butter
1 pound cod fillets, cubed
1 tbs chopped fresh parsley
3 tablespoons oil for frying

Directions

Put the potatoes in a large saucepan of water and bring to a boil. Allow the potatoes to simmer until almost tender.
Add the fish to the saucepan and boil until both the fish and the potatoes are tender. Drain well and place the potatoes and fish in a large mixing dish.
Mash together the butter, onion, parsley, and egg in mixing dish

Chicken-Cheese-Fish

Prep time: 18 minutes **Cooking time:** 20 minutes
Serve: 1

Ingredients

2 pounds skinless, boneless chicken breast halves

4 (3 ounces) cans of tuna packed in olive oil

2 cups crumbled feta

2 cups ricotta cheese

1 (8 ounces) package cream cheese, softened

2 eggs, beaten

2 tbs butter, cut small pieces

1 cup shredded Swiss cheese

4 cups shred Cheddar cheese

2 cups heavy whipping cream 4 eggs, beaten

1 cup shredded mozzarella cheese

3 cups Italian seasoned breadcrumbs

2 (16 ounces) cans pink salmon, drained

Directions

Preheat the oven carefully to 350°F (175 degrees C). Fill a large baking dish halfway with chicken breasts. Sprinkle with Cheddar and Swiss cheeses. Layer the tuna and salmon on the cheese in an equal layer. In a mixing bowl, combine the whipped cream and the 4 beaten eggs; pour over the top of the dish.

In a mixing dish, combine the feta, mozzarella, and ricotta cheeses; distribute over the fish. Next, combine the cream cheese, 2 beaten eggs, and breadcrumbs; spread evenly over the cheese. Finally, arrange little slices of butter evenly throughout the entire dish. Wrap with aluminum foil. Bake for 1 1/2 hours, or until cooked through and golden brown on top, in a preheated oven.

Fish Batter with Newcastle™ Brown Ale

Prep time: 15 minutes **Cooking time:** 25 minutes
Serve: 1

Ingredients

1-quart vegetable oil for frying

½ cup cornmeal

½ teaspoon garlic powder

1 cup brown ale (such as Newcastle™ brown ale)

½ cup flour

1 pound cod fillets, cut into pieces

1 teaspoon garlic salt

½ tbsp ground cinnamon

Directions

Heat the oil in a deep fryer to 325°F (165 degrees C). Combine the flour, cornmeal, garlic salt, garlic powder, and cinnamon in a large mixing bowl. Mix in the beer until there are no dry lumps left. Dip the fish into the batter, allowing some of the excess to run out before gently placing it in the deep fryer. Cook for 8 minutes, or until the fish is golden brown and crispy on the exterior and easily flaked. To prevent overcrowding the deep fryer, cook the fish in batches.

Traditional fish and chips

Prep time: 20 minutes **Cooking time:** 20 minutes
Serve: 1

Ingredients

4 large potatoes, peeled and cut into strips

1 teaspoon ground black pepper

1 egg

1 ½ pounds cod fillets

1 cup all-purpose flour

1 teaspoon baking powder

1 cup milk

1 teaspoon salt

1-quart vegetable oil for frying

Directions

Place the potatoes in a medium dish of cool water. In a medium-sized mixing basin, combine the flour, baking powder, salt, and pepper separately. Whisk in the milk and egg and continue to stir until the mixture is smooth. Allow the mixture to stand for 20 minutes.

Preheat the oil to 350°F in a big pot or electric skillet (175 degrees C). Fry the potatoes until they are soft in heated oil. They should be drained on paper towels.

Dredge the fish in the batter, one piece at a time, and fry in heated oil. Fry the fish till golden brown. Increase the heat as needed to keep the temperature at 350 degrees F (175 degrees C). Drain well on paper towels. Fry the potatoes for another 1 to 2 minutes to enhance crispness.

Fish and Things Teriyaki Marinade

Prep time: 15 minutes **Cooking time:** 25 minutes
Serve: 1

Ingredients

2 cups soy sauce

1 cup honey

¾ cup white sugar, divided

8 green onions

¾ cup brown sugar, divided

1 clove garlic, chopped

4 slices fresh ginger root

Directions

In a 2-quart saucepan, combine soy sauce, 1/2 cup brown sugar, 1/2 cup white sugar, green onions, ginger, and garlic. Bring the mixture to a simmer. Reduce the heat to low and continue to cook for 15 minutes.

Pour in the remaining whites and brown sugar, as well as the honey. Bring the water to a boil. When the mixture rises and foams and doubles in size, take it from the fire and set it aside to cool.

Air Fryer Blackened Fish Tacos

Prep time: 20 minutes **Cooking time:** 25 minutes
Serve: 1

Ingredients

1 (15 ounces) can seasoned black beans, rinsed, and drained
½ teaspoon salt
1 teaspoon Louisiana-style hot sauce (Optional)
¼ cup blackened seasoning
4 (6 inches) corn tortillas

1 tablespoon olive oil
1 tablespoon lime juice
2 ears corn, kernels
1 pound tilapia fillets cooking spray
1 lime, cut into wedges

Directions

Preheat the oven carefully to 400 degrees Fahrenheit (200 degrees C). Combine black beans, corn, olive oil, lime juice, and salt in a mixing dish. Set aside after gently stirring until the beans and corn are uniformly covered.

Place the fish fillets on a clean work area and pat with paper towels to dry. Spray each fillet lightly with cooking spray and sprinkle with ½ of the blackened seasoning. Turn the fillets over, spray with cooking spray, and season with the rest of the spice.

Place the fish in the air fryer basket in a single layer, working in batches if required. 2 minutes in the oven, cook for 2 minutes more on the other side before transferring to a platter. Cook for 10 minutes, stirring halfway through, in the bean and corn mixture, in the air fryer basket. Fill corn tortillas with fish and top with bean and corn mixture. **Serve:** with lime wedges and spicy sauce on the side.

Baked Fish Fillets

Prep time: 15 minutes **Cooking time:** 25 minutes
Serve: 1

Ingredients

1 tablespoon vegetable oil, or to taste
⅛ tbsp ground black pepper
2 tablespoons lemon juice

1 teaspoon salt
2 pounds mackerel fillets
¼ cup butter, melted

⅛ teaspoon ground paprika

Directions

Preheat the oven carefully to 350°F (175 degrees C). Vegetable oil should be used to grease a baking pan. Season the mackerel fillets in the baking pan with salt and pepper.

Combine the butter, lemon juice, and paprika in a mixing dish. **Serve:** with mackerel fillets. Cook in a preheated oven for 20 to 25 minutes or until the mackerel flakes easily with a fork.

Curry with Tamarind Sauce for Fish

Prep time: 15 minutes **Cooking time:** 20 minutes
Serve: 1

Ingredients

2 pounds white carp
1 tablespoon vegetable oil
1 cup warm water
1 ½ teaspoons salt
½ teaspoon cumin seeds
1 large onion, minced

2 tablespoons red chili powder
2 tablespoons ground coriander

¼ cup oil
1 tablespoon red chili powder
¼ cup tamarind pulp
1 ½ tablespoon garlic paste
1 pinch salt to taste
1 tablespoon chopped fresh coriander
1 tbs ground turmeric

Directions

Place the fish in a bowl and toss with 1 tablespoon vegetable oil, 1 tablespoon chili powder, turmeric, and 1 1/2 teaspoons salt for about 10 minutes. Pour warm water over the tamarind pulp in a dish.

To obtain the juice from the tamarind, squeeze it. In a pan over medium heat, heat 1/4 cup oil; add cumin seeds and stir. Cook, constantly stirring, until the onion is transparent, 5 to 10 minutes. Cook for 3 minutes after adding the garlic paste.

Cover the skillet and cook the carp for 5 minutes. Bring the fish mixture to a boil with the tamarind juice. Turn the carp pieces over and season with 2 teaspoons red chili powder, coriander, and salt. Cook over low heat for 10 minutes or until the sauce thickens and the oil separates. Garnish with coriander leaves if desired.

Baja Sauce for Fish or Shrimp Tacos

Prep time: 15 minutes **Cooking time:** 25 minutes
Serve: 1

Ingredients

¼ cup sour cream
1 teaspoon lime juice
¾ teaspoon seafood seasoning (such as Old Bay®)

¼ cup mayonnaise
1 tbsp chopped cilantro
¼ teaspoon ground ancho chili pepper

Directions

Combine the sour cream, mayonnaise, lime juice, cilantro, seafood seasoning, and ancho chili pepper in a mixing bowl. Refrigerate for at least 1 hour, covered with plastic wrap.

Twice Fried Fish

Prep time: 10 minutes **Cooking time:** 18 minutes
Serve: 1

Ingredients

1 tablespoon hoisin sauce	1 tablespoon canned
1 tablespoon dry sherry	tomato sauce
1 teaspoon ground black	1 teaspoon white sugar
pepper	1 teaspoon salt
1 ½ pounds cod fillets	3 tablespoons vegetable oil
2 tbs dark soy sauce	1 tablespoon lard
1 teaspoon cornstarch	4 tablespoons water

Directions

Mix hoisin sauce, tomato sauce, sherry, pepper, soy sauce, sugar, and salt in a mixing bowl. Allow for a 20-minute resting period.

1 tablespoon of oil should be rubbed into the filets of fish. Heat the remaining 2 tablespoons of oil in a large pan. Fry the fish for 2 minutes on both sides, then drain on paper towels.

Remove the skillet's oil and replace it with 1 tablespoon of lard. Melt over medium heat and toss in the soy sauce mixture. Dissolve the cornstarch in the water and pour it into the skillet, continually swirling. Cook until the sauce thickens.

Return the fish to the skillet and cook for another minute on each side.

Grilled Tuna Fish Steaks

Prep time: 20 minutes **Cooking time:** 20 minutes
Serve: 1

Ingredients

8 (3 ounces) fillets fresh	½ cup soy sauce
tuna steaks, 1 inch thick	1 tablespoon fresh lime
	juice
⅓ cup sherry	¼ cup vegetable oil
1 clove garlic, minced	

Directions

In a shallow baking dish, place the tuna steaks. Combine the soy sauce, sherry, vegetable oil, fresh lime juice, and garlic in a medium mixing bowl. Turn the tuna steaks in the soy sauce mixture to coat. Refrigerate for at least one hour, covered.

Preheat the grill to high. Grease the grill grate lightly. Place the tuna steaks on the grill and discard the marinade. Grill for 3 to 6 minutes per side, or until done to preference.

Fish Croquettes Baked

Prep time: 15 minutes **Cooking time:** 25 minutes
Serve: 1

Ingredients

2 cups leftover cooked	1 cup soft
steelhead trout	breadcrumbs
½ sweet onion, minced	½ cup mayonnaise
½ cup sour cream	½ lemon, juiced
½ teaspoon	½ teaspoon seasoned salt,
Worcestershire sauce	or more to taste
½ teaspoon garlic powder	½ cup panko
ground black pepper to	breadcrumbs, or as
taste	needed

Directions

Preheat the oven carefully to 425°F (220 degrees C). Then, using parchment paper or aluminum foil, line a baking pan.

Remove the skin, bones, and crust from the trout and flake it with a fork. In a mixing bowl, combine flaked fish, soft breadcrumbs, onion, mayonnaise, sour cream, lemon juice, Worcestershire sauce, salt, garlic powder, and black pepper. Form the mixture into balls, then roll each one in the panko. Place the balls on the baking sheet that has been prepared.

Bake for 15 to 20 minutes, or until the croquettes are gently browned and crispy.

Accidental Fish

Prep time: 15 minutes **Cooking time:** 20 minutes
Serve: 1

Ingredients

4 ounces fillets Mahi Mahi	½ cup salted butter
2 drops Louisiana-style	1 Roma tomato, seeded
hot sauce	and chopped
1 tablespoon lemon juice	1 clove garlic, minced
1 green onion, chopped	2 teaspoons olive oil

Directions

Preheat the oven carefully to 450°F (230 degrees C). Place the mahi-mahi fillets on a baking dish and brush with olive oil. Bake for 20 minutes in a preheated oven or until the fish flakes easily with a fork. Melt the butter in a skillet over medium heat while the mahi-mahi bakes.

Simmer the garlic, lemon juice, and spicy sauce in the melted butter for 1 minute. Cook and stir the tomato and green onion into the butter mixture until heated. To **Serve:**, spoon the sauce over the cooked fish.

Pretzel Coated Fried Fish1-quart oil for frying

Prep time: 15 minutes **Cooking time:** 20 minutes
Serve: 1

Ingredients

1-quart oil for frying	¾ cup all-purpose flour
½ tbs ground black pepper	¾ cup crushed pretzels
1-pound frozen cod fillets, thawed	1 teaspoon salt
	2 eggs

Directions

Heat the oil in a deep fryer to 350°F (175 degrees C). In a large resealable plastic bag, combine the flour, salt, and pepper. Place the cod in the bag and shake gently to coat. Separate the eggs and crumbled pretzels into two small bowls. Coat the fish in eggs, then with broken pretzels.
Fry coated fish in hot oil for 10 minutes, rotating once, until golden brown and readily flaked with a fork.

Fiery Fish Tacos with Crunchy Corn Salsa

Prep time: 10 minutes **Cooking time:** 18 minutes
Serve: 1

Ingredients

2 cups cooked corn kernels	½ cup diced red onion
1 cup peeled, diced jicama	½ cup diced red bell pepper, 1 cup cilantro leaves chopped
1 lime, juiced, and zested	
2 tablespoons olive oil	
2 tablespoons cayenne pepper, or to taste	2 tbs salt, or to taste
	6 (4 ounces) fillets of tilapia
1 tbso ground black pepper	2 tbs sour cream, or to taste
12 corn tortillas, warmed	

Directions

Preheat the grill to high. Combine corn, red onion, jicama, red bell pepper, and cilantro in a medium mixing bowl. Mix in the lime juice and zest. Combine cayenne pepper, ground black pepper, and salt in a small bowl. Brush each fillet with olive oil and season with salt and pepper to taste. Place the fillets on the grill grate and cook for 3 minutes on each side. Top two corn tortillas with fish, sour cream, and corn salsa for each spicy fish taco.

Soup with Spicy Fish

Prep time: 18 minutes **Cooking time:** 20 minutes
Serve: 1

Ingredients

½ onion, chopped	1 clove garlic, minced
1 tablespoon chili powder	1 ½ cups chicken broth
1 (4 ounces) can canned green chili peppers, chopped	1 ½ cups canned peeled and diced tomatoes
½ cup chopped green bell pepper	½ cup shrimp
	1 teaspoon ground cumin
½ pound cod fillets	¾ cup plain nonfat yogurt

Directions

Over medium-high heat, coat a large pot with vegetable cooking spray. Sauté the onions for about 5 minutes, stirring often. Cook for 2 minutes more after adding the garlic and chili powder.
Then, add the chicken broth, chili peppers, and cumin while stirring constantly. Bring to a boil, then lower to low heat, cover, and leave to simmer for 20 minutes.

Add the tomatoes, green bell pepper, prawns, and fish next. Return to a boil, lower to low heat, cover, and continue cooking for 5 minutes. Stir in the yogurt gradually until it is cooked completely.

Air Fryer Fish Sticks

Prep time: 15 minutes **Cooking time:** 25 minutes
Serve: 1

Ingredients

1 pound cod fillets	¼ cup all-purpose flour,
½ cup panko breadcrumbs	¼ cup grated Parmesan cheese
1 egg	
1 teaspoon paprika	½ teaspoon black pepper
1 tablespoon parsley flakes	cooking spray

Directions

Preheat an air fryer to 400°F (200 degrees C).
Pat the fish dry using paper towels before slicing it into 1x3-inch pieces.
In a small bowl, combine the flour and salt. In a separate shallow dish,
beat the egg. In a third shallow dish, combine panko, Parmesan cheese, parsley, paprika, and pepper.
Each fish stick should be coated in flour, then dipped in beaten egg, and then coated in seasoned panko mixture.
Spray the air fryer basket with nonstick cooking spray. Arrange half of
the sticks in the basket, ensuring none of them is a contact. Cooking spray should be sprayed on the top of each stick.
Cook for 5 minutes in a hot air fryer. Cook for a further 5 minutes after
flipping the fish sticks. Rep with the rest of the fish sticks.

Snacks, Sides & Appetizers

Chips with Dill Mayonnaise on Root Vegetables

(**Ready in about** 40 minutes | **Servings:** 4)

Ingredients

1/2 pound red beetroot, julienned
1/2 pound golden beetroot, julienned
1/2 cup mayonnaise
Sea salt and ground black pepper, to taste
1 teaspoon olive oil
1/4 pound carrot
1 teaspoon garlic, minced
1/4 teaspoon dried dill weed

Directions

Toss your veggies with salt, black pepper and olive oil.

Arrange the veggie chips in a single layer in the Air Fryer cooking basket.

Cook the veggie chips in the preheated Air Fryer at 340 degrees F for 20 minutes; tossing the basket occasionally to ensure even cooking. Work with two batches.

Meanwhile, mix the mayonnaise, garlic and dill until well combined.

Serve: the vegetable chips with the mayo sauce on the side. Bon appétit!

Parmesan Squash Chips

(**Ready in about** 20 minutes | **Servings:** 3)

Ingredients

3/4 pound butternut squash, cut into thin rounds
1 teaspoon butter
1/2 cup ketchup
Sea salt and ground black pepper, to taste
1 teaspoon Sriracha sauce
1/2 cup Parmesan cheese, grated

Directions

Toss the butternut squash with Parmesan cheese, salt, black pepper and butter.

Transfer the butternut squash rounds to the Air Fryer cooking basket.

Air Fryer at 400 degrees F for 12 minutes. Shake the Air Fryer basket periodically to ensure even cooking. Work with batches.

While the parmesan squash chips are baking, whisk the ketchup and sriracha and set it aside.

Serve: the parmesan squash chips with Sriracha ketchup and enjoy!

Crunchy Mexican Cheese Straws

(**Ready in about** 15 minutes | **Servings:** 3)

Ingredients

1/2 cup almond flour
1/4 teaspoon shallot powder 1/4 teaspoon garlic powder
1 ounce Manchego cheese, grated
1/4 teaspoon xanthan gum 1/4 teaspoon ground cumin
1 egg yolk, whisked
2 ounces Cotija cheese, grated

Directions

Mix all Ingredients until everything is well incorporated.

Twist the batter into straw strips and place them inside your Air Fryer on a baking mat.

Cook the cheese straws in your Air Fryer at 360°F for 5 minutes, then flip them over and cook for another 5 minutes.

Before serving, allow the cheese straws to cool. Enjoy!

Greek-Style Zucchini Rounds

(**Ready in about** 15 minutes | **Servings:** 3)

Ingredients

1/2 pound zucchini, cut into thin rounds
1/2 teaspoon oregano
Coarse sea salt and ground black pepper, to taste
Greek dipping sauce
1/2 teaspoon fresh lemon juice
2 tablespoons mayonnaise
1/2 teaspoon dried sage, crushed
1/4 tbs ground bay leaf
1/2 cup Greek yogurt
1 teaspoon extra-virgin olive oil
1/2 teaspoon garlic, pressed

Directions

Toss the zucchini rounds with olive oil and spices and place them in the Air Fryer cooking basket.

Cook in the preheated Air Fryer at 400 degrees F for 10 minutes; shaking the basket halfway through the cooking time.

Let it cool slightly and cook an additional minute or so until crispy and golden brown.

Meanwhile, make the sauce by whisking all the sauce Ingredients; place the sauce in the refrigerator until ready to **Serve:**.

Serve: the crispy zucchini rounds with Greek dipping sauce on the side. Enjoy!

French Fries with Paprika and Cheese

(**Ready in about** 15 minutes | **Servings:** 2)

Ingredients

8 ounces French fries, frozen	1/2 cup Monterey-Jack cheese, grated
Sea salt, to taste	1 teaspoon paprika

Directions

Cook the French fries in your Air Fryer at 400 degrees F for about 7 minutes. Shake the basket and continue to cook for a further 6 minutes.

Top the French fries with cheese, paprika and salt cheese. Continue to cook for 1 minute more or until the cheese has melted. **Serve:** warm and enjoy!

Beer-Battered Vidalia Onion Rings

(**Ready in about** 15 minutes | **Servings:** 2)

Ingredients

1/2 cup all-purpose flour 1	1/4 tbsp cayenne pepper
1/4 teaspoon dried oregano	Kosher salt and ground black pepper, to taste
/2 teaspoon baking powder	
1/4 cup beer	1 cup crushed tortilla chips
1/2 pound Vidalia onions, cut into rings	1 large egg, beaten

Directions

In a mixing bowl, thoroughly combine the flour, baking powder, cayenne pepper, oregano, salt, black pepper, egg and beer; mix to combine well.

In another shallow bowl, place the crushed tortilla chips.

Dip the Vidalia rings in the beer mixture; then, coat the rings with the crushed tortilla chips, pressing to adhere.

Transfer the onion rings to the Air Fryer cooking basket and spritz them with a nonstick spray. Cook the onion rings at 380 degrees F for about 8 minutes, shaking the basket halfway through the **Cooking time:**to ensure even browning. Bon appétit!

Cinnamon Pear Chips

(**Ready in about** 10 minutes | **Servings:** 2)

Ingredients

1 large pear, cored and sliced	1 teaspoon apple pie spice blend
1 teaspoon honey	1 teaspoon coconut oil

Directions

Toss the pear slices with the spice blend, coconut oil and honey. Then, place the pear slices in the Air Fryer cooking basket and cook at 360 degrees F for about 8 minutes.

Shake the basket once or twice to ensure even cooking. Pear chips will crisp up as it cools

Italian-Style Tomato Chips

(**Ready in about** 20 minutes | **Servings:** 2)

Ingredients

2 tomatoes, cut into thick rounds	Sea salt and fresh ground pepper, to taste
1 teaspoon Italian seasoning mix	1 teaspoon extra-virgin olive oil
1/4 cup Romano cheese, grated	

Directions

Start by preheating your Air Fryer to 350 degrees F.

Toss the tomato sounds with remaining Ingredients. Transfer the tomato rounds to the cooking basket without overlapping.

Cook your tomato rounds in the preheated Air Fryer for 5 minutes. Flip them over and cook an additional 5 minutes. Work with batches. Bon appétit!

Bacon Chips with Chipotle Dipping Sauce

(**Ready in about** 15 minutes | **Servings:** 3)

Ingredients

6 ounces bacon, cut into strips	6 tablespoons sour cream
Chipotle Dipping Sauce	1/2 teaspoon chipotle chili powder

Directions

Place the bacon strips in the Air Fryer cooking basket.

Cook the bacon strips at 360 degrees F for 5 minutes; turn them over and cook for another 5 minutes.

Meanwhile, make the chipotle dipping sauce by whisking the sour cream and chipotle chili powder; re**Serve:**.

Serve: the bacon chips with the chipotle dipping sauce and enjoy!

Bites of Mexican Cheesy Zucchini

Prep time: 15 minutes **Cooking time:** 10 minutes
Servings: 4

Ingredients

1 large-sized zucchini, thinly sliced
1/2 cup tortilla chips, crushed
1/2 cup Queso Añejo, grated

1/4 cup yellow cornmeal
1 egg, whisked
Salt and cracked pepper, to taste
1/2 cup flour

Directions

Pat dry the zucchini slices with a kitchen towel. Mix the remaining Ingredients in a shallow bowl; mix until everything is well combined. Dip each zucchini slice in the prepared batter. Cook in the preheated Air Fryer at 400 degrees F for 12 minutes.

Homemade Apple Chips

Prep time: 5 minutes **Cooking time:** 15 minutes
Servings: 4

Ingredients

2 cooking apples, cored and thinly sliced
1 teaspoon peanut oil
1 tablespoon smooth peanut butter

1/4 teaspoon ground cloves 1/4 teaspoon ground cinnamon

Directions

Toss the apple slices with the peanut oil. Bake at 350 degrees F for 5 minutes; shake the basket to ensure even cooking and continue to cook an additional 5 minutes.
Spread each apple slice with a little peanut butter and sprinkle with ground cloves and cinnamon. **Serve:** and enjoy!

Toasted Nuts

Prep time: 5 minutes **Cooking time:** 15 minutes
Servings: 4

Ingredients

1/2 Cup Macadamia Nuts
1/2 Cup Pecans
1 Tablespoon Olive Oil

1/4 Cup Walnuts
1/4 Cup Hazelnuts
1 Teaspoon Sea Salt, Fine

Directions

Start by turning your air fryer to 32, and then place your nuts in your air fryer. Cook your nuts for eight minutes, and then stir. Cook for another four minutes.

Sprinkle them with oil and salt before shaking them. Cook for one more minute before serving.

Easy and Delicious Pizza Puffs

Prep time: 5 minutes **Cooking time:** 10 minutes
Servings: 6

Ingredients

6 ounces crescent roll dough
3 ounces pepperoni
3 ounces mushrooms, chopped
1/4 cup Marina sauce, for dipping

1/2 cup mozzarella cheese, shredded

1 teaspoon garlic powder
1 teaspoon oregano

Directions

Unroll the crescent dough. Set out the dough using a rolling pin; cut into 6 pieces. Place the cheese, pepperoni, and mushrooms in the center of each pizza puff.
Sprinkle with oregano and garlic powder. Fold each corner over the filling using wet hands. Press together to cover the filling entirely and seal the edges. Now, spritz the bottom of the Air Fryer basket with cooking oil.
Lay the pizza puffs in a single layer in the cooking basket. Work in batches. Bake at 370 degrees F for 5 to 6 minutes or until golden brown. **Serve:** with the marinara sauce for dipping.

Parmesan Sticks

Prep time: 10 minutes **Cooking time:** 15 minutes
Servings: 3

Ingredients

1/4 Teaspoon Black Pepper
4 Tablespoons Almond Flour
8 Ounces Parmesan Cheese

1/2 Cup Heavy Cream
1 Egg

Directions

Crack your egg into a bowl, beating it. Add in your almond flour and cream, mixing well. Sprinkle your cream mixture with black pepper, whisking well.

Cut your cheese into short, thick sticks, and then dip it in the cream mixture. Place these sticks in a plastic bag and place them in the freezer. Let them freeze.

Turn your air fryer to 400, and then place your frozen sticks on the air fryer rack, and then cook for eight minutes.

Traditional Zucchini Chips

Prep time: 5 minutes **Cooking time:** 35 minutes
Servings: 6

Ingredients
3 zucchinis thinly sliced   1 teaspoon salt

Directions

Put the zucchini in the air fryer and sprinkle with salt. Cook them at 350F for 35 minutes. Shake the zucchini every 5 minutes.

Seaweed Crisps

Prep time: 10 minutes **Cooking time:** 5 minutes
Servings: 4

Ingredients
3 nori sheets   1 teaspoon nutritional
2 tablespoons water   yeast

Directions

Cut the nori sheets roughly and put in the air fryer basket.
Sprinkle the nori sheets with water and nutritional yeast and cook at 375F for 5 minutes.

Avocado Sticks

Prep time: 10 minutes **Cooking time:** 14 minutes
Servings: 4

Ingredients
1 avocado, pitted, halves   1 tablespoon coconut
1 egg, beaten   shred

Directions

Cut the avocado halves into 4 wedges and dip in the egg.
Then coat the avocado in coconut shred and put in the air fryer. Cook the avocado sticks at 375F for 7 minutes per side.

Mozzarella Sticks

Prep time: 10 minutes **Cooking time:** 4 minutes
Servings: 4

Ingredients
1 egg, beaten   4 tbsp almond flour
9 oz. Mozzarella, cut into
sticks

Directions

Dip the mozzarella sticks in the egg and they coat in the almond flour. Then put the mozzarella sticks in the air fryer basket and cook at 400F for 4 minutes.

Lettuce Wraps

Prep time: 10 minutes **Cooking time:** 4 minutes
Servings: 12

Ingredients
12 bacon strips   12 lettuce leaves
1 tablespoon mustard   1 tablespoon apple cider
    vinegar

Directions

Set the bacon in the air fryer in one layer and cook at 400f for 2 minutes per side.

Then sprinkle the bacon with mustard and apple cider vinegar and put on the lettuce. Wrap the lettuce into rolls.

Carrot Chips

Prep time: 10 minutes **Cooking time:** 13 minute
Servings: 8

Ingredients
3 carrots, thinly sliced   1 teaspoon avocado oil

Directions

Set the carrots in the air fryer basket, sprinkle with avocado oil. Cook the carrot chips for 30 minutes at 355F. Shake the carrot chips every 5 minutes.

Crunchy Bacon

Prep time: 5 minutes **Cooking time:** 8 minutes
Servings: 4

Ingredients
8 bacon slices   1 teaspoon Erythritol
Directions

Sprinkle the bacon with Erythritol and put in the air fryer basket in one layer. Cook it for 4 minutes per side or until the bacon is crunchy.

Keto Granola

Prep time: 10 minutes **Cooking time:** 12 minutes
Servings: 4

Ingredients
1 teaspoon monk fruit   1 teaspoon pumpkin pie
2 teaspoons coconut oil   spices
3 pecans, chopped   1 tbsp coconut shred
3 oz. almonds, chopped   1 tablespoon flax seeds

Directions

In the mixing bowl, mix all Ingredients from the list above. Make the small balls from the mixture and put them in the air fryer. Cook the granola for 6 minutes per side at 365F. Cool the cooked granola.

Air Fryer Cinnamon-Sugar Doughnuts

Prep time: 10 minutes **Cooking time:** 18 minutes
Serve: 1

Ingredients

¼ cup butter, melted
¼ cup brown sugar
¼ teaspoon ground nutmeg (optional)
½ cup white sugar
1 tbs ground cinnamon
1 (16.3 ounces) package refrigerated flaky biscuit dough (such as Pillsbury™ Grands! ™ Flaky Layers)

Directions

Melt the butter in a basin. Combine the white sugar, brown sugar, cinnamon, and nutmeg in a separate dish.

Separate the biscuit dough into individual biscuits and use a biscuit cutter to cut out the centers to make a doughnut shape. Fill the air fryer basket halfway with doughnuts.

4 to 6 minutes in an air fryer at 350°F (175°C) until golden brown. Cook for a further 1 to 3 minutes after flipping the doughnuts.

Take the doughnuts out of the air fryer. Dip each doughnut into melted butter (coating top, bottom, and sides), then into the sugar-cinnamon mixture until completely coated. **Serve:** right away.

Rosemary Potato Wedges for the Air Fryer

Prep time: 18 minutes **Cooking time:** 20 minutes
Serve: 1

Ingredients

2 russet potatoes, sliced into 12 wedges, each with skin on
1 tablespoon finely chopped fresh rosemary
2 teaspoons seasoned salt
1 tbsp extra-virgin olive oil

Directions

Preheat an air fryer carefully to 380°F (190 degrees C). Toss the potatoes with the olive oil in a large mixing basin. Toss with the seasoned salt and rosemary to mix.

Once the air fryer is heated, place the potatoes in a uniform layer in the fryer basket; you may need to cook them in batches.

Air fried the potatoes for 10 minutes before flipping them with tongs. Continue air frying until the potato wedges are done to your liking, about 10 minutes longer.

Fried Green Tomatoes in the Air Fryer

Prep time: 15 minutes **Cooking time:** 25 minutes
Serve: 1

Ingredients

2 green tomatoes, cut into 1/4-inch slices
½ cup buttermilk
1 cup plain panko breadcrumbs
½ teaspoon paprika
⅓ cup all-purpose flour
salt and black pepper
2 eggs, lightly beaten
1 teaspoon garlic powder
1 cup yellow cornmeal
1 tablespoon olive oil, or as needed

Directions

Season the tomato slices properly with salt and pepper to taste. Set up a breading station with three shallow dishes flour in the first, buttermilk and eggs in the second, and breadcrumbs, cornmeal, garlic powder, and paprika in the third.

Dredge tomato slices in flour and shake off excess. Dip the tomatoes into the egg mixture, then the bread crumb mixture, coating both sides.

Preheat the air fryer carefully to 400°F (200 degrees C). Brush olive oil into the frying basket. Place the breaded tomato slices in the fryer basket, making sure they don't touch; cook in batches if required. Brush olive oil over the tops of the tomatoes. Cook for 12 minutes, then turn the tomatoes and spray with olive oil one more. 3 to 5 minutes more, or until crisp and golden brown. To keep the tomatoes crisp, place them on a rack lined with paper towels. Rep with the remaining tomatoes.

Air Fryer French Toast Sticks

Prep time: 15 minutes **Cooking time:** 25 minutes
Serve: 1

Ingredients

2 large eggs
1 tablespoon butter, melted
4 slices of day-old bread, cut into thirds
1 teaspoon vanilla extract
⅓ cup milk
1 tbs ground cinnamon
1 teaspoon confectioners' sugar, or to taste

Directions

Combine the eggs, milk, butter, vanilla essence, and cinnamon in a mixing dish. Using parchment paper, line an air fryer basket. Place each slice of bread in the basket after dipping it in the milk mixture. Make sure they are not touching and, if required, cook in batches.

Preheat the air fryer carefully to 370°F (188 degrees C). Fry the bread for 6 minutes in the basket, then flips and cook for another 3 minutes. Confectioners' sugar should be sprinkled on each stick.

Air Fryer Rib-Eye Steak

Prep time: 20 minutes **Cooking time:** 20 minutes
Serve: 1

Ingredients

2 rib-eye steaks, cut 1
1/2- inch thick
¼ cup olive oil

4 teaspoons grill seasoning
(such as Montreal Steak
Seasoning®)
½ cup reduced-sodium soy
sauce

Directions

Combine the steaks, soy sauce, olive oil, and spice in a
large resealable bag. Marinate the meat for at least 2
hours before cooking. Take the steaks out of the bag
and discard the marinade. Next, remove any extra oil
from the steaks.

To prevent the air fryer pan from smoking throughout
the cooking process, add roughly 1 tablespoon of
water to the bottom. Preheat the air fryer carefully to
400°F (200 degrees C). Cook the steaks in the air fryer
for 7 minutes. Cook for another 7 minutes, or until
the steaks are medium-rare. Increase the overall cook
time to 16 minutes for a medium steak, turning after 8
minutes.

Remove the steaks from the pan, keep warm, and set
aside for 4 minutes before serving.

Air Fryer Roasted Broccoli and Cauliflower

Prep time: 15 minutes **Cooking time:** 25 minutes
Serve: 1

Ingredients

3 cups broccoli florets
½ teaspoon garlic powder
¼ teaspoon paprika
2 tablespoons olive oil

3 cups cauliflower florets
¼ teaspoon sea salt
⅛ teaspoon ground black
pepper

Directions

Heat an air fryer to 400°F (200°C) according to the
manufacturer's instructions. In a large microwave-safe dish,
combine broccoli florets. Cook for 3 minutes on high
power in the microwave. Any collected liquid should be
drained.

Combine the cauliflower, olive oil, garlic powder, sea salt,
paprika, and black pepper in the same bowl as the
broccoli. To blend, mix everything thoroughly. Fill the air
fryer basket halfway with the mixture. Cook for 12
minutes, turning the veggies halfway through to ensure
equal browning.

Cauliflower Roasted in the Air Fryer

Prep time: 15 minutes **Cooking time:** 20 minutes
Serve: 1

Ingredients

3 cloves garlic
½ teaspoon salt

1 tablespoon peanut oil
½ teaspoon smoked
paprika
4 cups cauliflower florets

Directions

Preheat an air fryer carefully to 400°F (200 degrees C).
Cut the garlic in half and pound it with a knife blade.

Air Fryer Lemon Pepper Shrimp

Prep time: 20 minutes **Cooking time:** 25 minutes **Serve:**
1

Ingredients

1 tablespoon olive oil
¼ teaspoon paprika
12 ounces uncooked
medium shrimp, peeled
and deveined
1 lemon, sliced

1 teaspoon lemon pepper
¼ teaspoon garlic powder
1 lemon, juiced

Directions

Preheat an air fryer carefully to 400 degrees F. (200
degrees C). Cut the garlic in half and smash it with the
blade of a knife. Combine in a bowl with the oil, salt,
and paprika. Add the cauliflower and toss to coat.
Place the coated cauliflower in the air fryer bowl and
cook until crisp, about 15 minutes total, shaking every
5 minutes.

Air Fryer Bacon

Prep time: 20 minutes **Cooking time:** 20 minutes
Serve: 1

Ingredients

½ (16 ounces) package
bacon

Directions

Preheat an air fryer carefully to 390°F (200 degrees C).
Lay the bacon in a single layer in the air fryer basket;
little overlap is OK. Cook for 8 minutes. Cook for
another 7 minutes, or until the bacon is crisp. Place
fried bacon on a dish lined with paper towels to
absorb extra fat.

Baby Back Ribs in the Air

Prep time: 15 minutes **Cooking time:** 20 minutes
Serve: 1

Ingredients

1 rack baby back ribs
1 tablespoon olive oil
½ teaspoon salt
1 tablespoon brown sugar
½ teaspoon garlic powder
½ teaspoon chili powder

1 tablespoon liquid smoke flavoring
½ teaspoon ground black pepper
½ teaspoon onion powder
1 cup BBQ sauce

Directions

Remove the membrane off the back of the ribs and pat dry with a paper towel. Cut the rack into four parts. In a small dish, combine the olive oil and liquid smoke and apply them on both sides of the ribs. Combine brown sugar, garlic powder, onion powder, salt, pepper, and chili powder in a mixing bowl. Season both sides of the ribs well with the seasoning mixture. Allow the ribs to rest for 30 minutes to allow the taste to develop.
Preheat an air fryer carefully to 375°F (190 degrees C). Place the ribs in the air fryer basket, bone side down, ensure they don't touch; cook in batches if required. The **Cooking time:** is 15 minutes. Cook for 10 minutes more after flipping the ribs (meat-side down). Remove the ribs from the air fryer and brush the bone-side with 1/2 cup BBQ sauce. Return the basket to the air fryer and cook for 5 minutes. Cook for a further 5 minutes, or until desired char is obtained, after flipping the ribs over and brushing the meat side with the remaining 1/2 cup BBQ sauce.

Roasted Rainbow Vegetables in the Air Fryer

Prep time: 15 minutes **Cooking time:** 18 minutes
Serve: 1

Ingredients

1 red bell pepper
1 zucchini cut in pieces
4 ounces fresh mushrooms, cleaned and halved
salt and pepper to taste

1 yellow summer squash, cut into 1-inch pieces
½ sweet onion, cut into 1-inch wedges
1 tbsp extra-virgin olive oil

Directions

Preheat an air fryer carefully according to the manufacturer's instructions.
Combine the red bell pepper, summer squash, zucchini, mushrooms, and onion in a large bowl. Toss in the olive oil, salt, and black pepper to taste.
In the air fryer basket, arrange the vegetables in an even layer. Cook until the veggies are roasted, approximately 20 minutes, stirring halfway through.

Air Fryer Flour Tortilla Bowls

Prep time: 15 minutes **Cooking time:** 22 minutes
Serve: 1

Ingredients

1 (8 inches) flour tortilla   1 (4 1/2-inch) souffle dish

Directions

Preheat the air fryer carefully to 375°F (190 degrees C).
Heat the tortilla in a big pan or directly on the gas stove grates until warm and malleable. Place the tortilla in the souffle dish, smoothing it down and fluting it up the sides.
4 to 5 minutes in the air fryer until the tortilla becomes golden brown.
Place the tortilla bowl upside down in the basket after removing it from the souffle dish. 1 to 2 minutes more air fry until golden brown.

Air Fryer Steak and Cheese Melts

Prep time: 10 minutes **Cooking time:** 18 minutes
Serve: 1

Ingredients

1 pound beef rib-eye steak, thinly sliced
1 medium onion, sliced into petals
½ green bell pepper, thinly sliced
1 tablespoon olive oil
½ teaspoon ground mustard
4 hoagie rolls
4 slices Provolone cheese

1 tablespoon reduced-sodium soy sauce
4 ounces sliced baby portobello mushrooms
½ teaspoon salt
2 tablespoons Worcestershire sauce
¼ teaspoon ground black pepper

Directions

Combine the steak, Worcestershire sauce, and soy sauce in a mixing bowl. Refrigerate for 4 hours to overnight. Remove from the refrigerator and set aside for 30 minutes to come to room temperature.
Preheat the air fryer carefully to 380°F (190 degrees C).
Combine the onion, mushrooms, and bell pepper in a large mixing basin. Stir in the olive oil, salt, ground mustard, and pepper to coat. Place the hoagie rolls in the air fryer basket and toast for about 2 minutes. Then, place the rolls on a platter.
Place the steak in the air fryer basket and cook for 3 minutes. Cook for 1 minute more after stirring. Place on a platter.
Cook for 5 minutes in the air fryer basket with the veggie mix. Cook until softened, approximately 5 minutes more.
Incorporate the meat into the veggie mixture. Place somewhat overlapping cheese slices on top. Cook for 3 minutes, or until the cheese is melted and bubbling.
Serve: immediately on toasted buns with the mixture.

Air Fryer Bacon-Wrapped Scallops with Sriracha Mayo

Prep time: 10 minutes **Cooking time:** 18 minutes
Serve: 1

Ingredients

½ cup mayonnaise

1 pound bay scallops
(about 36 small scallops),

1 pinch coarse
salt

1 serving olive oil

2 tablespoons Sriracha
sauce

12 slices bacon, cut into
thirds

1 pinch cracked black
pepper

cooking spray

Directions

In a small bowl, combine mayonnaise and Sriracha sauce. Refrigerate the Sriracha mayonnaise until ready to use. Preheat the air fryer carefully to 390°F (200 degrees C). Spread the scallops on a plate or cutting board and wipe dry with a paper towel. Season with salt and pepper to taste. Wrap a third of a slice of bacon around each scallop and fasten with a toothpick.
Cooking spray should be sprayed on the air fryer basket. Place the bacon-wrapped scallops in a single layer in the basket; if required, divide them into two groups.
Cook for 7 minutes in the air fryer. Check for doneness; the scallops should be opaque and the bacon crispy. Cook for an additional 1 to 2 minutes, checking every minute. With tongs, carefully remove the scallops and lay them on a paper towel-lined dish to soak any extra oil from the bacon. Toss with Sriracha mayonnaise and **Serve:.**

Air Fryer Prosciutto and Mozzarella Grilled Cheese

Prep time: 15 minutes **Cooking time:** 20 minutes
Serve: 1

Ingredients

2 tbs unsalted butter

2 ounces prosciutto

2 slices sourdough bread

3 ounces fresh mozzarella

Directions

Preheat the oven to 360° F. (180 degrees C).
Butter one side of a slice of bread and set it greased side down on a platter. Top with prosciutto and mozzarella slices in an even layer. Butter the second slice of bread and set it on top, buttered side out. Place in the air fryer and cook for 8 minutes, or until gently browned and toasted.

Beignets in the Air Fryer

Prep time: 18 minutes **Cooking time:** 20 minutes
Serve: 1

Ingredients

cooking spray

¼ cup white sugar

1 large egg, separated

½ teaspoon baking powder

2 tablespoons
confectioners' sugar, or to
taste

½ cup all-purpose flour

⅛ cup water

1 ½ teaspoon melted
butter

½ teaspoon vanilla extract

1 pinch salt

Directions

Preheat the air fryer carefully to 370°F (185 degrees C). Nonstick cooking sprays a silicone egg-bite mold. Combine the flour, sugar, water, egg yolk, butter, baking powder, vanilla extract, and salt in a large mixing basin. To blend, stir everything together.
In a small mixing basin, beat the egg white with an electric hand mixer on medium speed until soft peaks form. Incorporate into the batter. Transfer the batter to the prepared mold using a tiny, hinged ice cream scoop.
Fill the silicone mold and place it in the air fryer basket.
Fry for 10 minutes in a hot air fryer. Carefully remove the mold from the basket; pop the beignets out and flip them onto a parchment paper circle.
Return the parchment round containing the beignets to the air fryer basket. Cook for another 4 minutes. Remove the beignets from the air fryer basket and sprinkle them with confectioners' sugar.

Air-Fryer Potato-Skin Wedges

Prep time: 15 minutes **Cooking time:** 20 minutes **Serve:** 1

Ingredients

4 medium russet potatoes

1 cup water

¼ teaspoon ground black
pepper

3 tablespoons canola oil

1 teaspoon paprika

¼ teaspoon salt

Directions

Fill a big saucepan halfway with salted water and bring to a boil. Reduce the heat to medium-low and cook until the potatoes are fork- tender, about 20 minutes. Drain. Refrigerate in a bowl for 30 minutes or until totally cold.
Combine the oil, paprika, black pepper, and salt in a mixing dish. Toss the quartered cold potatoes into the mixture.
Preheat an air fryer carefully to 400°F (200 degrees C). Place half of the potato wedges in the air fryer basket, skin side down, being careful not to overcrowd.
13 to 15 minutes, or until golden brown. Rep with the remaining wedges.

Air Fryer To stones

Prep time: 20 minutes **Cooking time:** 20 minutes
Serve: 1

Ingredients

2 green (unripe) plantains
olive oil cooking spray

3 cups water, or as
needed, salt to taste

Directions

Preheat an air fryer carefully to 400°F (200 degrees C). Remove the plantain tips. Make a vertical cut from end to end in the skin, careful not to cut through the thick skin and into the plantain flesh. Plantain, still in its peel, should be cut into 1-inch segments. Peel the skin off each portion, beginning with the slit you formed.

Spray the plantain pieces with olive oil spray and place them in the air fryer basket. 5 minutes in the air fryer. Prepare a dish of salted water in the meantime.

Using tongs, remove the plantain pieces from the air fryer. Using a Costanera, pound to a thickness of about 1/2-inch (plantain smasher). While the remainder of the two stones is being broken, soak them in a dish of salted water.
After removing the two stones from the salted water, blot them dry using a paper towel.

Return to stones to the air fryer in batches, each time filling the basket with a single layer. Season the tops with salt and coat with olive oil spray; air fry for 5 minutes. With tongs, flip the pan over and coat the opposite side with olive oil spray. Season with salt and pepper. 4 to 5 minutes longer air fry until golden brown and crunchy.

Air Fryer Rosemary Garlic Baby Potatoes

Prep time: 15 minutes **Cooking time:** 18 minutes
Serve: 1

Ingredients

1 ½ pounds multi-colored
new potatoes, halved
1 teaspoon finely chopped
fresh rosemary
½ teaspoon lemon zest

2 cloves garlic, minced
2 tablespoons olive oil
½ teaspoon kosher salt

Directions

Preheat the air fryer carefully to 400°F (200 degrees C).
Combine the potatoes, oil, garlic, rosemary, and salt in a large mixing basin. Arrange the potatoes in the air fryer basket in a single layer, not overcrowded; work in batches if required. Cook for 20 minutes, or until potatoes are golden brown and soft. Before serving, sprinkle with lemon zest.

Zesty Cheddar Biscuits in the Air Fryer

Prep time: 15 minutes **Cooking time:** 20 minutes
Serve: 1

Ingredients

1 cup self-rising flour
1 pinch white sugar
½ cup milk,
2 tablespoons canned
chopped green chili
peppers
¾ teaspoon garlic powder
1 serving cooking spray

¾ cup freshly shredded
sharp Cheddar cheese
¾ teaspoon taco
seasoning mix
2 tbsp taco seasoning mix
¼ teaspoon ground cumin
¼ cup salted butter,
melted

Directions

Preheat an air fryer carefully for 5 minutes at 350 degrees F (175 degrees C).
Combine the flour, Cheddar cheese, milk, green chili peppers, taco seasoning, garlic powder, cumin, and sugar in a medium mixing bowl. Combine all of the Ingredients in a mixing bowl until a dough forms. Line the air fryer basket with a ring of parchment paper. Coat the pan with nonstick cooking spray. Using a spring-hinged scoop, place dough in the basket. 12 minutes in the air fryer
Meanwhile, make the taco spice topping by combining melted butter and seasoning mix. Brush biscuits with taco-seasoned butter after separating them. **Serve:** right away.

Air Fryer Sriracha-Honey Shrimp

Prep time: 15 minutes **Cooking time:** 25 minutes
Serve: 1

Ingredients

1 tablespoon Sriracha
sauce
½ tablespoon soy sauce
½ pound large raw tail-on
shrimp

½ tablespoon lime juice
½ teaspoon minced garlic
2 green onions, chopped
1 tablespoon honey

Directions

According to the manufacturer's instructions, preheat the air fryer carefully to 400°F (200°C). Combine the Sriracha, honey, lime juice, soy sauce, and garlic in a large mixing bowl. Stir in the shrimp until evenly coated.

Place the shrimp in the air fryer basket with tongs and cook for 3 minutes. Return the shrimp to the sauce and toss to combine. Return the shrimp to the basket and cook for 3 minutes more. Garnish with green onions, if desired.

Air Fryer Mini Pizza Calzones

Prep time: 18 minutes **Cooking time:** 20 minutes
Serve: 1

Ingredients

1 (13.8 ounces) package refrigerated pizza dough (such as Pillsbury®)
4 ½ tablespoons shredded mozzarella cheese avocado oil cooking spray

1 (1.75 ounces) package pepperoni (such as Hormel®)
9 teaspoons pizza sauce

Directions

On a lightly floured board, roll out the pizza dough. Then, using a 2 1/8-inch biscuit cutter, cut out 9 circles. Each circular should be rolled into a 4 1/2-inch disc. 1 teaspoon pizza sauce, 3 slices pepperoni, and 1/2 tablespoon mozzarella cheese in each disc. Fold over, seal the edges by folding, and crimp with fork tines.

Preheat an air fryer carefully to 375°F (190 degrees C). Spray the air fryer basket with avocado oil after lining it with parchment paper. Mist a batch of calzones with avocado oil and place them in the basket. Cook for 6 to 8 minutes in an air fryer. Turn the calzones over, spritz

with avocado oil, and air fry for another 2 to 3 minutes, or

Air Fryer Pumpkin Seeds

Prep time: 15 minutes **Cooking time:** 25 minutes
Serve: 1

Ingredients

1 ¾ cups pumpkin seeds
2 teaspoons avocado oil
1 teaspoon salt

1 teaspoon smoked paprika

Directions

Rinse the pumpkin seeds well in a small colander.
On a plate, place two sheets of paper towels. Cover two additional paper towels after placing the pumpkin seeds on the towels. Press down to get rid of the majority of the water. Allow at least 15 minutes for drying.
Preheat the air fryer carefully to 350°F (180 degrees C). Place the seeds in a medium mixing basin. Mix in the avocado oil, paprika, and salt. Mix with a medium spoon. Cook for 35 minutes, stirring the basket periodically, in the air fryer basket with the seeds. Keep an eye on the pumpkin seeds for the last 5 minutes; they may easily go from nicely cooked to burnt.

Spanish Potato Wedges in the Air Fryer

Prep time: 15 minutes **Cooking time:** 25 minutes
Serve: 1

Ingredients

1 ½ pounds russet potatoes, unpeeled cooking spray,
½ teaspoon paprika
¼ teaspoon garlic powder
2 tablespoons vegetable oil

1 teaspoon chili powder,
1 teaspoon ground cumin
½ tbs ground coriander
⅛ teaspoon ground cinnamon salt to taste

Directions

To avoid breaking, cut potatoes into 8 equal wedges less than 5 inches long.
Soak potato wedges in a dish of boiling tap water for about 10 minutes.
Take the potatoes out of the water, rinse them, and wipe them dry with a paper towel.
Preheat an air fryer carefully to 375°F (190 degrees C). Cooking oil spray should be sprayed on the air fryer basket.
Drizzle oil over the potatoes in a large mixing basin. Combine chili powder, cumin, paprika, coriander, garlic powder, and cinnamon; sprinkle over potatoes and mix thoroughly. Place the potatoes in the air fryer basket without crowding them. If necessary, cook in two batches.
10 minutes in the air fryer. Open the air fryer and delicately turn the wedges with tongs. Cook for another 10 to 15 minutes, or until crispy and golden brown. Season with salt and pepper and **Serve:** immediately.

Air Fryer Oreos

Prep time: 20 minutes **Cooking time:** 25 minutes
Serve: 1

Ingredients

½ cup complete pancake mix
9 chocolate sandwich cookies (such as Oreo®)

⅓ cup water cooking spray
1 tablespoon confectioners' sugar, or to taste

Directions

In a mixing bowl, combine the pancake mix and water. Line an air fryer basket with parchment paper. On parchment paper, apply the nonstick cooking spray. After dipping each cookie in the pancake mixture, place it in the basket. Make sure they don't touch and, if necessary, cook in batches.
Preheat the air fryer to 400°F on a low setting (200 degrees C). Cook for 4 to 5 minutes on one side, then turn and cook for another 2 to 3 minutes on the other side, or until golden brown. On top, confectioners' sugar is strewn.

Stuffed Air Fryer Potatoes

Prep time: 15 minutes **Cooking time:** 20 minutes
Serve: 1

Ingredients

4 baking potatoes, peeled and halved
½ yellow onion diced fine
2 slices bacon

½ cup Cheddar cheese, divided
3 teaspoons olive oil, divided

Directions

Preheat the air fryer carefully to 350°F (175 degrees C).

Brush potatoes lightly with 1 teaspoon oil; place in the air fryer basket and cook for 10 minutes. Brush potatoes with 1 teaspoon more oil and cook in the air fryer for 10 minutes. Cook until soft, approximately 10 minutes more, after coating with the remaining oil. Cooked potatoes should be cut in half. Spoon the insides into a mixing basin; stir in 1/4 cup Cheddar cheese.

In a pan, sauté the onion and bacon over medium-high heat, rotating periodically until the bacon is uniformly browned, about 10 minutes.

Stuff potato-Cheddar cheese mixture, onion, bacon into the skins. Top with the remaining cheese. Return the filled potatoes to the air fryer and cook for 6 minutes

Air Fryer Blueberry Muffins

Prep time: 15 minutes **Cooking time:** 20 minutes
Serve: 1

Ingredients

1 cup self-rising flour

¼ teaspoon ground cinnamon
3 tablespoons melted butter
½ cup blueberries

2 ½ tablespoons white sugar
⅓ cup milk
1 egg
2 teaspoons vanilla extract

Directions

Preheat the air fryer carefully for 5 minutes at 340 degrees F (170 degrees C).

In a mixing basin, combine the flour, sugar, and cinnamon. Combine the milk, melted butter, egg, and vanilla essence in a mixing bowl. Blend until everything is properly incorporated. Blueberries should be folded in. Fill silicone cupcake liners 3/4 full of the mixture, using a tiny scoop. Carefully place in the air fryer basket. Muffins should be cooked in the oven for 14 minutes.

Air Fryer Sourdough Bread

Prep time: 15 minutes **Cooking time:** 18 minutes
Serve: 1

Ingredients

1 cup bread flour
½ cup sourdough starter

½ teaspoon fine sea salt

½ cup spelled flour
1 tbsp extra-virgin olive oil
½ cup water

Directions

In the bowl of a stand mixer, combine bread flour, spelled flour, sourdough starter, oil, and salt. Begin kneading with the dough hook. Add water until all Ingredients come together and start to pull together; you may not need all of the water. Knead for 5 minutes at low speed.

Form the dough into a ball by folding it in half. Place in a baking dish that can be used in an air fryer. Cover with plastic wrap and set aside for 5 hours to overnight to double in volume. Preheat the air fryer carefully to 390°F (200 degrees C). Remove the plastic wrap off the bread and score it.

Place the baking dish in the air fryer and cook for 20 minutes, or until the loaf is golden. In the middle, an instant-read thermometer should read at least 190 degrees F. (88 degrees C). Allow cooling completely before slicing.

Air Fryer Asparagus Tots

Prep time: 15 minutes **Cooking time:** 22 minutes
Serve: 1

Ingredients

12 ounces asparagus, trimmed and diced
¼ cup finely shredded Parmesan cheese

½ cup panko breadcrumbs
1 serving cooking spray

Directions

Over medium-high heat, bring a saucepan of salted water to a boil. Cook the asparagus for 5 minutes. Drain in a colander and set aside to cool for 5 minutes, or until easily handled.

Combine the asparagus, breadcrumbs, and Parmesan cheese in a large mixing dish. Knead the Ingredients with your hands until it resembles dough. 1 tablespoon of the mixture should be formed into a tot. **Serve:** on a platter. Repeat with the rest of the mixture. Freeze the tater tots for 30 minutes.

Preheat the air fryer carefully to 400°F (200 degrees C).

Spray the air fryer basket with nonstick cooking spray. Next, spray the tops of the tots with cooking spray before placing them in the basket. Fry for 10 minutes, shaking once halfway through.

Tofu in the Air Fryer

Prep time: 20 minutes **Cooking time:** 20 minutes
Serve: 1

Ingredients

1 (14 ounces) package extra-firm tofu	1 cup mayonnaise
½ cup sweet chili sauce	2 tbs. toasted sesame oil
1 ½ cups panko breadcrumbs	1 ½ tbs. Sriracha sauce
	1 green onion, chopped

Directions

Place the tofu on a dish lined with paper towels. Cover with additional paper towels and a second plate. Press the tofu for 30 minutes with a 3- to 5-pound weight on top. Drain and discard any remaining liquid, then cut the tofu into 1/2-inch pieces.

Toss the cubed tofu in a dish with the sesame oil. Allow for a 20- minute resting period after gently stirring.

Meanwhile, create the bang bang sauce by whisking together the mayonnaise, sweet chili sauce, and Sriracha sauce until smooth. Then, in a separate dish, combine the panko.

Preheat the air fryer carefully to 400°F (200 degrees C).

Tofu should be mixed with 1/2 cup bang bang sauce until evenly incorporated. Coat the tofu in the panko breadcrumbs and set it in the air fryer basket, ensuring the tofu pieces do not overlap. You may need to perform this in batches depending on the size of your air fryer.

5 minutes in the oven. Cook for 3 minutes more after shaking. **Serve:** with the leftover bang bang sauce and garnished with green onion.

Air Fryer Butternut Squash Home Fries

Prep time: 15 minutes **Cooking time:** 25 minutes
Serve: 1

Ingredients

1 pound butternut squash	1 tbs. extra-virgin olive oil
2 teaspoons bagel seasoning (such as Trader Joe's Everything but the Bagel Sesame Seasoning Blend)	1 teaspoon chopped fresh rosemary

Directions

Preheat an air fryer carefully to 400°F (200 degrees C). Toss the butternut squash with the olive oil in a large mixing basin. Place the squash pieces in the air fryer basket. Cook until gently browned, approximately 22 minutes total, stirring every 3 to 4 minutes.

Transfer to a dish or serving plate and evenly sprinkle with the spice blend. Garnish with fresh rosemary if desired.

Air Fryer Lobster Tails with Lemon-Garlic Butter

Prep time: 15 minutes **Cooking time:** 20 minutes
Serve: 1

Ingredients

2 (4 ounces) lobster tails	4 tablespoons butter
1 teaspoon lemon zest	salt and ground black pepper to taste
1 clove garlic, grated	
2 wedges lemon	1 teaspoon chopped fresh parsley

Directions

Butterfly lobster tails by using kitchen shears to cut longitudinally through the hard upper shells and flesh. Cut to the bottoms of the shells, but not all the way through. Separate the tail halves. Place the lobster tails in the air fryer basket, lobster flesh facing up.

In a small saucepan over medium heat, melt the butter. Heat the lemon zest and garlic for 30 seconds, or until the garlic is soft. Brush 2 tablespoons of the butter mixture onto the lobster tails; remove any excess brushed butter to avoid contamination with raw lobster. Season the lobster with salt and pepper to taste. Cook for 5 to 7 minutes in an air fryer at 380°F (195°C) until lobster flesh is opaque.

Spicy Homemade Breakfast Sausage in the Air Fryer

Prep time: 15 minutes **Cooking time:** 25 minutes
Serve: 1

Ingredients

1 pound ground pork	1 teaspoon rubbed sage
1 teaspoon crushed red pepper	½ teaspoon dried marjoram
	1 teaspoon sea salt
½ teaspoon onion powder	½ teaspoon ground black pepper
¼ teaspoon dried thyme	

Directions

Preheat an air fryer carefully to 400°F (200 degrees C). In a large mixing bowl, combine ground pork, sea salt, sage, red pepper, marjoram, onion powder, pepper, and thyme. Mix thoroughly with your hands until everything is equally incorporated. Make 8 patties out of the mixture.

Cook for 5 minutes with 4 patties in the air fryer basket. Cook for 5 minutes longer after carefully flipping the burgers. Repeat with the remaining patties on a plate lined with paper towels.

Wedges of Rosemary Potatoes

Prep time: 10 minutes **Cooking time:** 25 minutes
Serve: 4

Ingredients

3 potatoes, cut into wedges
1 tsp garlic powder
1 tbsp parsley, chopped
Salt

3 tbsp olive oil

1 tbsp fresh rosemary, chopped Pepper

Directions

Preheat the air fryer to 390 F. Soak potato wedges into the water for 30 minutes. Drain well and pat dry with paper towels.

In a mixing bowl, toss potato wedges with parsley, oil, garlic powder, rosemary, pepper, and salt.
Place potato wedges into the air fryer basket and cook for 15 minutes. Stir well and cook for 10 minutes more. **Serve:** and enjoy.

Healthy Mixed Nuts

Prep time: 10 minutes **Cooking time:** 9 minutes
Serve: 4

Ingredients

1/4 cup hazelnuts
1/2 cup pecans
1/4 cup walnuts

1/2 cup macadamia nuts
1 tbsp olive oil
1 tsp salt

Directions

Preheat the air fryer to 320 F. In a bowl, toss nuts with oil and salt. Add nuts into the air fryer basket and cook for 9 minutes. Stir halfway through. **Serve:** and enjoy.

Stuff Mushrooms

Prep time: 10 minutes **Cooking time:** 5 minutes
Serve: 6

Ingredients

9 oz mushrooms, cut stems
6 oz mozzarella cheese, shredded
1/2 tsp salt

1 tsp dried parsley

1 tbsp butter

Directions

Preheat the air fryer to 400 F. In a small bowl, mix together cheese, butter, parsley, and salt until well combined. Stuff cheese mixture into the mushroom caps and place in the air fryer basket and cook for 5 minutes.
Serve: and enjoy.

Crispy Broccoli Popcorn

Prep time: 10 minutes **Cooking time:** 6 minutes
Serve: 4

Ingredients

4 eggs yolks
1/4 cup butter, melted

Salt

2 cups broccoli florets
2 cups coconut flour
Pepper

Directions

Preheat the air fryer to 400 F. In a small bowl, whisk egg yolks with butter, pepper, and salt. In a separate bowl, add coconut flour.

Dip each broccoli floret with egg mixture and coat with coconut flour. Place coated broccoli florets into the air fryer basket and cook for 6 minutes. **Serve:** and enjoy.

Zucchini Bites

Prep time: 10 minutes **Cooking time:** 10 minutes
Serve: 6

Ingredients

1 egg, lightly beaten
4 zucchinis, grated and squeezed
Salt

1 tsp Italian seasoning
1/2 cup parmesan cheese, grated Pepper
1 cup shredded coconut

Directions

Preheat the air fryer to 400 F. Add all Ingredients into the bowl and mix until well combined.

Make small balls from the zucchini mixture and place into the air fryer basket and cook for 10 minutes. Turn halfway through. **Serve:** and enjoy.

Air Fryer Almonds

Prep time: 5 minutes **Cooking time:** 6 minutes **Serve:** 6

Ingredients

1 cup almonds
1 tsp chili powder
1/4 tsp paprika Salt

1/4 tsp cumin
2 tsp olive oil

Directions

Preheat the air fryer to 320 F.
Add almond and remaining Ingredients into the bowl and toss to coat.
Transfer almonds into the air fryer basket and cook for 6 minutes.
Serve: and enjoy.

Air Fryer Cheese-Stuffed Mini Italian Meatloaves

Prep time: 10 minutes **Cooking time:** 18 minutes
Serve: 1

Ingredients

⅓ cup milk
1 egg, lightly beaten
2 ounces small fresh mozzarella balls
2 tablespoons purchased basil pesto
¼ teaspoon ground black pepper
1 pound 90% lean ground beef

⅓ cup Italian-seasoned panko breadcrumbs
½ cup marinara sauce, warmed
1 clove garlic, minced
8 slices pepperoni
1 tablespoon chopped fresh basil

Directions

Combine the milk, pesto, egg, garlic, and pepper in a medium mixing bowl. Next, combine the ground beef and breadcrumbs, being careful not to overmix. Divide the meat mixture into four equal halves. Make a well in the center of each section, leaving a 1/2-inch border around the edge. Fill each well with 2 slices of pepperoni, overlapping to span the whole length of the well. Top with a quarter of the mozzarella balls. Enclose the filling by pressing the meat mixture around it; shape each chunk into an oblong loaf shape. Loaves should be placed in the air fryer basket in batches.
Cook in the air fryer at 370°F (190°C) for 15 minutes, or until an instant-read thermometer inserted into the thickest part of the meat registers 165°F (75°C).
Serve: the meatloaves with warm marinara sauce and fresh basil on top.

Air Fryer Mahi Mahi with Brown Butter

Prep time: 15 minutes **Cooking time:** 25 minutes
Serve: 1

Ingredients

4 (6 ounces) mahi-mahi fillets
⅔ cup butter

salt and ground black pepper
to taste cooking spray

Directions

Preheat an air fryer carefully to 350°F (175 degrees C). Season the mahi-mahi fillets with salt and pepper and coat both sides with cooking spray. Place the fillets in the air fryer basket, leaving space between them.
Cook for 12 minutes, or until the fish flakes easily with a fork and has a golden tint.
Melt butter in a small saucepan over medium-low heat while the fish cooks. Bring the butter to a boil and cook for 3 to 5 minutes, or until it becomes foamy and deep brown. Turn off the heat.
Place the fish fillets on a platter and top with brown butter.

Air Fryer Black Garlic-Cauliflower Patties

Prep time: 18 minutes **Cooking time:** 20 minutes
Serve: 1

Ingredients

1 medium head cauliflower, cut into florets
¼ cup Italian-seasoned breadcrumbs
½ teaspoon ground black pepper to taste

½ teaspoon dried parsley
½ teaspoon dried rosemary
½ teaspoon onion powder
cooking spray

½ cup all-purpose flour
2 eggs, beaten
1 teaspoon salt
4 solo black garlic bulbs
½ teaspoon dried basil
2 teaspoons baking powder
½ teaspoon dried oregano
½ tbs red pepper flakes

4 slices Swiss cheese, torn into 4 pieces each

Directions

Combine cauliflower and black garlic; process until finely "riced." Transfer to a mixing basin. In a large mixing bowl, combine the flour, eggs, breadcrumbs, baking powder, salt, black pepper, basil, parsley, oregano, rosemary, red pepper flakes, and onion powder. Stir until everything is completely blended.
Preheat an air fryer carefully to 400°F (200 degrees C). Spray the air fryer basket with cooking spray and line it with parchment paper.
Using a big cookie scoop, drop the cauliflower mixture onto the parchment paper and flatten gently with your fingertips.
Cook for 4 to 6 minutes in the air fryer, turn with a spatula, and continue cooking until patties are set, about 1 minute more. Remove each burger from the air fryer and top with 1/4 slice Swiss cheese. Return to the air fryer and cook for 30 to 40 seconds more, or until the cheese is melted.

Air Fryer Tajin Apple Chips

Prep time: 10 minutes **Cooking time:** 18 minutes
Serve: 1

Ingredients

1 apple, cored

½ tablespoon chili-lime seasoning (such as Tajin®), or more to taste

Directions

Preheat the air fryer carefully to 180°F (82 degrees C). Using a mandolin, thinly slice the apple.
Place as many apple slices as you can in the air fryer basket, ensuring they don't touch.
Cook for 12 minutes in the air fryer, working in batches as required. Remove the basket and heat until the apple slices are gently browned on the other side, 8 to 12 minutes longer. Sprinkle with chili-lime seasoning right away.

Desserts Recipes

Chelsea Currant Buns from scratch

(**Ready in about** 50 minutes | **Servings:** 4)

Ingredients

1/2 pound cake flour
1 teaspoon dry yeast
A pinch of sea salt
1/2 cup milk, warm
1 egg, whisked

1 tablespoons granulated sugar
4 tablespoons butter
1/2 cup dried currants
1 ounce icing sugar

Directions

Mix the flour, yeast, sugar and salt in a bowl; add in milk, egg and 2 tablespoons of butter and mix to combine well. Add lukewarm water as necessary to form a smooth dough.

Knead the dough until it is elastic; then, leave it in a warm place to rise for 30 minutes.

Roll out your dough and spread the remaining 2 tablespoons of butter onto the dough; scatter dried currants over the dough.

Cut into 8 equal slices and roll them up. Brush each bun with a nonstick

cooking oil and transfer them to the Air Fryer cooking basket.

Cook your buns at 330 degrees F for about 20 minutes, turning them over halfway through the cooking time.

Dust with icing sugar before serving. Bon appétit!

Old-Fashioned Pinch-Me Cake with Walnuts

(**Ready in about** 20 minutes | **Servings:** 4)

Ingredients

1 (10-ounces) can crescent rolls
1 teaspoon pumpkin pie spice blend

1/2 cup caster sugar
1/2 stick butter
1/2 cup walnuts, chopped
1 tablespoon dark rum

Directions

Start by preheating your Air Fryer to 350 degrees F.

Roll out the crescent rolls. Spread the butter onto the crescent rolls; scatter the sugar, spices and walnuts over the rolls. Drizzle with rum and roll them up.

Using your fingertips, gently press them to seal the edges.

Bake your cake for about 13 minutes or until the top is golden brown. Bon appétit!

Genuine Swedish Kärleksmums

(**Ready in about** 20 minutes | **Servings:** 3)

Ingredients

2 tablespoons Swedish butter, at room temperature
1 tablespoon lingonberry jam
5 tbs all-purpose flour

A pinch of coarse sea salt

1 egg
4 tablespoons brown sugar

2 tablespoons cocoa powder A pinch of grated nutmeg
1/2 tbs baking powder

Directions

Using an electric mixer, cream the butter and sugar together. Fold in the egg and lingonberry jam until well combined. Mix in the flour, baking powder, cocoa powder, grated nutmeg, and salt until well combined. Pour the batter into a baking dish that has been lightly buttered.

Bake your cake for about 15 minutes, or until a tester inserted into the centre comes out dry and clean. Good appetite!

Air Grilled Peaches with Cinnamon-Sugar Butter

(**Ready in about** 25 minutes | **Servings:** 2)

Ingredients

2fresh peaches pitted halved
1/4 tbsp ground cinnamon

2 tablespoons caster sugar
1 tablespoon butter

Directions

Mix the butter, sugar and cinnamon. Spread the butter mixture onto the peaches and transfer them to the Air Fryer cooking basket. Cook your peaches at 320 degrees F for about 25 minutes or until the top is golden.

Serve: with vanilla ice cream, if desired. Bon appétit!

Chocolate Apple Chips

(**Ready in about** 15 minutes | **Servings:** 2)

Ingredients

1 large Pink Lady apple, cored and sliced
2 teaspoons cocoa powder

A pinch of kosher salt
1 tbs light brown sugar
2 tablespoons lemon juice

Directions

Toss the apple slices in with the remaining Ingredients. Bake at 350°F for 5 minutes, then shake the basket to ensure even cooking and cook for another 5 minutes. Good appetite!

Favorite Apple Crisp

(**Ready in about** 40 minutes | **Servings:** 4)

Ingredients

4 cups apples, peeled, cored and sliced
1 tablespoon cornmeal
1/2 teaspoon ground cinnamon
1/2 cup quick-cooking oats 1/2 cup all-purpose flour

1 tablespoon honey
1/2 cup brown sugar
1/4 teaspoon ground cloves 1/4 cup water
1/2 cup caster sugar
1/2 tbs baking powder
1/3 cup coconut oil, melted

Directions

Toss the sliced apples with the brown sugar, honey, cornmeal, cloves, and cinnamon. Divide between four custard cups coated with cooking spray.

In a mixing dish, thoroughly combine the remaining Ingredients. Sprinkle over the apple mixture.

Bake in the preheated Air Fryer at 330 degrees F for 35 minutes. Bon appétit!

Cocktail Party Fruit Kabobs

(**Ready in about** 10 minutes | **Servings:** 6)

Ingredients

1 pears, diced into bite-sized chunks
2 apples, diced into bite-sized chunks
1 tbs fresh lemon juice
1 tbs ground cinnamon

2 mangos, diced into bite-sized chunks
1 teaspoon vanilla essence
1/2 tbsp ground cloves
2 tablespoons maple syrup

Directions

Toss all Ingredients in a mixing dish. Tread the fruit pieces on skewers. Cook at 350 degrees F for 5 minutes.

Bon appétit!

Peppermint Chocolate Cheesecake

(**Ready in about** 40 minutes | **Servings:** 6)

Ingredients

1 cup powdered sugar
1/2 cup all-purpose flour
1/2 cup butter
2 drops peppermint extract
1 teaspoon vanilla extract

1 cup mascarpone cheese, at room temperature
4 ounces semisweet chocolate, melted

Directions

In a mixing bowl, combine the sugar, flour, and butter. Press the mixture into the bottom of a baking pan that has been lightly greased.

Bake for 18 minutes at 350 degrees F. Set it in the freezer for 20 minutes. Then, combine the remaining Ingredients to make the cheesecake topping.

Place this topping on top of the crust and place it in the freezer for another 15 minutes to cool. Chill before serving.

Baked Coconut Doughnuts

(**Ready in about** 20 minutes | **Servings:** 6)

Ingredients

1 ½ cups all-purpose flour
1 teaspoon baking powder
A pinch of kosher salt
2 eggs
1/4 tbs ground cardamom
2 tbsp coconut oil, melted
1 teaspoon coconut essence
1 cup coconut flakes

A pinch of freshly grated nutmeg
1/2 cup white sugar
2 tablespoons full-fat coconut milk
1/4 tbs ground cinnamon
1/2 teaspoon vanilla essence

Directions

In a mixing bowl, thoroughly combine the all-purpose flour with the baking powder, salt, nutmeg, and sugar.

In a separate bowl, beat the eggs until frothy using a hand mixer; add the coconut milk and oil and beat again; lastly, stir in the spices and mix again until everything is well combined.

Then, stir the egg mixture into the flour mixture and continue mixing until a dough ball forms. Try not to over-mix your dough. Transfer to a lightly floured surface.

Roll out your dough to a 1/4-inch thickness using a rolling pin. Cut out the doughnuts using a 3-inch round cutter; now, use a 1-inch round cutter to remove the center.

Bake in the preheated Air Fryer at 340 degrees F approximately 5 minutes or until golden. Repeat with remaining doughnuts. Decorate with coconut flakes and **Serve:**.

Mug Cake with Chocolate

(**Ready in about** 10 minutes | **Servings:** 2)

Ingredients

1/2 cup self-rising flour
5 tablespoons coconut milk
4 tablespoons unsweetened cocoa powder
2 eggs
6 tablespoons brown sugar
4 tablespoons coconut oil
A pinch of grated nutmeg
A pinch of salt

Directions

Mix all the Ingredients together; divide the batter between two mugs. Place the mugs in the Air Fryer cooking basket and cook at 390 degrees F for about 10 minutes. Bon appétit!

Easy Plantain Cupcakes

(**Ready in about** 10 minutes | **Servings:** 4)

Ingredients

1 teaspoon baking powder
1/4 teaspoon ground cloves
1 cup all-purpose flour
2 ripe plantains, peeled and mashed with a fork
1 egg, whisked
1/4 cup brown sugar
1/4 tbs ground cinnamon
A pinch of salt
2 tablespoons raisins, soaked
4 tablespoons coconut oil, room temperature
4 tablespoons pecans, roughly chopped

Directions

In a mixing bowl, thoroughly combine all Ingredients until everything is well incorporated. Spoon the batter into a greased muffin tin.

Bake the plantain cupcakes in your Air Fryer at 350 degrees F for about 10 minutes or until golden brown on the top. Bon appétit!

Strawberry Dessert Dumplings

(**Ready in about** 10 minutes | **Servings:** 3)

Ingredients

9 wonton wrappers
1/3 strawberry jam
2 ounces icing sugar

Directions

Start by laying out the wonton wrappers. Divide the strawberry jam between the wonton wrappers. Fold the wonton wrapper over the jam; now, seal the edges with wet fingers.

Cook your wontons at 400 degrees F for 8 minutes; working in batches. Bon appétit!

Crunchy French Toast Sticks

(**Ready in about** 10 minutes | **Servings:** 3)

Ingredients

1 egg
1 tablespoon brown sugar
1/4 teaspoon ground cloves
1/4 vanilla paste
1/4 cup milk
1/4 cup double cream
1/4 teaspoon ground cinnamon

3 thick slices of brioche bread, cut into thirds
1 cup crispy rice cereal

Directions

Thoroughly combine the egg, cream, milk, sugar, ground cloves, cinnamon and vanilla.

Dip each piece of bread into the cream mixture and then, press gently into the cereal, pressing to coat all sides.

Arrange the pieces of bread in the Air Fryer cooking basket and cook them at 380 degrees F for 2 minutes; flip and cook on the other side for 2 to 3 minutes longer.

Bon appétit!

Old-Fashioned Apple Crumble

(**Ready in about** 35 minutes | **Servings:** 4)

Ingredients

2 baking apples, peeled, cored and diced
1/4 teaspoon grated nutmeg 1/4 teaspoon ground cloves 1/2 teaspoon ground cinnamon
1/2 teaspoon vanilla essence
1/4 cup coconut oil
1 tablespoon cornstarch
2 tablespoons brown sugar
1/2 cup quick-cooking oats 1/4 cup self-rising flour
1/4 cup brown sugar
1/4 cup apple juice
1/2 teaspoon baking powder

Directions

Toss the apples with 2 tablespoons brown sugar and 2 tablespoons cornstarch. Place the apples in a baking pan that has been lightly greased with nonstick cooking spray. Spray with cooking spray.

Combine the remaining topping Ingredients in a mixing bowl. Over the apple layer, sprinkle the topping Ingredients.

Bake your apple crumble for 35 minutes in a preheated Air Fryer at 330 degrees F. Good appetite!

Authentic Spanish Churros

(**Ready in about** 20 minutes | **Servings:** 4)

Ingredients

1/2 cup water
1 tablespoon granulated sugar A pinch of ground cinnamon
1/2 teaspoon lemon zest
2 ounces dark chocolate
1/2 cup milk

1/4 cup butter, cut into cubes A pinch of salt
1/2 cup plain flour

1 egg Chocolate Dip
1 teaspoon ground cinnamon

Directions

Boil the water in a saucepan over medium-high heat; now, add the butter, sugar, cinnamon, salt and lemon zest; cook until the sugar has dissolved.

Next, remove the pan from the heat. Gradually stir in the flour, whisking continuously until the mixture forms a ball; let it cool slightly.

Fold in the egg and continue to beat using an electric mixer until everything comes together.

Pour the dough into a piping bag with a large star tip. Squeeze 4-inch strips of dough into the greased Air Fryer pan.

Cook your churros at 380 degrees F for about 10 minutes, shaking the basket halfway through the cooking time.

In the meantime, melt the chocolate and milk in a saucepan over low heat. Add in the cinnamon and cook on low heat for about 5 minutes. **Serve:** the warm churros with the chocolate dip and enjoy!

Classic Brownie Cupcakes

(**Ready in about** 25 minutes | **Servings:** 3)

Ingredients

1/3 cup all-purpose flour
1/4 teaspoon baking powder
1/2 teaspoon rum extract
1/3 cup caster sugar
3 tablespoons cocoa powder

2 ounces butter, room temperature
1 large egg
A pinch of ground cinnamon A pinch of salt

Directions

In a mixing bowl, combine the dry Ingredients. Combine the wet Ingredients in a separate bowl. Stir in the wet Ingredients gradually into the dry mixture.

Divide the batter evenly among the muffin cups and place them in the Air Fryer cooking basket.

Bake the cupcakes at 330°F for 15 minutes, or until a tester comes out dry and clean. Allow your cupcakes to cool for 10 minutes on a wire rack before unmolding. Good appetite!

Salad with Baked Fruit

(**Ready in about** 15 minutes | **Servings:** 2)

Ingredients

1 banana, peeled
1 tablespoon freshly squeezed lemon juice
1/2 teaspoon ground star anise
1/2 teaspoon granulated ginger

1 cooking pear, cored
1/4 teaspoon ground cinnamon
1 cooking apple, cored
1/4 cup brown sugar
1 tablespoon coconut oil, melted

Directions

Toss your fruits with lemon juice, star anise, cinnamon, ginger, sugar and coconut oil.

Transfer the fruits to the Air Fryer cooking basket.

Bake the fruit salad in the preheated Air Fryer at 330 degrees F for 15 minutes.

Serve: in individual bowls, garnished with vanilla ice cream. Bon appétit

Red Velvet Pancakes

(**Ready in about** 35 minutes | **Servings:** 3)

Ingredients

1 cup all-purpose flour

1/8 teaspoon sea salt
1/2 teaspoon baking soda
1/2 cup powdered sugar

1 small-sized egg, beaten
1/2 cup milk
2 ounces cream cheese, softened
1 tablespoon butter, softened

1 teaspoon granulated sugar
1/8 teaspoon freshly grated nutmeg
2 tablespoons ghee, melted
1 teaspoon red paste food color

Directions

Thoroughly combine the flour, baking soda, granulated sugar, salt and nutmeg in a large bowl.

Gradually add in the melted ghee, egg, milk and red paste food color, stirring into the flour mixture until moistened. Allow your batter to rest for about 30 minutes.

Spritz the Air Fryer baking pan with cooking spray. Pour the batter into the pan using a measuring cup. Set the pan into the Air Fryer cooking basket.

Cook at 330 degrees F for about 5 minutes or until golden brown. Repeat with the other pancakes.

Meanwhile, mix the remaining Ingredients until creamy and fluffy. Decorate your pancakes with cream cheese topping. Bon appétit!

Clove Crackers

Prep time: 20 minutes **Cooking time:** 33 minutes
Servings: 8

Ingredients
1 cup almond flour
1 teaspoon flax meal
1 teaspoon baking powder
2 tablespoons Erythritol
3 tbs coconut oil, softened

1 teaspoon xanthan gum
1/2 teaspoon salt
1 egg, beaten
1 teaspoon lemon juice
1/2 tbsp ground clove

Directions

In the mixing bowl mix up almond flour, xanthan gum, flax meal, salt, baking powder, and ground clove. Add Erythritol, lemon juice, egg, and coconut oil. Stir the mixture gently with the help of the fork. Then knead the mixture till you get a soft dough. Line the chopping board with parchment. Put the dough on the parchment and roll it up in a thin layer. Cut the thin dough into squares (crackers). Preheat the air fryer to 360F.

Line the air fryer basket with baking paper. Put the prepared crackers in the air fryer basket in one layer and cook them for 11 minutes or until the crackers are dry and light brown. Repeat the same steps with remaining uncooked crackers.

Sage Cream

Prep time: 5 minutes **Cooking time:** 30 minutes
Servings: 4

Ingredients
7 cups red currants
6 sage leaves

1 cup water
1 cup swerve

Directions

In a pan that fits your air fryer, mix all the Ingredients, toss, put the pan in the fryer and cook at 330 degrees F for 30 minutes. Discard sage leaves, divide into cups and **Serve:** cold.

Currant Vanilla Cookies

Prep time: 5 minutes **Cooking time:** 30 minutes
Servings: 6

Ingredients
2 cups almond flour
1/2 cup ghee, melted
1 teaspoon vanilla extract
1/2 cup currants

2 teaspoons baking soda
1/2 cup swerve

Directions

In a bowl, mix all the Ingredients and whisk well. Spread this on a baking sheet lined with parchment paper put the pan in the air fryer and cooks at 350 degrees F for 30 minutes. Cool down, cut into rectangles and **Serve:**.

Fudge Chocolate

Prep time: 15 minutes **Cooking time:** 30 minutes
Servings: 8

Ingredients
1/2 cup butter, melted
2 tbsp cocoa powder
3 tbsp coconut flour
3 tablespoons Splenda
1 teaspoon vanilla extract

1 oz. dark chocolate, chopped, melted
2 eggs, beaten
Cooking spray

Directions

In the bowl mix up melted butter and dark chocolate. Then add vanilla extract, eggs, and cocoa powder. Stir the mixture until smooth and add Splenda, and coconut flour. Stir it again until smooth. Then preheat the air fryer to 325F.

Line the air fryer basket with baking paper and spray it with cooking spray. Pour the fudge mixture in the air fryer basket; flatten it gently with the help of the spatula. Cook the fudge for 30 minutes. Then cut it on the serving squares and cool the fudge completely.

Cranberries Pudding

Prep time: 5 minutes **Cooking time:** 20 minutes
Servings: 6

Ingredients
1 cup cauliflower rice
1/2 cup cranberries

1 teaspoon vanilla extract
2 cups almond milk

Directions

In a pan that fits your air fryer, mix all the Ingredients, whisk a bit, put the pan in the fryer and cook at 360 degrees F for 20 minutes. Stir the pudding, divide into bowls and **Serve:** cold.

Merengues

Prep time: 15 minutes **Cooking time:** 65 minutes
Servings: 6

Ingredients
2 egg whites
4 tablespoons Erythritol

1 tbs lime zest, grated
1 teaspoon lime juice

Directions

Whisk the egg whites until soft peaks. Then add Erythritol and lime juice and whisk the egg whites until you get strong peaks. After this, add lime zest and carefully stir the egg white mixture. Preheat the air fryer to 275F.

Line the air fryer basket with baking paper. With the help of the spoon make the small merengues and put them in the air fryer in one layer. Cook the dessert for 65 minutes.

Chocolaty Banana Muffins

Prep time: 5 minutes **Cooking time:** 25 minutes Serving 12

Ingredients

3/4 cup whole wheat flour
3/4 cup plain flour
1teaspoon baking soda
1/4 teaspoon salt
1cup sugar
1/3 cup canola oil
1egg
1cup mini chocolate chips
1/4 cup of cocoa powder
1/4 teaspoon baking powder
2large bananas, peeled and mashed
1/2 teaspoon vanilla essence

Directions

In a large bowl, mix flour, cocoa powder, baking powder, baking soda, and salt. In another bowl, add bananas, sugar, oil, egg, and vanilla extract and beat till well combined. Slowly, add flour mixture to egg mixture and mix till just combined.

Fold in chocolate chips. Preheat the air fryer oven to 345 degrees F. Grease 12 muffin molds. Transfer the mixture into prepared muffin molds evenly and cooks for about 20-25 minutes or till a toothpick inserted in the center comes out clean.

Remove the Air fryer's muffin molds and keep on a wire rack to cool for about 10 minutes. Carefully turn on a wire rack to cool completely before serving.

Air Fryer Oreos

Prep time: 5 minutes **Cooking time:** 14 minutes Serving 4

Ingredients

1/2 cup total pancake mixture
9 chocolate sandwich cookies (like Oreo®)
cooking spray
1/3 cup water
1tbsp confectioners' sugar or to flavor

Directions

Mix pancake mix and water until well blended. Using parchment paper, Line-up the air fryer basket. Spray parchment paper with non-stick cooking spray.

Dip each cookie into the pancake mix and put it in the jar.
Be sure they're not touching; cook in batches if needed.
Preheat the air fryer to 400 degrees F (200 degrees C).

Insert basket and cook 4 to 5 minutes; reverse and cook till golden brown, 2-3 minutes longer. Sprinkle with confectioners' sugar.

Churros

Prep time: 8 minutes **Cooking time:** 15 minutes Serving 4

Ingredients

1/4 cup butter
1/2 cup milk
2eggs
1/2 teaspoon ground cinnamon
1/4 cup white sugar
1pinch salt
1/2 cup flour

Directions

Melt butter in a saucepan over medium-high water. Pour milk and then add salt. Reduce heat to mild and carry to a boil, still stirring with a wooden spoon. Instantly add flour all at one time. Keep mixing until the dough comes together.

Remove from heat and let cool for 5 to 7 minutes. Mix in eggs together with the wooden spoon till choux pastry comes together. Spoon dough to a pastry bag fitted with a large star tip—pipe dough into pieces directly into the air fryer bowl.

Air fry churros in 340 degrees F (175 degrees C) for 5 minutes. Meanwhile, blend sugar and cinnamon in a small bowl and then pour on a shallow plate. Eliminate fried churros from the air fryer and roll from the cinnamon- sugar mix.

Fluffy Blueberry Fritters

Prep time: 5minutes **Cooking time:** 15 minutes Serving 4

Ingredients

3/4 cup all-purpose flour
1teaspoon baking powder
A pinch of sea salt
2tablespoons melted butter
1 egg
1/2 cup coconut milk 2 tbsp coconut sugar
2 ounces fresh blueberries

Directions

In a mixing bowl, thoroughly combine all the Ingredients.
Drop a spoonful of batter onto the greased Air Fryer pan. Cook in the preheated Air Fryer at 360 degrees F for 10 minutes, flipping them halfway through the cooking time.
Repeat with the remaining batter and **Serve:** warm. Enjoy!

Brownie Muffins

Prep time: 10 minutes **Cooking time:** 10 minutes
Servings: 12

Ingredients

1package Betty Crocker fudge brownie mix
1/3 cup vegetable oil
Egg
1/4 cup walnuts, chopped
2 teaspoons water

Directions

Grease 12 muffin molds. Set aside. In a bowl, put all Ingredients together. Place the mixture into the prepared muffin molds. Press "Power Button" of Air Fry Oven and turn the dial to select the "Air Fry" mode. Press the Time button and again turn the dial to set the **Cooking time:** to 10 minutes.

Now push the Temp button and rotate the dial to set the temperature at 300 degrees F. Press "Start/Pause" button to start. When the unit beeps to show that it is preheated, open the lid. Arrange the muffin molds in "Air Fry Basket" and insert in the oven. Place the muffin molds onto a wire rack to cool for about 10 minutes. Carefully, invert the muffins onto the wire rack to completely cool before serving.

Mug Cake with Chocolate

Prep time: 15 minutes **Cooking time:** 13 minutes
Servings: 1

Ingredients

1/4 cup self-rising flour
3tablespoons coconut oil
1tablespoon cocoa powder
5 tablespoons caster sugar
3tablespoons whole milk

Directions

In a shallow mug, add all the Ingredients and mix until well combined. Press "Power Button" of Air Fry Oven and turn the dial to select the "Air Fry" mode.

Press the Time button and again turn the dial to set the **Cooking time:** to 13 minutes. Now push the Temp button and rotate the dial to set the temperature at 392 degrees F.

Press "Start/Pause" button to start. When the unit beeps to show that it is preheated, open the lid. Arrange the mug in "Air Fry Basket" and insert in the oven. Place the mug onto a wire rack to cool slightly before serving.

Grilled Peaches

Prep time: 10 minutes **Cooking time:** 10 minutes
Servings: 2

Ingredients

2 peaches, cut into wedges and remove pits
1/4 cup graham cracker crumbs
1/4 cup brown sugar
1/4 cup butter, diced into pieces

Directions

Arrange peach wedges on air fryer oven rack and air fry at 350 F for 5 minutes. In a bowl, put the butter, graham cracker crumbs, and brown sugar together.

Turn peaches skin side down. Spoon butter mixture over top of peaches and air fry for 5 minutes more.
Top with whipped cream and **Serve:**.

Simple and Delicious Spiced Apples

Prep time: 10 minutes **Cooking time:** 10 minutes
Servings: 4

Ingredients

4 apples, sliced
2tbsp. ghee, melted
1tsp apple pie spice
2tbsp. sugar

Directions

Add apple slices into the mixing bowl.
Add remaining Ingredients on top of apple slices and toss until well coated.
Transfer apple slices on instant vortex air fryer oven pan and air fry at
350 F for 10 minutes.
Top with ice cream and **Serve:**.

Peanut Butter Cookies

Prep time: 10 minutes **Cooking time:** 5 minutes
Servings: 24

Ingredients

1egg, lightly beaten
1 cup creamy peanut butter
1 cup of sugar

Directions

In a big bowl, combine sugar, egg, and peanut butter together until well mixed. Spray air fryer oven tray with cooking spray.

Using ice cream scooper scoop out cookie onto the tray and flattened them using a fork. Bake cookie at 350 F for 5 minutes. Cook remaining cookie batches using the same temperature. **Serve:** and enjoy.

Lemon Coconut Bars

Prep time: 10 minutes **Cooking time:** 20 minutes
Servings: 12

Ingredients
1cup coconut cream	1/4 cup cashew butter, soft
1 egg, whisked Juice of 1 lemon	1 teaspoon lemon peel, grated
1 teaspoon baking powder	3/4 cup swerve

Directions

In a bowl, combine all the Ingredients gradually and stir well. Spoon balls this on a baking sheet lined with parchment paper and flatten them. Put the sheet in the fryer and cook at 350 degrees F for 20 minutes. Cut into bars and **Serve:** cold.

Orange Cinnamon Cookies

Prep time: 15 minutes **Cooking time:** 24 minutes
Servings: 10

Ingredients
3 tablespoons cream cheese	1 teaspoon vanilla extract
1/2 teaspoon ground cinnamon	1 egg, beaten
3 tablespoons Erythritol	1 cup almond flour
1/2 tbs baking powder	1 teaspoon butter, softened
	1/2 tbs orange zest, grated

Directions

Put the cream cheese and Erythritol in the bowl. Add vanilla extract, ground cinnamon, and almond flour. Stir the mixture with the help of the spoon until homogenous. Then add egg, almond flour, baking powder, and butter. Add orange zest and stir the mass until homogenous. Then knead it with the help of the fingertips.

Roll up the dough with the help of the rolling pin. Then make the cookies with the help of the cookies cutter. Preheat the air fryer to 365F. Line the air fryer basket with baking paper. Put the cookies on the baking paper and cook them for 8 minutes. The time of cooking depends on the cooking size.

Mini Almond Cakes

Prep time: 10 minutes **Cooking time:** 20 minutes
Servings: 4

Ingredients
3 ounces dark chocolate, melted	2 tablespoons swerve
	1/4 cup coconut oil, melted
2 eggs, whisked	1/4 teaspoon vanilla extract Cooking spray
1tablespoon almond flour	

Directions

In bowl, combine all theIngredients except the cooking spray and whisk really well. Divide this into 4 ramekins greased with cooking spray, put them in the fryer and cook at 360 degrees F for 20 minutes.**Serve:** warm.

Chia Bites

Prep time: 15 minutes **Cooking time:** 8 minutes
Servings: 2

Ingredients
1/2 scoop of protein powder	3 tbsp almond flour
1 oz. hazelnuts, grinded	1 egg, beaten
1 tablespoon flax meal	1 teaspoon butter, softened 1 teaspoon chia seeds, dried
1/4 teaspoon ground clove	1 teaspoon Splenda

Directions

In the mixing bowl mix up protein powder, almond flour, grinded hazelnuts, flax meal, chia seeds, ground clove, and Splenda. Then add egg and butter and stir it with the help of the spoon until you get a homogenous mixture.

Espresso Cinnamon Cookies

Prep time: 5 minutes **Cooking time:** 15 minutes
Servings: 12

Ingredients
tablespoons ghee, melted	1/4 cup brewed espresso
1cup almond flour	1/4 cup swerve
1/2 tablespoon cinnamon powder	2eggs, whisked
	2teaspoons baking powder

Directions

In a bowl, mix all the Ingredients and whisk well. Spread medium balls on a cookie sheet lined parchment paper, flatten them, put the cookie sheet in your air fryer and cook at 350 degrees F for 15 minutes. **Serve:** the cookies cold.

Delicious Apple Crisps

Prep time: 10 minutes **Cooking time:** 25 minutes
Serve: 2

Ingredients

For filling
½ tbsp fresh lime juice
½ tsp cinnamon For
1 tsp whole wheat flour
1 tbsp maple syrup
1 tbsp butter, melted

1 apple, diced
½ tbsp maple syrup
½ tsp cinnamon
 topping
1/3 cup rolled oats

Directions

Mix together apple, lime juice, maple syrup, and cinnamon and divide into two ramekins. Mix together topping Ingredients and spread on top of the apple mixture.

Cover ramekin with foil and place into the air fryer basket and cook at 350 F for 15 minutes. Remove foil and cook for 10 minutes more. **Serve:** and enjoy.

Moist Orange Muffins

Prep time: 10 minutes **Cooking time:** 15 minutes
Serve: 12

Ingredients

4 eggs
1 orange zest
1/2 cup butter, melted

3 cups almond flour
1 orange juice
1 tsp baking soda

Directions

Preheat the air fryer to 350 F. Add all Ingredients into the mixing bowl and mix until well combined. Spoon mixture into the silicone muffin molds. Place muffin molds into the air fryer basket and cook for 12-15 minutes. **Serve:** and enjoy.

Sliced Apples

Prep time: 10 minutes **Cooking time:** 10 minutes
Serve: 6

Ingredients

4 small apples sliced
1 tsp apple pie spice

2 tbsp butter melted
1/2 cup erythritol

Directions

Preheat the air fryer to 350 F. In a mixing bowl, toss apple slices with butter, apple pie spice, and sweetener. Transfer apple slices into the baking dish. Place baking dish into the air fryer basket and cook for 10 minutes.**Serve:** and enjoy.

Baked Pears

Prep time: 10 minutes **Cooking time:** 10 minutes
Serve: 4

Ingredients

2 medium pears, cut in
half & cored
½ tsp cinnamon

2 tbsp butter, melted
1 tbsp honey
1 tbsp sugar

Directions

Mix together sugar and cinnamon and sprinkle over pears.
Place pears into the air fryer basket and cook at 370 F for 10 minutes.Drizzle butter and honey over pears and **Serve:**.

Gooey Chocolate Cake

Prep time: 10 minutes **Cooking time:** 10 minutes
Serve: 4

Ingredients

2 eggs
1 cup dark chocolate chips
3 ½ tbsp sugar

1 ½ tbsp self-rising flour
7 tbsp butter

Directions

Add butter and chocolate chips into the bowl and microwave for 30 seconds or until butter and chocolate chips melted. Stir well. In a separate bowl, whisk eggs and sugar. Add melted chocolate mixture and flour and stir until smooth. Spoon batter into the four greased ramekins.

Chocolate Brownies

Prep time: 10 minutes **Cooking time:** 12 minutes
Serve: 4

Ingredients

1 egg
¼ cup butter, melted
½ cup sugar
6 tbsp flour

¼ cup cocoa powder
½ tsp vanilla
¼ tsp salt

Directions

In a bowl, beat eggs with vanilla, sugar, and salt until light.
Add butter and mix well. Add cocoa powder and flour and stir until well combined. Pour batter into the greased air fryer baking dish. Place baking dish into the air fryer basket and cook at 330 F for 12 minutes. Slice and **Serve:**.

Chocolate Banana Packets

Prep time: 5 minutes **Cooking time:** 15 minutes
Servings: 1

Ingredients

Miniature marshmallows
(2 tablespoons)
Banana, peeled (1 piece)
Chocolate chips, semi-
sweet (2 tablespoons)

Cereal, cinnamon,
crunchy, slightly crushed
(2 tablespoons)

Directions

Preheat air fryer to 390 degrees Fahrenheit. Slightly
open banana by cutting lengthwise. Place on sheet of
foil. Fill sliced banana with chocolate chips and
marshmallows. Close foil packet. Air-fry for fifteen to
twenty minutes.
Open packet and top banana with crushed cereal.

Creamy Strawberry Mini Wraps

Prep time: 10 minutes **Cooking time:** 15 minutes
Servings: 12

Ingredients

Cream cheese, softened (4
ounces)
Powdered sugar (1/3 cup)

Pie crust, refrigerated (1
box)
Strawberry jam (12 tbs)

Directions

Preheat air fryer to 350 degrees Fahrenheit. Roll out
pie crusts and cut out 12 squares. Beat together
powdered sugar and cream cheese.

Shape each dough square into a diamond before filling
with cream cheese mixture (1 tablespoon). Top each
with strawberry jam (1 teaspoon) and cover with
dough sides. Place mini wraps on baking sheet and air-
fry for fifteen minutes.

Tasty Shortbread Cookies

Prep time: 25 minutes **Cooking time:** 1 hour 35 minutes
Servings: 4

Ingredients

Powdered sugar (3/4 cup)
Butter softened (1 cup)
Vanilla (1 teaspoon)

Flour all purpose (2 1/2
cups)

Directions

Preheat air fryer to 325 degrees Fahrenheit. Combine
butter, vanilla and powdered sugar with flour to form
a soft dough. Roll out dough and cut out 4 circles.
Place on cookie sheet. Air-fry for fourteen to sixteen
minutes.

Heavenly Butter Cake Bars

Prep time: 15 minutes **Cooking time:** 35 minutes
Servings: 12

Ingredients

Butter, melted (1/2 cup)
Cream cheese (8 ounces)
Vanilla (1 teaspoon)
Powdered sugar (1 pound)

Cake mix, super moist,
French vanilla (15 1/4
ounces)
Eggs (3 pieces)

Directions

Preheat air fryer to 325 degrees Fahrenheit. Use
parchment to line baking dish. Combine cake mix with
egg and melted butter to form soft dough. Press into
baking dish. Beat together 2 eggs, cream cheese,
vanilla, and sugar. Spread on top of cake mix layer.
Air-fry for forty-five minutes. Let cool before slicing.

Air-Fried Mini Pies

Prep time: 20 minutes **Cooking time:** 55 minutes
Servings: 4

Ingredients

Pie filling (4 cups)
Egg, whisked (1 piece)

Pie crusts, refrigerated (2
packages)

Directions

Preheat air fryer to 325 degrees Fahrenheit.
Mist cooking spray onto 12 muffin cups.
Roll out pie crust and cut out twelve 4-inch circles.
Press each onto bottom of a muffin cup. Cut
remaining dough into thin strips. Add pie filling (1/4
cup) to each dough cup. Cover each with dough strips
laid in a lattice pattern. Brush whisked egg on tops of
pies and air-fry for thirty to forty minutes.

Pumpkin Pie Minis

Prep time: 25 minutes **Cooking time:** 20 minutes
Servings: 12

Ingredients

Nutmeg (1/4 teaspoon)
Brown sugar (3/8 cup)
Heavy cream (1
tablespoon) Egg, large (1
piece)

Pie crust, refrigerated (1
package)
Pumpkin puree (1 cup)
Cinnamon (1/2 teaspoon)

Directions

Preheat air fryer to 325 degrees Fahrenheit.
Combine pumpkin, heavy cream, spices, and brown
sugar. Unroll dough pieces and cut out twenty-four
2.5-inch circles. Place 12 circles on sheet of
parchment. Top each with pie filling (1 tablespoon)
and cover with another circle. Press to seal and brush
all mini pies with whisked egg (1 piece). Dust all over
with mixture of cinnamon and sugar. Air-fry for
twenty minutes.

Easy Air Fryer French Toast Sticks

Prep time: 15 minutes **Cooking time:** 25 minutes
Serve: 1

Ingredients

4 slices of slightly stale thick bread, such as Texas toast parchment paper
¼ cup milk

2 eggs, lightly beaten
1 teaspoon cinnamon
1 pinch ground nutmeg
1 teaspoon vanilla extract

Directions

To make sticks, cut each slice of bread into thirds. Then, to fit the bottom of the air fryer basket cut a piece of parchment paper.

Preheat the air fryer carefully to 360°F (180 degrees C).
Combine the eggs, milk, vanilla extract, cinnamon, and nutmeg in a mixing dish until thoroughly blended. Dip each slice of bread into the egg mixture, ensuring sure it is well immersed. Shake each breadstick to remove extra liquid before placing it in the air fryer basket in a single layer. If necessary, cook in batches to avoid overflowing the fryer.

Fry for 5 minutes, then flip the bread slices and cook for another 5 minutes.

Air Fryer Pull-Apart Pepperoni-Cheese Bread

Prep time: 15 minutes **Cooking time:** 20 minutes
Serve: 1

Ingredients

cooking spray
1tbs grated Parmesan cheese
1-ounce sliced turkey pepperoni
dried oregano to taste
1 teaspoon melted butter
½ cup shredded mozzarella cheese

1 ½ pound fresh pizza dough

ground red pepper to taste
garlic
salt to taste

Directions

To fit the bottom of your air fryer, shape a big piece of aluminum foil into a pan with 2-inch-high edges. Coat the pan with nonstick cooking spray. Preheat the air fryer carefully to 390°F (200°C) for 15 minutes.

Roll the pizza dough into 1-inch balls and set them in an aluminum foil pan in a single layer. Season with pepperoni, oregano, red pepper flakes, and garlic salt to taste. Brush with melted butter, then top with Parmesan cheese. Cook for 15 minutes with the pan at the bottom of the air fryer. Cook until the mozzarella cheese is melted and bubbling on the bread, about 2 minutes longer. Remove from the air fryer by pulling the sides of the pan up and out of the machine using tongs.

Air Fryer Asian-Inspired Deviled Eggs

Prep time: 20 minutes **Cooking time:** 25 minutes
Serve: 1

Ingredients

6 large eggs
1 ½ tbs sriracha sauce
1 tbs low-sodium soy sauce
1 teaspoon Dijon mustard
toasted sesame seeds

2 tablespoons mayonnaise
1 ½ tbs sesame oil
1 tbs finely grated ginger root
1 teaspoon rice vinegar
1 green onion, thinly sliced

Directions

Place the eggs on an air fryer rack or trivet, leaving enough room between them for air to circulate. Set the air fryer to 260 degrees Fahrenheit (125 degrees Celsius) and the timer for 15 minutes. The air fryer should be closed. Place the eggs in a dish of cold water for 10 minutes after being removed from the air fryer. Then, remove the eggs from the water, peel them, and cut them half. Scoop out the yolks and set them in a tiny food processor. In a mixing bowl, combine the mayonnaise, sriracha, sesame oil, low-sodium soy sauce, Dijon mustard, ginger root, and rice vinegar. Process until the mixture is well blended and creamy, mousse-like consistency. Fill a piping bag halfway with the yolk mixture and evenly spread it into the egg white halves until they are overflowing full; you can also do this with a spoon. Garnish with sesame seeds and green onion, if desired.

Air Fryer Steak Tips and Portobello Mushrooms

Prep time: 15 minutes **Cooking time:** 18 minutes
Serve: 1

Ingredients

¼ cup olive oil
½ teaspoon garlic powder
2 strip steaks
4 ounces portobello mushrooms, quartered

1 tbs coconut aminos
2 teaspoons Montreal steak seasoning

Directions

Combine the olive oil, coconut aminos, steak seasoning, and garlic powder in a small bowl. Mix well, then add the steak pieces and marinate for 15 minutes.

Carefully to 390°F (200 degrees C). The perforated parchment paper should line the bottom of the air fryer basket. Remove the meat from the marinade. Fill the air fryer basket halfway with steak and quartered portobello mushrooms.

Cook for 5 minutes in a hot air fryer. Remove the basket, stir the steak and mushrooms around, and cook for 4 minutes.

Air Fryer Garlic and Parsley Baby Potatoes

Prep time: 20 minutes **Cooking time:** 25 minutes
Serve: 1

Ingredients

1 pound baby potatoes, cut into quarters	¼ teaspoon salt
½ teaspoon granulated garlic	1 tablespoon avocado oil
	½ teaspoon dried parsley

Directions

Carefully to 350°F (175 degrees C). Toss the potatoes in a basin with the oil to coat. Toss in 1/4 teaspoon granulated garlic and 1/4 teaspoon parsley to coat. Rep with the rest of the garlic and parsley. Place the potatoes in the air fryer basket.

Place the basket in the air fryer and cook, stirring regularly, for 20 to 25 minutes, or until golden brown.

Air Fryer Salmon Cakes with Sriracha Mayo

Prep time: 15 minutes **Cooking time:** 20 minutes
Serve: 1

Ingredients

¼ cup mayonnaise	1 tablespoon Sriracha
1-pound skinless salmon fillets	⅓ cup almond flour
1 ½ teaspoon seafood seasoning	1 egg, lightly beaten
1 green onion, coarsely chopped cooking spray	1 pinch seafood seasoning (such as Old Bay®) (Optional)

Directions

In a small mixing dish, combine mayonnaise and sriracha. 1 tablespoon Sriracha mayo in a food processor; chill the remainder until ready to use To the Sriracha mayo, add the salmon, almond flour, egg, 1 ½ teaspoons seafood spice, and green onion; pulse quickly for 4 to 5 seconds, or until Ingredients are barely mixed but tiny bits of salmon remains. (Be careful not to overprocess the mixture, or it will turn mushy.)

Line a plate with waxed paper and squirt cooking spray on your hands. Transfer the salmon mixture to a dish and shape it into 8 tiny patties. Refrigerate for 15 minutes or until cool and stiff. Preheat the air fryer carefully to 390°F (200 degrees C). Cooking spray should be sprayed on the air fryer basket. Take the salmon cakes out of the refrigerator. Spray both sides with frying spray and place in the air fryer basket, working in batches as required to minimize congestion. Cook for 6 to 8 minutes in a preheated air fryer. **Serve:** with the remaining Sriracha mayo and a small dusting of Old Bay seasoning, if preferred, on a serving dish.

Air Fryer Spicy Dill Pickle Fries

Prep time: 15 minutes **Cooking time:** 18 minutes
Serve: 1

Ingredients

1 ½ (16 ounces) jars spicy dill pickle spears	½ teaspoon paprika
¼ cup milk	1 cup all-purpose flour
1 cup panko breadcrumbs cooking spray	1 egg, beaten

Directions

Drain and pat dry the pickles. In a mixing dish, combine the flour and paprika. In a separate dish, whisk together the milk and the beaten egg. In a third bowl, combine the panko.

Carefully to 400°F (200°C) according to the manufacturer's instructions. Place a pickle on a dish after dipping it in the flour mixture, then the egg mixture, and finally the breadcrumbs. Rep with the remaining pickles. Lightly spray the covered pickles with cooking spray.
Place the pickles in the air fryer basket in a single layer; cook in batches if required to avoid overflowing the fryer. Set a timer for 14 minutes and flip the pickles halfway through.

Air Fryer Brown Sugar and Pecan Roasted Apples

Prep time: 15 minutes **Cooking time:** 22 minutes
Serve: 1

Ingredients

2 tablespoons coarsely chopped pecans	1 teaspoon all-purpose flour
	1 tablespoon brown sugar
¼ teaspoon apple pie spice 2 medium apples	1 tablespoon butter

Directions

Preheat the air fryer carefully to 360°F (180 degrees C).

Combine pecans, brown sugar, flour, and apple pie spice in a small mixing bowl. In a medium mixing bowl, combine apple wedges and drizzle with butter, tossing to coat. Arrange the apples in the air fryer basket in a single layer and top with the pecan mixture.

Cook in a hot air fryer for 10 to 15 minutes, or until apples are soft.

Air Fryer Chocolate Chip Cookie Bites

Prep time: 15 minutes **Cooking time:** 20 minutes
Serve: 1

Ingredients

½ cup butter softened

¼ cup white sugar
½ teaspoon salt,
1 egg
1 cup miniature semisweet
chocolate chips
1 ⅓ cups all-purpose flour

½ cup packed brown
sugar
½ teaspoon baking soda
1 ½ teaspoons vanilla
extract
⅓ cup finely chopped
pecans, toasted

Directions

To fit an air fryer basket, cut a piece of parchment
paper.

In a large mixing basin, beat the butter for 30 seconds
on medium to high-speed using an electric mixer. Mix
in the brown sugar, white sugar, baking soda, and salt
for 2 minutes on medium speed, scraping the bowl
regularly. Mix in the egg and vanilla essence until well
mixed. Mix in as much flour as possible. Combine the
remaining flour, chocolate chips, and pecans in a
mixing bowl.

Drop the dough by teaspoonfuls onto the parchment
paper, 1 inch apart. Transfer the parchment paper to
the air fryer basket with care.

Preheat the air fryer carefully to 300°F (150°C) and
cook until golden

brown and firm, about 8 minutes. Cool the parchment
paper on a wire rack. Repeat with the rest of the
cookie dough.

Chocolate Cake in an Air Fryer

Prep time: 20 minutes **Cooking time:** 20 minutes
Serve: 1

Ingredients

cooking spray
3 ½ tablespoons butter,
softened
6 tablespoons all-purpose
flour

¼ cup white sugar
1 tablespoon apricot jam
1 egg
1 tablespoon unsweetened
cocoa powder salt to taste

Directions

Carefully to 320°F (160 degrees C). Coat a small,
fluted tube pan with nonstick cooking spray. In a
mixing bowl, beat the sugar and butter with an electric
mixer until light and fluffy. Mix in the egg and jam
until well mixed. Sift in the flour, cocoa powder, and
salt and thoroughly combine.

Crispy Air Fryer Cod

Prep time: 15 minutes **Cooking time:** 22 minutes
Serve: 1

Ingredients

1 pound cod, about 1-inch
thick
1 ½ tbs seafood seasoning
½ tbsp paprika olive oil
1 ½ teaspoon garlic salt
1 teaspoon onion powder

¼ cup all-purpose
flour
¼ cup polenta
cooking spray
½ teaspoon ground black
pepper

Directions

Carefully to 380°F (195 degrees C). Using paper
towels, pat the codpieces dry. Combine the polenta,
flour, seafood seasoning, garlic salt, onion powder,
pepper, and paprika in a shallow dish. Coat each piece
of cod with the breading mixture, pressing the
breading into each side of the fish until well coated.

Spray the air fryer basket with olive oil cooking spray.
Arrange the cod in the basket, leaving enough space
between each piece to allow air to flow. Cooking spray
should be sprayed on the top of each piece of fish.
8 minutes in the oven cook for 4 minutes longer after
turning each piece and spraying with cooking spray.

Air Fryer Fried Mushrooms

Prep time: 10 minutes **Cooking time:** 18 minutes
Serve: 1

Ingredients

3 eggs
½ cup plain breadcrumbs
½ tablespoon kosher salt
1 teaspoon onion powder
1 teaspoon garlic powder
1 teaspoon seafood
seasoning (such as Old
Bay®)
1-pound small cremini
mushrooms

1 cup all-purpose flour
½ cup panko breadcrumbs
1 teaspoon ground black
pepper
1 teaspoon paprika
1 serving nonstick cooking
spray

Directions

Preheat the air fryer carefully to 400°F (200 degrees
C). In a mixing dish, whisk together the eggs. Then,
combine the flour, breadcrumbs, kosher salt, onion
powder, garlic powder, pepper, paprika, and seafood
seasoning in a separate bowl.

Dip the mushrooms in the eggs first, then in the
seasoned flour. Dip into the eggs again, then into the
seasoned flour. **Serve:** on a platter. Place a batch of
mushrooms in the air fryer basket, being careful not to
overlap them. Coat the pan with nonstick cooking spray.
6 minutes in the oven Shake the basket and apply
nonstick cooking spray on chalky places. Cook for
another 6 minutes. Rep with the remaining mushrooms

Air Fryer Frog Legs

Prep time: 15 minutes **Cooking time:** 20 minutes
Serve: 1

Ingredients

1 pound frog legs
2 cups milk
2 tablespoons seafood seasoning
2 cups yellow cornmeal
1 cup all-purpose flour
cooking spray

Directions

Pour milk over the top of the frog legs in a dish. Refrigerate for 1 hour, covered. Carefully to 400°F (200°C) according to the manufacturer's instructions. Meanwhile, add cornmeal, flour, and seafood seasoning in a gallon- sized resealable plastic bag. To blend, seal the container and shake it vigorously. Remove 1 frog leg from the milk, allowing the excess to drip into the dish. Shake the bag with the seasoned cornmeal mixture to coat. Return the frog legs to the cornmeal mixture after dipping them back in the milk. Shake again to coat, then transfer to a dish. Rep with the remaining frog legs.
Cooking sprays the air fryer basket and puts as many frog legs as you can without overlapping. Coat the tops in cooking spray. If necessary, work in bunches. 5 minutes in the air fryer. Cooking spray should be used to remove any chalky patches. Cook for another 3 minutes, or until the bacon is crispy. Repeat with the remaining batches on a platter.

Air Fryer Churros

Prep time: 15 minutes **Cooking time:** 25 minutes **Serve:** 1

Ingredients

¼ cup butter
2 eggs
½ cup all-purpose flour
½ teaspoon ground cinnamon
½ cup milk
1 pinch salt
¼ cup white sugar

Directions

In a saucepan over medium-high heat, melt the butter. Pour in the milk and season with salt. Reduce the heat to medium and bring to a boil, constantly stirring with a wooden spoon. Add the flour all at once. Continue to whisk until the dough comes together.
Remove from the fire and set aside for 5 to 7 minutes to cool. With a wooden spoon, mix the eggs until the pastry comes together. Fill a pastry bag with a big star tip with the dough. Pipe dough strips directly into the air fryer basket. For 5 minutes, air-fried churros at 340 degrees F (175 degrees C).

Air Fryer Hush Puppies

Prep time: 15 minutes **Cooking time:** 18 minutes
Serve: 1

Ingredients

nonfat cooking spray
1 ½ teaspoons baking powder
¼ teaspoon cayenne pepper, or more to taste
2 tablespoons minced onion
¾ cup low-fat buttermilk
¾ cup all-purpose flour
½ teaspoon salt
1 cup yellow cornmeal
¼ teaspoon garlic powder
2 tablespoons minced green bell pepper
1 large egg

Directions

Carefully to 390°F (198°C) according to the manufacturer's instructions. Spray the bottom of the air fryer basket with nonfat cooking spray and line with aluminum foil. In a large mixing bowl, combine cornmeal, flour, baking powder, salt, cayenne pepper, and garlic powder. Next, combine the onion and bell pepper.

In a separate dish, whisk together the buttermilk and egg. Mix into the cornmeal mixture. Allow the mixture to sit for 5 minutes. Using a 2-tablespoon cookie scoop, scoop the cornmeal mixture into the foil-lined basket, making sure not to overlap. Coat the pan with nonfat cooking spray.
9 to 10 minutes in a preheated air fryer, until golden brown, crispy, and cooked through. **Serve:** immediately.

Chinese Five-Spice Air Fryer Butternut Squash Fries

Prep time: 20 minutes **Cooking time:** 20 minutes **Serve:** 1

Ingredients

1 large butternut squash
2 tablespoons olive oil
2 teaspoons sea salt
1 tablespoon minced garlic
1 tablespoon Chinese five-spice powder
2 teaspoons black pepper

Directions

Preheat the air fryer carefully to 400°F (200 degrees C).
In a large mixing basin, combine the chopped squash. Toss in the oil, five-spice powder, garlic, salt, and black pepper to coat. Cook butternut squash fries in a preheated air fryer for 15 to 20 minutes, shaking every 5 minutes, until crisp. Remove the fries and season with sea salt to taste.

Air Fryer Mini Bean and Cheese Tacos

Prep time: 20 minutes **Cooking time:** 20 minutes
Serve: 1

Ingredients

1 (16 ounces) can refried beans
cooking spray

1 (1 ounce) envelope taco seasoning mix
12 slices American cheese, cut in half 12 (6 inches) flour tortillas

Directions

Preheat the air fryer carefully to 400°F (200 degrees C).
In a bowl, combine the refried beans. Stir in taco seasoning until evenly blended.

1 slice of cheese in the center of a tortilla 1 spoonful of the bean mixture should be spooned over the cheese. On top of the beans, place another piece of cheese. To seal the taco, fold the tortilla over and press down. Continue with the remaining tortillas, beans, and cheese.

Nonstick frying spray should be sprayed on all sides of the tacos. Place tacos in the air fryer basket, ensuring sure none overlap. 3 minutes in the oven cook for 3 minutes longer after flipping the tacos. Rep with the remaining tacos.

Sweet Potato Chips in the Air Fryer

Prep time: 15 minutes **Cooking time:** 25 minutes
Serve: 1

Ingredients

1 teaspoon avocado oil
½ teaspoon Creole seasoning

1 medium sweet potato, peeled and sliced crossways into 1/8-inch slices

Directions

Preheat the air fryer carefully to 400°F (200 degrees C).
In a large mixing basin, combine the sweet potato pieces. Mix with the avocado oil, covering each piece equally.

Stir in the Creole seasoning until well combined. Spread the slices on the bottom of the air fryer basket in a thin layer.

Cook for 7 minutes in a preheated air fryer. Shake and flip the slices to ensure consistent frying. Cook for another 6 minutes, or until the desired crispness is attained. Allow the potato slices to cool on a rack.

Skinny Air Fryer Funnel Cakes

Prep time: 15 minutes **Cooking time:** 20 minutes
Serve: 1

Ingredients

nonstick cooking spray
1 tablespoon almond flour
4 tablespoons erythritol confectioners' sweetener
1 ½ teaspoons baking powder
1 teaspoon ground cinnamon

1 teaspoon vanilla extract
1 cup almond flour
1 cup nonfat plain Greek yogurt
½ teaspoon salt

Directions

Carefully to 325°F (165°C) according to the manufacturer's instructions. Line the basket with parchment paper and sprinkle it with nonstick cooking spray.
Combine almond flour, Greek yogurt, 2 tablespoons sweetener, baking powder, cinnamon, vanilla extract, and salt in a mixing dish. Make the dough come together by kneading it with your hands.
Flour your work surface, divide the dough into four equal pieces, and form into balls. Using a bench scraper, cut each ball into 8 equal pieces. Roll each piece in flour and roll into a long, thin rope between your palms. Place all 8 ropes, one by one, into the preheated air fryer basket in a circular mound. Repeat with the rest of the dough balls. Cooking spray should be sprayed on each funnel cake.
5 to 6 minutes in the air fryer until golden brown. Flip each funnel cake over, coat with cooking spray, and continue to air fry for 3 to 4 minutes. Finish with the remaining 2 teaspoons of sweetener.

Air-Fried Jalapeno Poppers

Prep time: 20 minutes **Cooking time:** 25 minutes
Serve: 1

Ingredients

6 medium jalapeno peppers, halved and seeded
3 slices salami, dry or hard, pork, beef
6 slices bacon, cut in half lengthwise

1-ounce shredded Cheddar cheese
6 ounces cream cheese, softened

Directions

Carefully to 390°F (199°C) according to the manufacturer's instructions.
Fill each half of jalapeño with cream cheese and Cheddar cheese. If
desired, place 1/2 a slice of salami on top of each pepper, wrap with bacon, and fasten with a toothpick.
Layer the jalapeño poppers in the preheated air fryer and cook for 10 to 12 minutes, or until the bacon is browned and the cheese is melted.

Air-Fried Ratatouille, Italian-Style

Prep time: 15 minutes **Cooking time:** 22 minutes
Serve: 1

Ingredients

½ small eggplant, cut into cubes
½ large yellow bell pepper, cut into cubes
½ onion, cut into cubes
1 zucchini, cut into cubes
5 sprigs fresh basil, stemmed and chopped
salt and ground black pepper to taste
1 teaspoon vinegar

1 medium tomato, cut into cubes
½ large red bell pepper, cut into cubes
1 fresh cayenne pepper, diced
2 sprigs of fresh oregano, stemmed and chopped
1 tablespoon white wine
1 clove garlic, crushed
1 tablespoon olive oil

Directions

Carefully to 400°F (200 degrees C).
Combine the eggplant, zucchini, tomato, bell peppers, and onion in a mixing dish. Next, combine the cayenne pepper, basil, oregano, garlic, salt, and pepper in a mixing bowl. To ensure that everything is distributed equally, combine all
Ingredients in a mixing bowl. Drizzle in the oil, wine, and vinegar and toss to cover all veggies.
Place the vegetable mixture in a baking dish and place it in the air fryer basket. 8 minutes in the oven cook for another 8 minutes, stirring occasionally. Stir once more and simmer until tender, 10 to 15 minutes more, stirring every 5 minutes. Turn off the air fryer but leave the dish inside. Allow for a 5-minute pause before serving.

Air-Fried Cauliflower with Almonds and Parmesan

Prep time: 20 minutes **Cooking time:** 25 minutes
Serve: 1

Ingredients

3 cups cauliflower florets
1 clove garlic, minced
⅓ cup finely shredded Parmesan cheese
¼ cup panko breadcrumbs

3 teaspoons vegetable oil, divided
¼ cup chopped almonds
½tsp dried thyme, crushed

Directions

In a medium mixing basin, combine cauliflower florets, 2 tablespoons oil, and garlic; toss to coat. Place in an air fryer basket in a single layer.
Cook for 10 minutes in the air fryer at 360°F (180°C), shaking the
basket halfway through.
Toss the cauliflower with the remaining 1 teaspoon oil in the basin. Toss in the Parmesan cheese, almonds, breadcrumbs, and thyme to coat. Return cauliflower mixture to air fryer basket and cook for another 5 minutes, or until crisp and golden

Air Fryer Corn Dogs

Prep time: 18 minutes **Cooking time:** 20 minutes
Serve: 1

Ingredients

parchment paper
1 (6.5 ounces) package cornbread mix
1 teaspoon white sugar

6 bamboo skewers
⅔ cup milk
1 egg
8 hot dogs, cut in half

Directions

Divide the soaking bamboo skewers into thirds. To properly fit the bottom of the air fryer basket, cut a piece of parchment paper.
Preheat the air fryer carefully to 400°F (200 degrees C).
In a mixing bowl, combine cornbread mix, milk, egg, and sugar until blended; pour into a tall glass.
Insert a skewer into the center of each hot dog piece. Remove the air fryer basket and lay the cut parchment paper on the bottom of the basket. Dip four hot dogs in the batter and set them on top of the parchment paper, alternating the direction of the stick ends.
Cook for 8 minutes in a preheated air fryer without turning, or until desired brownness. Repeat with the remaining hot dogs on a dish.

Air Fryer Salt and Vinegar Fries for One

Prep time: 15 minutes **Cooking time:** 20 minutes
Serve: 1

Ingredients

1 large Yukon Gold potato 1 cup distilled white vinegar
salt and ground black pepper to taste

½ tablespoon light vegetable oil

Directions

Peel the potato and cut it into 1/2-inch sticks lengthwise. For a few seconds, rinse the potato sticks under cold running water. Transfer to a large mixing bowl. Pour in just enough water to cover the potatoes with vinegar. Allow for a 30-minute soak.
Preheat the air fryer carefully to 320°F (160 degrees C).
Drain and pat dry the potatoes. Toss in a bowl with the oil, salt, and pepper and place in the air fryer basket.
Cook for 16 minutes in a hot air fryer until soft but not browned. Shake
the basket and heat it to 355 degrees Fahrenheit (180 degrees C). 6 minutes in the air fryer, shake, and check for doneness. Cook for another 6 minutes, or until the outsides of the fries are crispy and golden

Sweet Caramel Pineapple

Prep time: 10 minutes **Cooking time:** 12 minutes
Serve: 4

Ingredients

2 cups pineapple slices
1 tbsp butter, melted

2 tbsp maple syrup
1 tsp cinnamon

Directions

Preheat the air fryer to 380 F. In a mixing bowl, mix together pineapple slices, butter, maple syrup, and cinnamon until well coated. Place pineapple slices into the air fryer basket and cook for 12 minutes. Turn halfway through. **Serve:** and enjoy.

Blueberry Cobbler

Prep time: 10 minutes **Cooking time:** 15 minutes
Serve: 2

Ingredients

6 oz blueberries
For topping
½ tsp baking powder
2 tbsp sugar
½ tsp salt

1 tbsp fresh lemon juice
¼ cup milk
¼ cup all-purpose flour
1 tbsp sugar

Directions

Add blueberries, sugar, and lemon juice into the two ramekins and mix well. In a bowl, mix together topping Ingredients and pour over blueberry mixture. Place ramekins into the air fryer basket and cook at 320 F for 12-15 minutes. **Serve:** and enjoy.

Apple Pecan Carrot Muffins

Prep time: 10 minutes **Cooking time:** 10 minutes
Serve: 12

Ingredients

1 egg
½ cup pecans, chopped
1 cup apples, shredded
1 cup carrots, shredded
½ cup yogurt
¼ tsp nutmeg
2 tsp cinnamon
½ tsp salt

1 ½ cups all-purpose flour
½ cup raisins
2/3 cup honey
2 tsp vanilla
1/3 cup applesauce
½ tsp ginger
2 tsp baking powder

Directions

Preheat the air fryer to 350 F. In a mixing bowl, mix together flour, ginger, nutmeg, cinnamon, baking powder, and salt. Add egg, vanilla, honey, yogurt, and applesauce and mix until just combined. Add pecans, raisins, apples, and carrots and fold well.
Spoon batter into the silicone muffin molds. Place muffin molds into the air fryer basket and cook for 10 minutes. **Serve:** and enjoy.

Blueberry Muffins

Prep time: 10 minutes **Cooking time:** 12 minutes
Serve: 8

Ingredients

1 egg
3 tbsp butter, melted
2 tsp vanilla
¼ tsp cinnamon
1 cup self-rising flour

¾ cup blueberries
1/3 cup unsweetened
almond milk
¼ cup sugar

Directions

Preheat the air fryer to 340 F. In a mixing bowl, whisk egg with sugar, vanilla, butter, and almond milk.

Add flour and cinnamon and stir until well combined.
Add blueberries and fold well.

Spoon batter into the silicone muffin molds. Place muffin molds into the air fryer basket and cook for 12-14 minutes. **Serve:** and enjoy.

Air Fryer Kale Chips with Parmesan

Prep time: 15 minutes **Cooking time:** 25 minutes
Serve: 1

Ingredients

1 bunch kale
salt and ground black
pepper to taste
2 tablespoons grated
Parmesan cheese

1 tablespoon olive oil
1 ½ teaspoon chili-lime
seasoning

Directions

Carefully to 280°F (138°C) according to the manufacturer's instructions. Wash the kale and separate the leaves from the ribs. Dry the kale leaves
fully before tearing them into pieces. Ribs should be discarded.

In a large mixing bowl, combine the kale leaves and olive oil; toss with your hands until the kale is uniformly and lightly coated. Season with salt and pepper to taste. Mix in the chili-lime seasoning until equally distributed.

Place some kale in the hot air fryer in batches without overlapping. 5 minutes in the oven Shake the basket and continue to air-fry for 3 minutes. Sprinkle with Parmesan cheese to coat, shake, and air-fry for
another 2 minutes, or until crispy. Repeat with the remaining batches, keeping an eye on the air fryer and keeping the temperature low.

Air Fryer Breakfast Toad-in-the-Hole Tarts

Prep time: 15 minutes **Cooking time:** 20 minutes
Serve: 1

Ingredients

1 sheet frozen puff pastry, thawed	4 tablespoons shredded Cheddar cheese
4 eggs	1 tablespoon chopped fresh chives
4 tablespoons diced cooked ham	

Directions

Preheat the air fryer carefully to 400°F (200 degrees C). Unfold the pastry sheet and cut it into 4 squares on a level surface.

Cook 6 to 8 minutes with 2 pastry squares in the air fryer basket. Remove the basket from the air fryer. To make an indentation, lightly push each square with a metal tablespoon. Fill each hole with 1 tablespoon Cheddar cheese and 1 tablespoon ham, then top with 1 egg.

Return the basket to the air fryer. Cook until done, about 6 minutes more. Remove tarts from the basket and set them aside for 5 minutes to cool. Rep with the rest of the pastry squares, cheese, ham, and eggs. Tarts should be garnished with chives.

Air Fryer Roasted Brussels Sprouts with Maple-Mustard Mayo

Prep time: 15 minutes **Cooking time:** 18 minutes
Serve: 1

Ingredients

2 tablespoons maple syrup, divided	1 tablespoon olive oil - ¼ teaspoon kosher salt
¼ teaspoon ground black pepper	1 pound Brussels sprouts, trimmed and halved
⅓ cup mayonnaise	1 tablespoon stone-ground mustard

Directions

Preheat the air fryer carefully to 400°F (200 degrees C).
In a large mixing bowl, combine 1 tablespoon maple syrup, olive oil, salt, and pepper. Toss in the Brussels sprouts to coat. Arrange Brussels sprouts in an air fryer basket in a single layer, without overcrowded; work in batches if required. 4 minutes in the oven cook until the sprouts are deep golden brown and tender, 4 to 6 minutes longer.

Meanwhile, combine mayonnaise, the remaining 1 tablespoon maple syrup, and mustard in a small mixing dish. Toss the sprouts in a little sauce combination and **Serve:** as a dipping sauce.

Air Fryer Onion Bhaji

Prep time: 15 minutes **Cooking time:** 22 minutes **Serve:** 1

Ingredients

1 small red onion, thinly sliced	1 small yellow onion, thinly sliced
1 jalapeno pepper, seeded and minced	1 clove garlic, minced
1 tablespoon salt	1 teaspoon coriander
1 teaspoon ground turmeric	1 teaspoon chili powder
4 tbs water, or as needed	½ teaspoon cumin
cooking spray	⅔ cup chickpea flour (bean)

Directions

In a large mixing bowl, combine red onion, yellow onion, salt, jalapeño, garlic, coriander, chili powder, turmeric, and cumin. Stir until everything is well blended. Mix in the chickpea flour and water. To make a thick batter, put all
Ingredients in a mixing bowl. If required, add extra water. Allow the mixture to settle for 10 minutes.

Preheat the air fryer carefully to 350°F (175 degrees C).
Nonstick cooking spray should be sprayed on the air fryer basket. Flatten 2 tablespoons of batter into the basket. Repeat as many times as your basket permits without touching the bhajis.

Cook for 6 minutes in a hot air fryer. Cooking spray should be sprayed on the tops of each bhaji. Cook for 6 minutes more on the other side. Transfer to a plate lined with paper towels. Rep with the remaining batter.

Rice & Grains Recipes

Aromatic Seafood Pilaf

(**Ready in about** 45 minutes | **Servings:** 2)

Ingredients

1 cup jasmine rice

1 small yellow onion, chopped

1 bay leaf

4 tablespoons cream of mushroom soup

Salt and black pepper, to taste

1 small garlic clove, finely chopped

1 teaspoon butter, melted

1/2 pound shrimp, divined and sliced

Directions

Bring 2 cups of a lightly salted water to a boil in a medium saucepan over medium-high heat. Add in the jasmine rice, turn to a simmer and cook, covered, for about 18 minutes until water is absorbed.

Let the jasmine rice stand covered for 5 to 6 minutes; fluff with a fork and transfer to a lightly greased Air Fryer safe pan.

Stir in the salt, black pepper, bay leaf, yellow onion, garlic, butter and cream of mushroom soup; stir until everything is well incorporated.

Cook the rice at 350 degrees F for about 13 minutes. Stir in the shrimp and continue to cook for a further 5 minutes.

Check the rice for softness. If necessary, cook for a few minutes more. Bon appétit!

Easy Pizza Margherita

(**Ready in about** 15 minutes | **Servings:** 1)

Ingredients

6-inch dough

1 teaspoon extra-virgin olive oil Coarse sea salt, to taste

2 tablespoons tomato sauce

2-3 fresh basil leaves

2 ounces mozzarella

Directions

Start by preheating your Air Fryer to 380 degrees F.

Stretch the dough on a pizza peel lightly dusted with flour. Spread with a layer of tomato sauce.

Add mozzarella to the crust and drizzle with olive oil. Salt to taste.

Bake in the preheated Air Fryer for 4 minutes. Rotate the baking tray and bake for a further 4 minutes. Garnish with fresh basil leaves and **Serve:** immediately. Bon appétit!

Famous Greek Tyrompiskota

(**Ready in about** 45 minutes | **Servings:** 3)

Ingredients

1 cup all-purpose flour

1 teaspoon baking powder

1/2 cup halloumi cheese, grated

1 egg

1 tablespoon flaxseed meal

1/2 stick butter

1 teaspoon Greek spice blend Salt to taste

Directions

Combine the flour, flaxseed meal, and baking powder in a mixing bowl. In a separate bowl, combine the butter, cheese, and egg. Incorporate the cheese mixture into the dry flour mixture.

Mix with your hands, then stir in the Greek spice blend; season with salt and stir again to combine thoroughly.

Form the batter into a log, wrap in cling film, and place in the refrigerator for about 30 minutes.

Using a sharp knife, cut the chilled log into thin slices. Cook your biscuits for 15 minutes in a preheated Air Fryer at 360 degrees F. Make use of batches.

Good appetite!

Bacon and Cheese Sandwich

(**Ready in about** 15 minutes | **Servings:** 1)

Ingredients

2 slices whole-wheat bread

2 ounces bacon, sliced

1 tablespoon ketchup

1/2 teaspoon Dijon mustard

1 ounce cheddar cheese, sliced

Directions

Spread the ketchup and mustard on a slice of bread. Add the bacon and cheese and top with another slice of bread.

Place your sandwich in the lightly buttered Air Fryer cooking basket.

Now, bake your sandwich at 380 degrees F for 10 minutes or until the cheese has melted. Make sure to turn it over halfway through the cooking time.

Bon appétit!

Basmati Rice

Prep time: 15 minutes **Cooking time:** 25 minutes
Serve: 1

Ingredients

1 ¾ cups water	1 cup basmati rice
¼ cup frozen green peas	1 teaspoon cumin seeds

Directions

Bring water to a boil in a saucepan. Stir in the rice. Reduce the heat to low, cover, and leave to simmer for 20 minutes.
When the rice is done, add the peas and cumin. Allow to stand for 5 minutes, covered.

Almond Wild Rice

Prep time: 18 minutes **Cooking time:** 20 minutes
Serve: 1

Ingredients

cooking spray	2 ½ cups chicken broth
1 ½ cups brown and wild rice mix	1 cup slivered almonds
2 tablespoons dried parsley	3 tablespoons butter
¼ teaspoon salt	1 cup sweetened dried cranberries
	¼ teaspoon ground black pepper

Directions

Preheat the oven carefully to 375°F (190 degrees C). Coat an 8-inch square baking dish with nonstick cooking spray.
In a saucepan, bring chicken broth to a boil.

Place the rice mixture in the prepared baking dish. Pour the boiling chicken stock over the rice with care. Wrap the dish with aluminum foil. Bake it in a preheated oven for 1 hour or until the rice is soft.

In a pan over medium heat, melt the butter. Cook and stir almonds in heated butter for 3 to 5 minutes, or until they brown. Continue to simmer and stir until the almonds are lightly toasted, about 3 to 5 minutes more.

In a large mixing basin, combine the baked rice, almond mixture, cranberries, salt, and pepper; toss to combine.

Thai Fried Rice

Prep time: 20 minutes **Cooking time:** 20 minutes
Serve: 1

Ingredients

6 slices bacon, sliced crosswise into 1/2-inch pieces	1 onion, finely chopped
½ cup chopped fresh pineapple	1 large tomato, cubed
2 tablespoons light soy sauce 1 tablespoon white sugar	2 cloves garlic, minced
½ cucumber, sliced	5 cups cooked jasmine rice, cooled
¼ cup chopped fresh cilantro	¼ teaspoon freshly ground white pepper
1 lime, cut into wedges	3 eggs, beaten
	2 green onions, chopped
	4 green Thai chili peppers
	2 tablespoons ketchup

Directions

Cook the bacon in a large pan or wok over medium heat until it is browned and crisp, about 5 minutes. Drain, saving the bacon fat in a separate basin. Return 2 tablespoons of the fat to the skillet.

Increase the heat to medium-high and sauté the garlic for 30 seconds, or until fragrant. Cook often turns until the onion is softened, 2 to 3 minutes. Stir in the tomato and pineapple and cook for 2 minutes, or until heated through. 1 cup bacon grease 1 tablespoon bacon grease 1 tablespoon bacon grease 1 tablespoon bacon grease 1 Stir in the rice, breaking it up with a spatula so that it is fully covered with the bacon oil. Cook for approximately 3 minutes. Ketchup, soy sauce, sugar, and white pepper to taste. Place the rice mixture on one side of the skillet or wok and pour the beaten eggs on the other. Stir-fry for 2 to 3 minutes, or until the eggs are almost set. Combine eggs and rice mixture. Fold in the bacon pieces. Cucumber, green onions, cilantro, lemon wedges, and chili peppers

Sweet Coconut Rice

Prep time: 15 minutes **Cooking time:** 20 minutes
Serve: 1

Ingredients

1 ½ cups long-grain white rice	1 ¼ cups water
1 teaspoon white sugar	1 tbsp shredded coconut
	1 (14 ounces) can of coconut milk

Directions

In a saucepan, bed by the rice. Turn off the heat and leave the pot on the fire for another 5 to 10 minutes to allow the rice to simmer until sticky. Garnish with shredded coconut if desired.

Baked "Fried" Rice

Prep time: 15 minutes **Cooking time:** 20 minutes
Serve: 1

Ingredients

2 cups long-grain white rice 2 tablespoons canola oil	1 tablespoon sesame oil, or to taste
½ cup sliced green onions	½ cup diced red bell
3 cloves garlic, crushed	peppers
½ cup diced carrots	½ cup green peas
1 pinch salt to taste (Optional)	3 tablespoons soy sauce
2 teaspoons chili paste	1 cup diced ham
	3 cups chicken broth

Directions

Preheat the oven carefully to 400 degrees Fahrenheit (200 degrees C). In a large baking dish, place the rice. Drizzle canola and sesame oils over rice and toss to cover fully. Combine the garlic, green onions, bell peppers, carrots, peas, and ham in a mixing bowl. Season with salt and pepper. Stir until everything is completely blended.

Combine the chicken broth, soy sauce, and chili paste in a saucepan over high heat. Bring to a boil, stirring constantly. Pour over the rice and give it a quick swirl. Wrap the top securely in heavy-duty aluminum foil. Bake for 32 minutes in a preheated oven. Remove from the oven and set aside for 10 minutes. Remove the lid and fluff the rice with a fork. Seasoning should be tasted and adjusted.

Raise the oven temperature to 475°F (245 degrees C). Return to the oven for 10 minutes or until the rice is toasted and crusted.

Mushroom Rice

Prep time: 15 minutes **Cooking time:** 22 minutes
Serve: 1

Ingredients

2 teaspoons butter	6 mushrooms, coarsely
1 clove garlic, minced	chopped
1 green onion, finely chopped	1 cup uncooked white rice
½ teaspoon chopped fresh parsley	2 cups chicken broth
salt and pepper to taste	

Directions

In a saucepan over medium heat, melt the butter. Cook the mushrooms, garlic, and green onion until the liquid has evaporated and the mushrooms are tender. Combine the chicken broth and rice in a mixing bowl. Season with parsley, salt, and pepper to taste. Reduce the heat to low, cover, and leave to simmer for 20 minutes.

Island-Style Fried Rice

Prep time: 18 minutes **Cooking time:** 20 minutes
Serve: 1

Ingredients

1 ½ cups uncooked jasmine rice	2 teaspoons canola oil
	3 cups water
1 (12 ounces) can fully cook luncheon meat (such as SPAM®), cubed	½ cup sliced Chinese sweet pork sausage (lap Cheong)
	3 eggs, beaten
2 tablespoons canola oil	1 (8 ounces) can pineapple chunks, drained
½ cup chopped green onion 3 tablespoons oyster sauce	½ teaspoon garlic powder

Directions

In a saucepan over high heat, bring the rice and water to a boil. Reduce the heat to medium-low, cover, and cook for 20 to 25 minutes, or until the rice is soft and the liquid has been absorbed. Allow the rice to cool fully.

Brown the luncheon meat and sausage in a pan with 2 tablespoons of oil over medium heat. Set aside the beaten eggs and pour them into the heated skillet. Set aside the scrambled eggs.

In a large nonstick pan over normal heat, heat 2 tablespoons of oil and toss in the rice. Toss the rice in the hot oil for approximately 2 minutes, or until cooked through and beginning to brown. Toss the rice for 1 minute longer to enhance the garlic flavor, then add the luncheon meat, sausage, scrambled eggs, pineapple, and oyster sauce. Cook and stir for 2 to 3 minutes, or until the oyster sauce covers the rice and other Ingredients. Stir in the green onions and **Serve:**.

Cindy's Yellow Rice

Prep time: 15 minutes **Cooking time:** 25 minutes
Serve: 1

Ingredients

2 cups water	1 cup white rice
¼ cup dried minced onion	1 teaspoon ground
2 tablespoons olive oil	turmeric 1 teaspoon garlic powder
1 teaspoon ground black pepper	1 teaspoon salt

Directions

In a saucepan, bring water to a boil. Combine the rice, onion, olive oil, turmeric, garlic powder, black pepper, and salt in a mixing bowl. Cover the pot, decrease the heat to low, and simmer for 20 minutes, or until the water is absorbed and the rice is tender. With a fork, fluff the rice.

Apple Oats

Prep time: 10 minutes **Cooking time:** 15 minutes
Serve: 1

Ingredients
½ cup gluten-free oats
1 tbsp Greek yogurt
½ tsp cream of tartar
2 tbsp date spread
¼ cup apple, chopped
½ cup unsweetened almond milk
½ tsp baking powder
1 tbsp protein powder

Directions

In a mixing bowl, mix together oats, baking powder, and protein powder. Add yogurt, milk, date spread, and cream of tartar and mix until well combined.

Add apple and fold well. Pour oat mixture into the greased air fryer baking dish. Place baking dish into the air fryer basket and cook at 330 F for 15 minutes. **Serve:** and enjoy.

Peanut Butter Oatmeal

Prep time: 10 minutes **Cooking time:** 15 minutes
Serve: 1

Ingredients
½ cup rolled oats
½ tsp baking powder
1/3 cup unsweetened almond milk
1 tsp maple syrup
¼ tsp vanilla
½ tbsp peanut butter
½ banana
1/8 tsp salt

Directions

Preheat the air fryer to 350 F. Add oats into the food processor and process until get flour like consistency. Add remaining Ingredients and process until well combined. Pour batter into the greased ramekin. **Serve:** and enjoy.

Oats Granola

Prep time: 10 minutes **Cooking time:** 30 minutes
Serve: 8

Ingredients
3 cups old-fashioned oats
3 tbsp brown sugar
½ cup maple syrup
1 tsp vanilla
1 tsp cinnamon
3 tbsp coconut oil, melted
½ tsp salt

Directions

In a mixing bowl, mix together oats, vanilla, cinnamon, brown sugar, oil, maple syrup, and salt until well combined.

Spread oats mixture into the parchment-lined air fryer basket and cook at 250 F for 30 minutes. Stir after every 10 minutes. **Serve:** and enjoy.

Berry Oatmeal

Prep time: 10 minutes **Cooking time:** 8 minutes **Serve:** 4

Ingredients
2 eggs
5 tbsp unsweetened almond milk
1 tbsp vanilla
2 tbsp mixed berries
7 oz banana
2 tbsp honey
2 tbsp Greek yogurt
4.5 oz quick oats

Directions

In a mixing bowl, add banana and mash using the fork.
Add oats, vanilla, honey, yogurt, milk, and eggs and mix until well combined. Add berries and fold well.

Spoon mixture into the four greased ramekins. Place ramekins into the air fryer basket and cook at 400 F for 8 minutes. **Serve:** and enjoy.

Chocolate Oats

Prep time: 10 minutes **Cooking time:** 15 minutes
Serve: 2

Ingredients
1 egg
½ tsp cinnamon
1 tsp vanilla
½ tsp baking powder
½ cup rolled oats
1 tbsp cocoa powder
¼ cup unsweetened almond milk
1 tbsp maple syrup
½ banana Pinch of salt

Directions

Add oats and remaining Ingredients into the blender and blend until smooth. Pour blended oat mixture into the greased ramekins.

Place ramekins into the air fryer basket and cook at 330 F for 13-15 minutes. **Serve:** and enjoy.

Curried Chickpeas

Prep time: 10 minutes **Cooking time:** 18 minutes
Serve: 4

Ingredients
30 oz can chickpeas, drained & rinsed
½ tbsp parsley, chopped
Salt
½ tsp chili powder
2 tbsp curry powder
2 tbsp canola oil

Directions

Add chickpeas and remaining Ingredients into the mixing bowl and toss until well coated. Spread chickpeas into the air fryer basket and cook at 375 F for 15-18 minutes. Stir after every 5 minutes. **Serve:** and enjoy.

Quinoa Fried Rice

Prep time: 20 minutes **Cooking time:** 25 minutes
Serve: 1

Ingredients

1 ½ cups water
1 ½ tablespoons teriyaki sauce
1 tablespoon olive oil, divided
3 scallions, chopped, divided 3 cloves garlic, minced
½ cup frozen peas

2 ½ tablespoons soy sauce
¾ teaspoon sesame oil
1 cup quinoa salt to taste
¼ onion, chopped
2 carrots, peeled chopped
½ teaspoon minced fresh ginger

2 eggs, beaten

Directions

Bring the quinoa and water to a boil, season with salt. Reduce the heat to medium-low, cover, and cook for 15 to 20 minutes, or until the quinoa is tender and the water is absorbed. Turn off the heat and put aside for 5 minutes before fluffing the quinoa with a fork. Refrigerate for at least 8 hours and up to overnight.

In a mixing bowl, combine soy sauce, teriyaki sauce, and sesame oil until equally combined. Heat 1 1/2 tsp oil and sauté carrots and onion in a large pan over high heat for 2 minutes. Sauté the remaining 2 scallions, garlic, and ginger for 2 minutes, or until aromatic. Cook until heated through, approximately 2 minutes, with the remaining 1 1/2 tablespoons oil and quinoa.

Cook and swirl the sauce into the quinoa mixture for 2 minutes or evenly covered. In the center of the quinoa mixture, make a well. Pour the eggs into the well; heat and stir for 2 to 3 minutes, or until the eggs are scrambled and cooked through. Cook for 2 to 3 minutes, or until peas are cooked through. Stir in the remaining scallions.

Cinnamon Rice

Prep time: 15 minutes **Cooking time:** 18 minutes
Serve: 1

Ingredients

1 cup uncooked rice
2 cups water
2 teaspoons margarine
1 teaspoon sugar

2 tablespoons nonfat milk
5 tablespoons raisins
½ teaspoon ground cinnamon

Directions

In a saucepan over medium-high heat, bring rice, water, milk, raisins, and margarine to a boil, stirring periodically. Reduce the heat to low, cover, and simmer for 15 minutes, or until the liquid has been absorbed and the rice is soft. To **Serve:**, combine cinnamon and sugar and sprinkle over rice.

One-Pot Rice and Beef Pilaf

Prep time: 15 minutes **Cooking time:** 20 minutes
Serve: 1

Ingredients

½ cup olive oil

2 pounds bone-in beef pot roast, boned and cubed
1 onion, peeled, halved, and thinly sliced
2 fresh red chili peppers hot water to cover

2 cups uncooked white rice
4 carrots, peeled and cut into matchsticks
2 teaspoons ground cumin salt to taste
1 head garlic, unpeeled (optional)

Directions

Place the rice in a bowl and cover with warm water to soak while the meat cooks. Heat the olive oil in a saucepan over medium-high heat and sauté the bones for 5 minutes, or until gently browned.

Place the bones on a platter. Cook until the onion is tender and translucent, about 5 minutes, in the same saucepan. Brown the meat on both sides, 5 to 10 minutes. Return the bones to the pan and add the carrots. Garnish with cumin. Stir in the entire chili peppers and garlic, then season with salt. Fill the container halfway with boiling water. Bring to a boil, then lower to low heat and continue to cook for 35 to 40 minutes, or until the flavors are fully integrated.

With kitchen tongs, remove the bones and add the rice. Pour in 2 cups hot water and level out the rice to sit flat on top, but do not stir. Cook, covered, over low heat for 20 to 25 minutes, or until tender rice. Before serving, mix everything.

Classic Fried Rice

Prep time: 18 minutes **Cooking time:** 20 minutes
Serve: 1

Ingredients

6 strips bacon, cut into 1/2-inch pieces
1 egg, beaten
1 tablespoon minced garlic

8 green onions and tops, sliced
4 cups cold, cooked rice
3 tablespoons Kikkoman Soy Sauce

Directions

In a large pan over medium heat, cook bacon until crisp. Transfer the bacon to the side of the pan; add the egg and scramble it. Move the egg to the skillet, add the green onions, cook for approximately a minute. Next, stir in the rice, followed by the garlic and soy sauce. Toss until the mixture is properly combined and thoroughly cooked.

Yellow Rice with Meat

Prep time: 15 minutes **Cooking time:** 25 minutes
Serve: 1

Ingredients

1 tablespoon olive oil
2 pork chops
1 onion, diced
2 green bell peppers
4 sprigs of fresh thyme
2 teaspoons cloves
1 (10 ounces) package
yellow rice
1 lemon, cut into wedges
chili sauce

2 boneless, skinless
chicken thighs
2 cloves garlic, finely
chopped
3 bay leaves
1 sprig of fresh rosemary
1 cup peas
1 fresh jalapeno pepper
diced

Directions

In a skillet over medium heat, heat the olive oil. Cook until the pork chops and chicken thighs are browned on both sides, the chicken juices run clear, and the pork chops are done. Set aside after removing from skillet.

Cook until the bell peppers are cooked in the pan, then put aside. Mix in the onion and garlic. Combine rosemary, thyme, cloves, and bay leaves in a mixing bowl. Add rice to the pan, along with the amount of water specified on the rice bag. Cook for another 10 minutes.

Combine the pork chops, chicken, rice, peppers, and peas in a pan. Cook for another 10 minutes, or until the rice is soft. Remove the rosemary, thyme, and bay leaves. To **Serve:**, pour lemon juice over the meats and rice, then top with chopped jalapeño and chili sauce.

Perfect White Rice

Prep time: 15 minutes **Cooking time:** 20 minutes
Serve: 1

Ingredients

2 teaspoons unsalted
butter
2 cups water
½ teaspoon salt

1 cup uncooked long-grain
white rice

Directions

In a medium saucepan over medium heat, melt the butter. Stir in the rice to coat it. Cook for 1 to 2 minutes, or until the rice grains become opaque; do not brown. Pour in the water and salt.

Bring to a boil, then lower to low heat. Allow boiling for 15 minutes, covered. Do not remove the cover. Remove from the heat and set aside for 5 minutes, covered. Before serving, fluff with a fork.

Jeera Rice

Prep time: 20 minutes **Cooking time:** 25 minutes
Serve: 1

Ingredients

1 cup basmati rice
4 whole cloves
4 whole black peppercorns
1 ½ cups water salt to
taste

2 teaspoons vegetable oil
1 teaspoon cumin seeds
1 bay leaf
2 cardamom pods

Directions

Rinse rice three to four times before placing it in a bowl; cover with water and soak for at least 30 minutes.
Cook and swirl cumin in a pan over medium heat until it begins to pop, 2 to 4 minutes. Cook and stir for 1 1/2 minutes, or until the cloves, peppercorns, cardamom pods, and bay leaf are aromatic.

Drain the rice and combine with spice mixture; add 1 1/2 cups water and salt to taste. Cook for 5 minutes, covered, over high heat. Reduce the heat to medium and cook for another 10 minutes. Reduce the heat to low and continue to cook for 15 minutes. Remove skillet from heat and set aside for 15 minutes with the lid on.

Remove the lid and fluff the rice with a fork. Remove the bay leaf, cardamom pods, cloves, and peppercorns from the mixture.

South Indian-Style Lemon Rice

Prep time: 15 minutes **Cooking time:** 20 minutes
Serve: 1

Ingredients

4 cups water

¼ cup raw peanuts
6 tablespoons vegetable oil
½ teaspoon mustard
seeds
¼ cup lemon juice
1 ½ teaspoons salt

2 cups uncooked white
rice
½ teaspoon ground
turmeric
4 green chili peppers,
chopped
15 fresh curry leaves
(Optional)

Directions

Bring water and rice to a boil in a saucepan. Reduce to medium-low heat, cover, and simmer for 20 to 25 minutes, or until the rice is mushy and the water has been absorbed.

In a large skillet over medium heat, heat the oil. Cook and stir the peanuts, turmeric, and mustard seeds for 2 to 3 minutes, or until the peanuts are browned.

Combine the green chili peppers, lemon juice, curry leaves, and salt in a mixing bowl. Fold the cooked rice into the lemon juice mixture.

Special Events

Flavorful Chicken Skewers

Prep time: 10 minutes **Cooking time:** 20 minutes
Serve: 4

Ingredients

1 1/2 lbs. chicken breast, cut into 1-inch cubes	For marinade
2 tbsp dried oregano	1/2 cup low-fat yogurt
2 tbsp fresh rosemary, chopped	1 tbsp red wine vinegar
1/2 cup lemon juice	1 cup olive oil
1/4 tsp cayenne Pepper	4 garlic cloves
	Salt
	1/4 cup fresh mint leaves

Directions

Add all marinade Ingredients into the blender and blend until smooth. Pour marinade into a mixing bowl.
Add chicken and coat well, cover and place in the refrigerator for 1 hour.

Thread marinated chicken onto the soaked wooden skewers. Place chicken skewers into the air fryer basket and cook at 400 F for 15-20 minutes. **Serve:** and enjoy.

Turkey Meatballs

Prep time: 10 minutes **Cooking time:** 18 minutes
Serve: 6

Ingredients

1 lb. ground turkey	1 tbsp dried onion flakes
1 tbsp garlic, minced	2 eggs, lightly beaten
1 tsp cumin	1/3 cup almond flour
2 cups zucchini, grated	1 tbsp basil, chopped
1 tsp dried oregano	Pepper
Salt	

Directions

Preheat the air fryer to 400 F. Add turkey and remaining Ingredients into the mixing bowl and mix until well combined.

Make small balls from the turkey mixture and place into the air fryer basket and cook for 15-18 minutes. Turn halfway through. **Serve:** and enjoy.

Tandoori Chicken Drumsticks

Prep time: 10 minutes **Cooking time:** 15 minutes
Serve: 4

Ingredients

4 chicken drumsticks	For marinade
1/2 tsp garam masala	1 tsp chili powder
1/2 tsp turmeric	1 tbsp fresh lime juice
1 tbsp ginger garlic paste	1 tsp salt
1/4 cup yogurt	1 tsp ground cumin

Directions

Preheat the air fryer to 360 F. In a mixing bowl, add marinade Ingredients and mix until well combined.

Add chicken in marinade and mix until well coated. Cover and place in the refrigerator for overnight. Place marinated chicken drumsticks into the air fryer basket and cook for 15 minutes. Turn halfway through. **Serve:** and enjoy.

Chicken Burger Patties

Prep time: 10 minutes **Cooking time:** 18 minutes
Serve: 4

Ingredients

1 lb. ground chicken	2 oz mozzarella cheese, shredded
3 oz almond flour	
1 tbsp oregano Pepper	Salt

Directions

Preheat the air fryer to 360 F. Add chicken and remaining Ingredients into the mixin bowl and mix until well combined. Make four patties from the chicken mixture.
Place chicken patties into the air fryer basket and cook for 18 minutes. Turn halfway through. **Serve:** and enjoy.

Asian Pork Chops

Prep time: 10 minutes **Cooking time:** 12 minutes
Serve: 2

Ingredients

2 pork chops, boneless	1 tbsp sesame oil
3 tbsp lemongrass, chopped	1 tbsp garlic, chopped
1 tsp soy sauce	1 tbsp fish sauce
1 tbsp shallot, chopped	1 tsp liquid stevia

Directions

Preheat the air fryer to 400 F. Add pork chops and remaining Ingredients into the mixing bowl and mix well. Cover and place in refrigerator for 2 hours.

Place marinated pork chops into the air fryer basket and cook for 12 minutes. Turn halfway through. **Serve:** and enjoy.

Air-Fried Sweet and Sour Chicken Wings

Prep time: 20 minutes **Cooking time:** 20 minutes
Serve: 1

Ingredients

2 pounds party chicken wings	1 tablespoon extra-virgin olive oil
½ teaspoon salt	¾ cup white sugar
⅔ cup distilled white vinegar	⅓ cup water
2 tablespoons reduced-sodium soy sauce	1 tablespoon ketchup
	2 tablespoons cornstarch

Directions

Preheat the air fryer carefully to 380°F (190 degrees C).
Place the wings in a large mixing basin. Drizzle the oil over the top, then sprinkle with the salt and mix until evenly blended. Place half of the wings, skin side down, in the air fryer basket.

10 minutes in the air fryer. Cook for 10 minutes longer after flipping the wings with tongs. Raise the temperature to 400°F (200 degrees C). Cook until the wings are crispy on the other side, about 5 minutes more. Rep with the remaining wings.

Meanwhile, add sugar, vinegar, water, soy sauce, cornstarch, and ketchup in a saucepan over medium-high heat. For 3 to 5 minutes, whisk until sauce has thickened. Turn off the heat and set it aside to cool somewhat.
Place the wings in a large mixing basin. Pour the sauce over the top, mix to coat, and **Serve:** right away.

Cheese Balls

Prep time: 10 minutes **Cooking time:** 12 minutes
Serve: 8

Ingredients

2 eggs	1/2 cup almond flour
1/4 cup parmesan cheese, shredded	1/2 cup cheddar cheese, shredded Pepper
1/2 tsp baking powder	1/4 cup mozzarella cheese, shredded
Salt	

Directions

Preheat the air fryer to 400 F. In a mixing bowl, whisk eggs. Add almond flour, parmesan cheese, mozzarella cheese, baking powder, cheddar cheese, pepper, and salt and mix until well combined. Make 8 equal shapes of balls from the cheese mixture and place into the air fryer basket and cook for 12 minutes. **Serve:** and enjoy.

Crumbed Chicken Tenderloins

Prep time: 15 minutes **Cooking time:** 25 minutes
Serve: 1

Ingredients

1 egg	½ cup dry breadcrumbs
2 tablespoons vegetable oil	8 chicken tenderloins

Directions

Preheat an air fryer carefully to 350°F (175 degrees C). In a small bowl, whisk the egg. Combine breadcrumbs and oil in a separate dish until the mixture is loose and crumbly. Dip each chicken tenderloin into the egg, then shake off any excess.

Dip the chicken into the crumb mixture, coating it evenly and completely. Place the chicken tenderloins in the air fryer basket. Cook until the center is no longer pink, approximately 12 minutes. In the middle, an instant-read thermometer should read at least 162 degrees F. (74 degrees C).

Gluten-Free Almond Flour Chicken Nuggets

Prep time: 10 minutes **Cooking time:** 18 minutes
Serve: 1

Ingredients

1 ¼ pounds ground chicken 2 teaspoons salt, divided
½ teaspoon dry mustard
½ tbs dried oregano
2 tablespoons olive oil
¼ cup cornstarch

2 teaspoons ground black pepper, divided
½ teaspoon paprika
2 cups King Arthur Almond Flour
¼ cup water

Directions

Preheat the oven to 375 degrees Fahrenheit. Set aside an oven-safe wire rack on top of a baking sheet. Combine the chicken, 1 teaspoon salt and pepper, and the other spices

in a large mixing basin. Set aside after thoroughly mixing.
Whisk the almond flour and the remaining salt and pepper in a separate basin. Set aside this dish as well. Combine the cornstarch and cold water in a third bowl to make a slurry.

Take roughly 2 teaspoons of chicken and form it into a tiny disk with damp palms. Coat in almond flour first, then dip in the cornstarch slurry, coat again in almond flour, and place on a wire rack to cool (which is on top of your baking sheet).

This technique should be repeated until no chicken remains. In a nonstick skillet, heat the 2 tablespoons olive oil. When the pan is heated, add half of the chicken nuggets. Cook for 1 minute or until the bottoms start to brown. Cook for another minute on the other side to brown. Return the nuggets to the wire rack.
Continue frying until all of the nuggets are golden. Bake for 10 minutes with the full baking sheet (with the wire rack on top) on the middle rack of the oven.

Remove the nuggets from the oven and place them on a cooling rack to cool. Toss with your favorite dipping sauce and **Serve:**. Enjoy!

Smoked Chicken Drumsticks

Prep time: 15 minutes **Cooking time:** 25 minutes
Serve: 1

Ingredients

12 chicken drumsticks
⅓ cup BBQ rub

¼ cup vegetable oil

Directions

Remove the drumsticks from the package and set them on a rack over a drip tray or baking sheet. Refrigerate for 8 hours to overnight to air dry. Preheat an electric smoker to 275°F (135 degrees C). Follow the manufacturer's Directions for adding wood chips. Brush the drumsticks with a little vegetable oil. Put the drumsticks in a resealable plastic bag with the rub and shake to coat. To coat evenly, toss everything together.

Air-Fried Popcorn Chicken Gizzards

Prep time: 18 minutes **Cooking time:** 20 minutes
Serve: 1

Ingredients

1 pound chicken gizzards
1 ½ teaspoon seasoned salt (such as LAWRY'S®)
½ teaspoon garlic powder
1 pinch cayenne pepper (Optional)

⅓ cup all-purpose flour
½ teaspoon ground black pepper
½ teaspoon paprika
cooking spray
1 large egg, beaten

Directions

A big pot of water should be brought to a boil. Add the gizzards, cut into bite-sized pieces, to the boiling water. 30 minutes at a boil Drain. Combine the flour, seasoned salt, pepper, garlic powder, paprika, and cayenne in a flat plastic container. Put the lid on and shake until everything is mixed.

Combine the seasoned flour with the gizzards. Replace the cover and shake until evenly coated. In a separate dish, beat the egg. Each gizzard piece should be dipped in the beaten egg and then into the seasoned flour. Snap the cover back on and give it one more shake. Allow resting for 5 minutes while the air fryer warms up.

Preheat the air fryer carefully to 400°F (200 degrees C).Spray the tops of the gizzards with cooking spray and place them in the basket. For 4 minutes in the oven, Shake the basket, and re-spray any chalky areas with cooking spray. Cook for another 4 minutes.

Air-Fried Peruvian Chicken Drumsticks with Green Crema

Prep time: 15 minutes **Cooking time:** 20 minutes **Serve:** 1

Ingredients

olive oil for brushing	1 tablespoon olive oil
2 cloves garlic, grated	1 teaspoon salt
1 teaspoon ground cumin	½ teaspoon smoked
1 tablespoon honey	paprika
½ teaspoon dried oregano	¼ teaspoon ground black
6 (4 ounces) chicken	pepper
drumsticks	1 clove garlic, smashed
1 cup baby spinach leaves,	¾ cup sour cream
stems removed	2 tbsp fresh lime juice
¼ cup cilantro leaves	¼ tbsp ground black
	pepper
½ jalapeno pepper, seeded	¼ teaspoon salt

Directions

Brush olive oil into an air fryer basket. In a large mixing bowl, combine garlic, honey, 1 tablespoon olive oil, salt, cumin, paprika, oregano, and pepper. Toss in the drumsticks to coat. Arrange the drumsticks in the prepared basket vertically, resting against the basket wall and one another.

Cook in the air fryer at 400 degrees F (200 degrees C) for 15 to 20 minutes, or until an instant-read thermometer placed into the thickest section of the drumstick registers 175 degrees F (80 degrees C). To ensure consistent cooking, rearrange the drumsticks using kitchen tongs halfway through.

Meanwhile, mix spinach, sour cream, cilantro, lime juice, garlic, jalapeño pepper, salt, and pepper; process until crème is smooth. Drizzle some cream sauce over the drumsticks and **Serve:** the rest of the crema.

Grandma Egan's Chicken Stock

Prep time: 18 minutes **Cooking time:** 20 minutes **Serve:** 1

Ingredients

1 (8 pounds) chicken	3 stalks celery, chopped
	1 onion, quartered

Directions

In a large stockpot, combine the chicken, celery, and onion. Fill the container halfway with water. Bring the water to a boil.

Remove any extra fat. Reduce the heat to a simmer and cook for 2 to 3 hours. Take out the chicken and veggies. Using a cheesecloth, strain the soup.

Dry-Rub Air-Fried Chicken Wings

Prep time: 20 minutes **Cooking time:** 25 minutes **Serve:** 1

Ingredients

1 tbs dark brown sugar	½ tablespoon kosher salt
1 tablespoon sweet	1 teaspoon garlic powder
paprika	1 teaspoon onion powder
½ tbs ground black	
pepper	
1 tbs poultry seasoning	½ tbs mustard powder
	8 chicken wings, or more
	as needed

Directions

Preheat the air fryer carefully to 350°F (175 degrees C).

In a large mixing bowl, combine brown sugar, paprika, salt, garlic powder, onion powder, poultry seasoning, mustard powder, and pepper. Toss in the chicken wings and work the spices into them with your hands until they are well covered.

Arrange the wings in the preheated air fryer basket, standing up on their ends and resting against each other and the basket wall. Cook for 35 minutes, or until the wings are soft on the inside and golden brown and crisp on the exterior. Place the wings on a dish and **Serve:** immediately.

Mustard Fried Chicken

Prep time: 15 minutes **Cooking time:** 20 minutes **Serve:** 1

Ingredients

5 pounds chicken wings,	2 tablespoons ground
separated at joints, tips	black pepper
discarded	1 tablespoon seasoned salt
2 tablespoons garlic	3 tablespoons prepared
powder	yellow mustard
2 tablespoons onion	
powder	
1-quart oil for frying, or as	3 cups all-purpose flour
needed	

Directions

Season both sides of the chicken wings with seasoned salt, garlic powder, onion powder, pepper, and MSG. I prefer to spread everything out on a large plastic bag for simpler cleanup. Apply a little coating of mustard on each slice. You may use a basting brush or your fingers to apply the sauce. Fill a plastic bag halfway with flour, add the chicken, and shake to coat. Heat the oil in a deep-fryer or heavy skillet to 350°F (175 degrees C). Cook the chicken for 6 minutes on each side, or until the juices run clear after the oil is heated. Cool for 5 minutes on paper towels before serving.

Flavorful Stew Meat

Prep time: 10 minutes **Cooking time:** 25 minutes
Serve: 4

Ingredients

1 lb. beef stew meat, cut into strips
1 tbsp garlic powder
1/2 tbsp ground cumin
Salt
1/2 tsp onion powder
1/2 fresh lime juice
1 tbsp olive oil
Pepper

Directions

Preheat the air fryer to 380 F. Add stew meat and remaining Ingredients into the mixing bowl and mix well.
Add stew meat into the air fryer basket and cook for 25 minutes. Stir halfway through **Serve:** and enjoy.

Cheesy Lamb Patties

Prep time: 10 minutes **Cooking time:** 8 minutes **Serve:** 4

Ingredients

1 lb. ground lamb
1 tsp dried oregano
1/2 tsp kosher salt
1 cup goat cheese, crumbled 1 tbsp garlic, minced
1/4 tsp pepper
1/4 cup mint leaves, minced 1/4 cup fresh parsley, chopped
8 basil leaves, minced
1 tsp chili powder

Directions

Preheat the air fryer to 400 F. Add ground lamb and remaining Ingredients into the mixing bowl and mix until well combined. Make four equal shape patties from the lamb mixture. Place patties into the air fryer basket and cook for 8 minutes. Turn halfway through. **Serve:** and enjoy.

Chipotle Rib-eye Steak

Prep time: 10 minutes **Cooking time:** 10 minutes
Serve: 3

Ingredients

1 lb. rib-eye steak
1/8 tsp cocoa powder
1/8 tsp coriander powder
1/4 tsp chipotle powder
1/4 tsp paprika
Salt
1/2 tsp coffee powder
1/4 tsp onion powder
1/4 tsp garlic powder
Pepper
1/4 tsp chili powder

Directions

Preheat the air fryer to 390 F. In a small bowl, mix together all Ingredients except steak. Rub spice mixture all over the steak and allow to sit steak for 30 minutes.
Place steak into the air fryer basket and cook for 10 minutes. Turn halfway through. **Serve:** and enjoy.

Yogurt Beef Kebabs

Prep time: 10 minutes **Cooking time:** 15 minutes
Serve: 8

Ingredients

1 1/2 lbs. beef, cut into 1-inch pieces
1 onion, cut into chunks
pepper
1/4 cup Greek yogurt
1 tsp garlic, minced
Salt
2 bell pepper, cut into chunks

Directions

Preheat the air fryer to 350 F. Add meat and remaining Ingredients into the mixing bowl and mix well. Cover and place in refrigerator for 30 minutes. Thread marinated beef pieces, bell pepper, and onion pieces onto the skewers.
Place meat skewers into the air fryer basket and cook for 15 minutes. Turn halfway through. **Serve:** and enjoy.

Amazing Buttermilk Air Fried Chicken

Prep time: 15 minutes **Cooking time:** 25 minutes
Serve: 1

Ingredients

1 cup buttermilk
1/3 cup tapioca flour
1/8 teaspoon ground black pepper
1 1/2 teaspoons brown sugar
1 teaspoon garlic powder
1/2 teaspoon onion powder
1/4 teaspoon black pepper
1/2 teaspoon hot sauce
1/2 teaspoon garlic salt
1/2 cup all-purpose flour
2 teaspoons salt
1/2 teaspoon paprika
1 egg

1/4 teaspoon oregano
1-pound skinless, boneless chicken thighs

Directions

Add buttermilk and spicy sauce; stir to blend. Shake together tapioca flour, garlic salt, and 1/8 teaspoon black pepper in a resealable plastic bag. In a small dish, beat the egg. In a gallon-sized resealable bag, add flour, salt, brown sugar, garlic powder, paprika, onion powder, oregano, and 1/4 teaspoon black pepper.

Dip the chicken thighs in the following order buttermilk mixture, tapioca mixture, egg mixture, and flour mixture, brushing off the excess after each dipping. Preheat an air fryer carefully to 380°F (190 degrees C). Then, using parchment paper, line the air fryer basket. Fry the coated chicken thighs in batches for 10 minutes in the air fryer basket.

Crispy Honey Sriracha Chicken Wings

Prep time: 15 minutes **Cooking time:** 20 minutes
Serve: 1

Ingredients

2 tablespoons baking powder	1 teaspoon freshly ground black pepper
1 tablespoon kosher salt	1 tsp smoked paprika
2 ½ pounds chicken wing sections	⅓ cup honey
⅓ cup sriracha sauce	¼ teaspoon sesame oil
	1 tbsp seasoned rice vinegar

Directions

Preheat the oven to 425°F (220 degrees C). Then line a baking sheet with aluminum foil and set an oven-safe wire rack on top. Combine the baking powder, salt, black pepper, and paprika in a small mixing bowl. In a large mixing basin, combine the chicken wings. Toss the wings in 1/2 of the baking powder mixture to coat. Toss the wings with the remaining baking powder mixture to coat. Place the wings on the rack of the baking sheet that has been prepared.

Bake for 20 minutes in a preheated oven. Bake the wings for another 20 minutes. Bake for another 15 minutes, or until the wings are golden and crispy. Place the wings in a large mixing basin. Combine honey, sriracha sauce, rice vinegar, and sesame oil in a mixing bowl until smooth. Drizzle glaze over wings and toss to coat evenly. Place the wings on a serving plate and garnish with sesame seeds.

Air Fryer Gluten-Free Fried Chicken

Prep time: 10 minutes **Cooking time:** 18 minutes
Serve: 1

Ingredients

1 ¼ cups gluten-free flour	salt and freshly ground black pepper to taste
6 large eggs	¼ cup vegetable oil
1 ¼ cups Gluten-free crackers	2 pounds boneless, skinless chicken breast

Directions

In a small dish, whisk together the eggs and season with salt and pepper. In a separate bowl, properly combine the flour and cracker crumbs.

Dredge the chicken pieces in flour, then in eggs, and then in cracker crumbs. Next, place the pieces on an air fryer rack, ensuring they don't touch. Finally, brush the tops of the birds with oil.

Air-fried chicken for 10 minutes at 375°F (190°C) until cooked through and crisp.

Restaurant-Style Extra Crispy Chicken

Prep time: 15 minutes **Cooking time:** 25 minutes
Serve: 1

Ingredients

4 cups water	1 tablespoon salt
½ teaspoon monosodium glutamate	4 cups oil for deep frying
1 (4 pounds) whole chicken	1 egg, beaten
	2 ½ teaspoons salt
1 cup milk	2 cups all-purpose flour
¾ tbsp monosodium glutamate	¾ tbsp ground black pepper

Directions

Mix the water, salt, and monosodium glutamate in a big glass dish or basin. Cover and refrigerate for 20 minutes, flipping a couple of times to marinate the chicken.

Combine the egg and milk in a shallow dish or bowl. Separately, combine the flour, salt, pepper, and monosodium glutamate in a shallow dish or basin. Drain the chicken after removing it from the marinade (discarding the excess marinade). Preheat the oil in a deep fryer to 350°F (175 degrees C).

Dip chicken pieces one at a time into the flour mixture, then the egg/milk mixture, and finally the flour mixture, ensuring sure each piece is fully coated. Place the coated pieces on a dish or baking sheet.

Place the chicken, one piece at a time, into the heated oil. Fry half of the chicken parts (4 pieces) for 12 to 15 minutes, or until golden brown, then repeat with the remaining pieces. (Note Stir the chicken halfway through the frying time to ensure that each piece cooks evenly.) Before serving, drain the fried chicken for 5 minutes on paper towels or a wire cooling rack.

Alphabetical Index